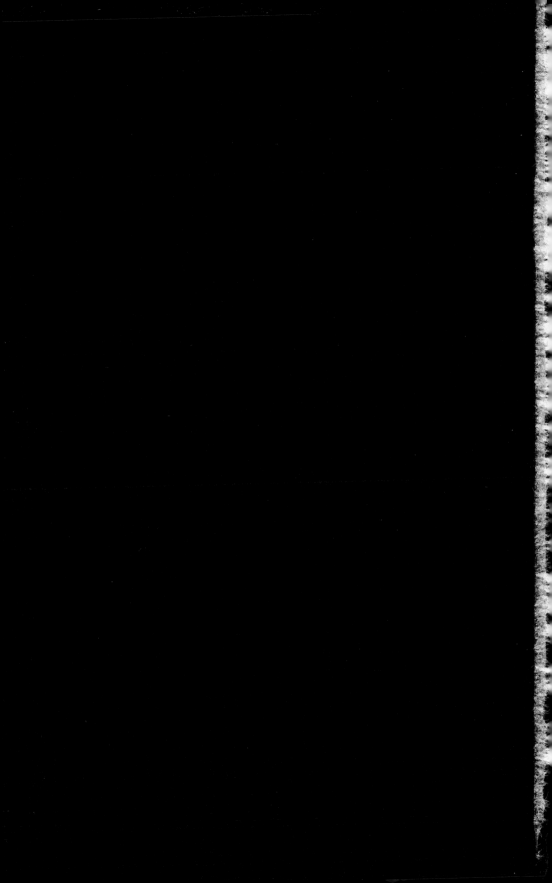

Black Square

Black Square

Adventures in the Post-Soviet World

Sophie Pinkham

WILLIAM HEINEMANN: LONDON

1 3 5 7 9 10 8 6 4 2

William Heinemann
20 Vauxhall Bridge Road
London SW1V 2SA

William Heinemann is part of the Penguin Random House group of companies
whose addresses can be found at global.penguinrandomhouse.com

Penguin
Random House
UK

Black Square is a work of non-fiction.
Certain names have been changed.

First published by William Heinemann in 2016

www.penguin.co.uk

A CIP catalogue record for this book is available from the British Library.

ISBN 9780434023516

Typeset in India by Thomson Digital Pvt Ltd, Noida, Delhi
Printed and bound in Great Britain by Clays Ltd, St Ives plc

Penguin Random House is committed to a sustainable future
for our business, our readers and our planet. This book is made
from Forest Stewardship Council® certified paper.

MIX
Paper from
responsible sources
FSC
www.fsc.org   FSC® C018179

For my friends in Ukraine and Russia,
with love and gratitude.

Contents

Preface

I was seven years old when the Berlin Wall fell. Watching the news with my parents in New York, I wondered how a simple concrete barrier could be so important. Why hadn't people just climbed over it? Newscasters discussed the "Iron Curtain," which sounded scary, but also confusing. Didn't curtains, by definition, ripple and fold?

I was sixteen when NATO bombed Yugoslavia during the Kosovo War. I assumed that Clinton had good reasons for intervening. Despite his sexual indiscretions, our president seemed like a kindly, paternal figure. At school I knew a nice Serbian boy who wrote poetry; he and his brother got into fights with the Albanian kids on the basketball court, but I couldn't quite understand why. Anyway, we were teenagers; we had better things to think about.

I graduated from high school in the year 2000. A year earlier the seniors had chanted *ninety-nine;* as we celebrated that June, my friends and I chanted *zero* and laughed. Panic about Y2K had come to nothing; the world hadn't ended with the old millennium. But disaster arrived the next year. From her high school classroom in downtown Manhattan, my younger sister saw two planes hit the Twin Towers. She and her classmates watched tiny figures leap from the burning buildings. A voice on the school intercom said *run north*: away from the fast-moving cloud of dust and death. Soon the United States was fighting a war, and then a series of wars, that became the permanent backdrop to our young adult lives.

It was an inauspicious start, and I often wished I'd been born in some other decade. But I had the idealism and longing for adventure common among young people. I wanted to fix something, to help someone. AIDS had gotten its name in the year I was born, and I had grown up with its threat; in high school and then in college, I volunteered with health groups. On a whim, I studied Russian. After college I applied to volunteer at the Red Cross in Siberia, in search of something I could not yet name.

My choice of destination, however haphazard, was deeply appropriate. When I arrived in Russia, the young countries of the former Soviet Union were still struggling to establish their places in the world, to define their identities. In Russia, as in the United States, the year 2000 had lived up to its millennial billing. It was the end of the 1990s, which had been a time of chaos, hope, and violence, and the beginning of the Putin era. Russia's new president stood for stability and prosperity, and he had wide support; in 2004, in Moscow, I was surprised to see Russian girls my age carrying Putin key chains. But this perceived stability came at the price of the civil liberties promised by the collapse of the USSR, and Russia was becoming an increasingly authoritarian state. In other countries of the former Soviet Union, the future looked brighter: "color revolutions"— Georgia's 2003 Rose Revolution,

Ukraine's 2004 Orange Revolution, Kyrgyzstan's 2005 Tulip Revolution—promised peaceful "transitions to democracy" led by activists, students, idealists.

After Siberia I got a job working for George Soros's Open Society Institute, a foundation dedicated to promoting democracy and "civil society" in the former Soviet Union (or overthrowing anti-Western governments, depending on your perspective; blamed for the "color revolutions," the Open Society Institute was pushed out of Russia and authoritarian Uzbekistan). I met activists who were only slighter older than I was, members of the first generation to come of age in a post-Soviet world. In 2008 I moved to Ukraine, where I became close friends with many other members of this generation— not only activists but doctors, musicians, artists, teachers.

My family and my friends at home had trouble understanding why I had fallen in love with Ukraine, a country that most Americans could hardly find on a map, famous only for Chicken Kiev and mail-order brides. I tried to explain that I loved the dreamlike quality of a place where the resolutely premodern—horse-drawn carts and babushkas afraid of the evil eye—survived amid the ruins of Soviet utopian modernism, a place that had not yet caught up with the anonymous global marketplace. I was fascinated with life on the other side of the Iron Curtain, in a world that had served for so long as America's nemesis, the mirror in which the United States confirmed its own identity. And then there was the charm of getting to know a foreign culture, as the unintelligible becomes the startlingly new.

I had already moved back to New York by the winter of 2013–14, when Ukraine had another revolution. This one wasn't assigned a color; more spontaneous than the Orange Revolution a decade earlier, it came to be known simply as Maidan, for Maidan Nezalezhnosti, Kiev's Independence Square, the site of mass protests that lasted for three months and ended with the flight of Ukraine's corrupt president, Viktor Yanukovych, to Russia. When I first lived in Ukraine, I was preoccupied with its ideas of the past and future. Once Maidan started, there was nothing but the present; every hour held the possibility of transformation, and of terrible violence.

Before Maidan, I had a lot of stories about Ukraine and about Russia, but I wasn't quite sure how they all fit together. After Maidan, a series of curious adventures became a historical trajectory, and the individual search for meaning—my own, and that of my Ukrainian and Russian friends—became a collective one. The *Bildungsroman* intersected with revolution, as tens of thousands of people converged on Kiev's central square.

In 1915, a century before Maidan, Kazimir Malevich painted a black square on a white background. When it was first exhibited, the painting hung in the upper corner of the room, the place traditionally reserved, in Russian homes, for a religious icon. The Black Square became the icon of the Russian avant-garde, hanging above Malevich's body when he lay in state in his Leningrad apartment in 1935. (He was lucky to die of natural causes before Stalin's 1937 Terror.) Malevich was born to Polish parents near Kiev; his work was influenced both by the black and red patterns of traditional Ukrainian textiles and by the stark black crosses on the garments of Russian saints. Today, like many heroes from the Soviet Union and the Russian Empire, he is claimed by Russians, Poles, and Ukrainians alike.

For Malevich, the Black Square represented the end of time, the culmination of history. He would have liked my high school graduation in the year 2000; for him, truth began at zero. (In 1915 he cofounded a journal called *Zero*.) His Black Square was meant to evoke "the experience of pure non-objectivity in the white emptiness of a liberated nothing." By the time the Russian Revolution and ensuing civil war were over, in 1922, this "emptiness of a liberated nothing" was painfully real, with everyday life shattered by the conflict between the Red Army and the anti-Communist White Guard.

Over the next decades, the Soviets built a new world, with millions of casualties along the way. But by 1991 the countries of the former Soviet Union found themselves at another zero point, forced to reinvent and rebuild yet again. And then there was Maidan. More than a hundred people were killed during the protests; some ten thousand died in the war that followed. Ukraine and Russia, which supported and prolonged the conflict, descended into paranoia and rage.

As a physical space and as a historical moment, Maidan was a kind of Black Square, a ground zero. Maidan is the place where history ends and returns and begins, the moment of liberation that lays bare the uncertainty of the future. The Black Square contrasts with Moscow's Red Square, the center of Russian power and the emblem of Communism, but black and red are also the colors of Ukraine's radical nationalism, of fertile earth and spilt blood. The Black Square evokes both utopian dreams and the threat of anarchy. Malevich's icon was worshipped by some, but denounced by others as a "sermon of nothingness and destruction."

For many Western observers, Maidan confirmed the ineluctable movement toward liberal democracy, the "end of history" that was celebrated after the fall of the Soviet Union but later slipped out of view. The Western idea of Maidan was the negative image of the Russian one: the Russian government and its media portrayed Ukraine's revolution as a neo-Nazi coup, a fascist junta. But history never ends; our world is composed of many colors, and many voices.

A Note on Transliteration

There are several ways of transliterating Ukrainian and Russian words. (The two languages use slightly different Cyrillic alphabets.) In the interest of legibility, I have used simplified versions of the Library of Congress transliteration systems. When someone has a clear preference about how his or her name should be transliterated, I have used that spelling (e.g., Klitschko rather than Klichko). In cases of personal names that have the same Cyrillic spelling in Russian and Ukrainian and are recognizable to English readers, I have chosen the familiar spelling rather than the Ukrainian transliteration (e.g., Igor rather than Ihor). For the names of places in contemporary Ukraine that have slightly different names in Russian, I have used the Ukrainian names and transliterations (e.g., Lviv rather than Lvov, Dnipropetrovsk rather than Dnepropetrovsk), except in the case of Kiev (rather than Kyiv) and Odessa (rather than Odesa), where I have chosen to use the spellings long familiar to English speakers.

Part I

New Worlds

Chapter 1

The Paris of Siberia

I was at an academic cocktail party, already tired of explaining why I was going to Siberia. As I refilled my glass of sherry, I was wrestled into conversation by my boyfriend's professor, a zaftig Renaissance scholar with a heavy southern accent.

I explained that I was going to Siberia for six weeks on a government exchange, to work at an HIV program at the Russian Red Cross.

"Now, is it *safe* to go to Russia?" she asked. It was 2004; the school massacre in Beslan had occurred a month earlier, the day after I agreed to take part in the program.

"Yes," I answered. "I mean, it's really not very dangerous, as countries go. And it's not like I'm going to Chechnya, or even Moscow. No terrorist would bother going all the way to Siberia."

"Well, I'm just concerned for your safety, honey." The Renaissance scholar looked tipsy. "Because I have a nephew, and he and his girlfriend went to South Africa to work there, okay?" She lurched forward and waved her glass at me. "And she was walking alone, and she was raped by ten men, all at once, okay?" She leaned back, satisfied that she had made her point. "That girl has never been the same."

"South Africa and Russia are pretty different," I said. I was thinking: *Christopher Columbus, Lewis and Clark didn't worry about getting raped!* On the other hand, I was not Christopher Columbus, or Lewis and Clark. My father had recently sent me an email asking if I was sure it was safe, and whether my trip would keep me from applying to graduate school. Lewis and Clark never went to graduate school! But I didn't say that to my father.

My first glimpse of Russia was through the fogged-up window of a tour bus: a stand of birches, slender and pale beside the long highway. Scattered among the trees were dilapidated barns, wooden shacks with tin roofs, rusted-out cars, scrap metal, and concrete buildings with opaque windows. These buildings seemed to be in the middle of nowhere, but still they declared CAFÉ, or ICE CREAM, or GROCERIES. I was pleased to be able to read the Russian words. I'd studied Russian in college for a year, just enough to learn the rudiments of grammar and a primitive vocabulary.

Our bus crossed a moatlike stream guarding a Holiday Inn on the outskirts of Moscow, a beige castle stranded in the barren landscape. We piled out of the bus and into the hotel, where neon signs and pinging noises wooed guests into a casino on the ground floor. At dinner, served in the hollow center of the building, I loaded my tray with lukewarm cabbage and dumplings and took a seat next to a shy man who was, as it turned out, one of the only Americans in the program who could actually speak Russian.

At the mansion of the American ambassador, we listened to speeches and mingled with reporters. The word *volunteerism* was used often, with enthusiasm. But in our case, the term *volunteer* wasn't quite accurate: our exchange program was organized and paid for by the United States and Russia, part of a friendship campaign.

During our orientation at the Holiday Inn, we Americans were given practical information about banks and doctors and common Russian scams. Our Russian counterparts, meanwhile, learned about the concept of "personal space", and were instructed not to stand too close to Americans or touch them without an invitation. The Russians later told us that they found this ridiculous. Why can't Americans stand close together? they asked. It was a good question. I found that I liked it when Russians invaded my personal space; it made it easier to make friends.

Some of the Russians—Vadim, Irina, and Olya—offered to take some of us Americans out to a club. We went to the center of the city, which looked to me like a bigger, glitzier, orientalized Paris, and through Red Square—where, a decade later, the conceptual artist Pyotr Pavlensky would nail his scrotum to the cobblestones—past the Kremlin and St. Basil's Cathedral and Lobnoye Mesto, which I was told was the place where people used to be executed, though this was just a myth, and where Pussy Riot would stage one of their first performances, a few years later. I found these tourist sites to be divinely beautiful. I loved the scale of Red Square, and the line of fir trees in front of the Kremlin's stone wall, and the coy, colorful onion domes of the cathedral. We drank Siberian Coronas, whose name delighted me, in an underground street crossing, which I learned was called a *perekhod*, or "go-across," and we watched some hooligans carouse, and then we walked down an avenue and onto a little mall full of shops, through a passageway with a velvet curtain, into a big café called Gogol, where we met Vadim's friends. I couldn't understand a word they said, though they were standing right beside me; their words ran together like paint in the rain.

After a few drinks we took the metro to a gay club.

"Why are we going to a gay club?" I asked Vadim. He was pretty cute: tall and skinny, with a brown cowlick that reminded me of Tintin's.

"Because I am MSM," he said. In AIDS lingo, MSM means "man who has sex with men." It's an epidemiological term meant to identify a risk behavior without assigning a sexual orientation, since some men have sex with men for strictly pragmatic reasons. I was a little surprised to hear that Vadim was gay, or maybe bisexual. (I assumed he wasn't doing it for pragmatic reasons.) I didn't know yet what signs indicated gayness in Russia, a country where every second man was wearing shiny, pointy shoes and carrying a man-purse, an item so ubiquitous that it had a special name, *barsetka*.

"People don't usually call themselves MSMs in conversation," I told him. "They say, 'I'm gay,' or 'I'm bisexual.'"

"I don't like labels," Vadim said serenely. A social worker who did HIV prevention work in Moscow, he had learned the language of the international AIDS movement, of epidemiology and "funding streams." But as people often do when learning a new language, he had made it his own, fitting it to his needs. A Russian "MSM" is faced with terrible options when he wants to find a name for himself. In mainstream discourse, popular choices include variants of the word *pederast*, including the cruel diminutive *pedik*; *gomoseksualist*, or "homosexual," shortened to the horrible *gomik*; *goluboi*, which literally means "light blue", less derisive than the others but derisive all the same; and *gei*, which is not derisive but is ostentatiously foreign. No wonder Vadim took refuge in acronyms.

The entrance of the club could have been the lobby of a shabby administrative building; the dimmed lights didn't conceal the linoleum floors, and the walls were bare. We followed the music into a basement crowded with dancers and techno. Two small, sturdy men with gelled hair and wicked grins danced in thongs onstage, lip-synching and beckoning others to join them. Men kept hopping up, stripping naked, and comparing the lengths of their penises. I learned the Russian word for "screwdriver" and danced with many Russians, feeling no concern for my personal space.

Along with three other young women, I had been assigned to work at the Red Cross in Irkutsk, in eastern Siberia, near the Mongolian border. (Many Americans have heard of Irkutsk because it was in the board game *Risk*.) As it turned out, I was the only one in our group who spoke any Russian at all, though one woman, who was about thirty, spoke Czech. She also had professional experience, having worked with crack-addicted sex workers in the Pacific Northwest.

The plane to Irkutsk was very old, with poorly anchored seats that smelled like dirty socks. Most of the male passengers were carrying plastic two-liter bottles of beer. By the time we landed, belches had turned to snores, and we were just in time to see the flat blue snow meet the lavender flush of sunrise. Moscow had been only as cold as New York in winter; Irkutsk felt arctic, like the beginning or end of the world, though it was only early November.

As we waited in the cold for a bus to take us to the terminal, we watched the Russians slip into full-length furs and bulky hats, like shape-shifters assuming their animal forms. They eyed our thigh-length down parkas with a mixture of pity and contempt. Russians can't stand to see a person underdressed. In this case, however, the sympathy was strictly abstract; we were elbowed aside by two busloads of Russian passengers and left to wait on the tarmac, shivering, for a third bus, on which we were the only passengers.

In the airport terminal we were greeted by Vika, a skinny woman with an angry bruise on the left side of her face, and by Tanya, our interpreter, a cheery, round-faced college student who was visibly excited to meet us. Vika and Tanya shepherded us into a clanking needle exchange van covered in cartoons of grinning, big-headed babies holding syringes. (I guess the babies were supposed to make the syringes seem less threatening.) We drove toward the apartment the Red Cross had rented for us in the center of the city, wondering who'd punched Vika in the face.

Vika told us that she had been robbed and beaten by junkies on her way home the night before.

"But please," she said, "I ask that you not tell anyone at the office, because I want to tell them myself." She barked directions at the driver, her brow furrowed.

Initially a remote colony, in the nineteenth century Irkutsk became one of the main destinations for exiles. These included political dissidents like the Decembrists, the idealistic noble-men who plotted an unsuccessful revolt against the tsar in December 1825. These homesick cosmopolitans, who were sometimes followed into exile by their wives or sisters, built mansions, theaters, and other reminders of St. Petersburg and Moscow, earning Irkutsk the half-ironic nickname "the Paris of

Siberia." But Irkutsk was also a place of exile for common criminals. Murders occurred daily, and homeowners fired rifles out of their palace windows to scare off the thieves and murderers lurking outside.

By the time we arrived, Irkutsk was still famous for its lowlifes, though the aristocrats were long gone. There were universities and research centers and factories, and quite a lot of foreign students. During the anarchic 1990s, the city had also been saturated with cheap Central Asian heroin, which was, at one point, available in the kiosks where you could buy beer. Heroin was cheaper than cigarettes. There was little knowledge about HIV or drug addiction; the government didn't provide education or prevention programs. Drug users often shared syringes, and HIV rates skyrocketed.

Our apartment was in the historic center of town, next to a mansion that had been converted into a synagogue and then burned down. (In 1994 an American visitor reported that the synagogue was functioning, but had been defaced by the words YELTSIN = YID.) The neighborhood was full of old log houses with once-colorful fretwork, unevenly repainted. These lopsided buildings didn't have proper foundations and sank into the earth at every thaw; by the time we arrived, the windowsills were at ground level. Compared to the grim, cement-block Soviet apartment buildings in other neighborhoods, though, they were picturesque.

At our ground-floor apartment, we took turns struggling to open our padded door with its long brass key. This was a ritual that would soon become familiar; in their zeal to prevent break-ins, Soviet door makers made it almost impossible to enter at all.

The apartment seemed huge, with what appeared to be two living rooms. The interior doors were decorated with stained-glass panes showing teapots and Donald Duck, and the wallpaper swarmed with glittering purple flowers. We oohed and ahhed, wanting to show Vika and Tanya that we weren't your usual spoiled, ungrateful Americans. Then we looked for the three bedrooms we'd been promised. As it turned out, this was a classic bedless Russian apartment, legacy of decades of communal living and chronic housing shortages. Every sofa and chair folded out into a lumpy bed. Our landlady told us that she was relieved to see how small we were; she'd been afraid we'd be too fat to sleep on the foldout chairs.

The next morning Tanya took us to the central market to buy blankets. We walked slowly, gaping at the most glamorous women in the world, with their high cheekbones, long fur coats, fur-lined stiletto boots, and tasseled fur hats. They strutted along the icy sidewalks as if they were on a Milanese catwalk. Like four Buster Keatons, we slipped again and again on the thick layer of ice that covered the unsalted pavement. Tanya helped us up, clucking in concern as the Russian women glided past us, their balance perfect, their effort enormous and invisible.

We started with the Red Cross anniversary party: toasts and speeches (it was disconcerting to watch doctors drinking at lunchtime), love-song-singing, and a strangely hilarious game, based on a fable, in which one of the nurses pretended to be a turnip stuck in the ground and others pretended to be a grandmother, grandfather, girl, cat, dog, and mouse, trying together to pull her out.

Then there was a party at the orphanage for the abandoned children of HIV-positive mothers. There were a lot of these children, in part because HIV-positive mothers were told that they were about to die and unfit to be parents, terrorized into giving up their children to orphanages. (Many were also urged to have abortions.) The orphanage was in the same complex as the AIDS Center, across the river, in the outskirts of the city. It looked like an abandoned factory, though the walls were freshly painted with cartoon characters, and there were clowns and a piano player and puppets playing the turnip game, again. Someone was pulling out all the stops, Irkutsk style, and I wondered if the party was for the children or for us. They'd led us rather quickly through the corridors of the orphanage, which looked, with the exception of the party room, to be gray and underfurnished. Still, the children seemed to be developing normally—not like the abandoned babies, stunted forever by lack of stimulation, that I'd read about in human rights reports. Even Potemkin couldn't fake cognitive development. Dressed in party outfits, the children crowed at the sight of us, holding out their arms to be lifted up, clutching our legs and asking, "Mama?"

We strolled along the paths around the orphanage with the children, escorted by the old doctor from the AIDS Center. He was wearing a big fur hat and a white coat: Dr. Santa Claus. We held the children's hands and lifted them up in the air. In the current system, they would never be allowed to go to school and would probably never be adopted. But the orphanage was only for children under five, and Irkutsk had no facility for older HIV-positive children. There was no plan for the children's future.

At the AIDS Center the next day, Dr. Santa told us that as far as Irkutsk's AIDS patients were concerned, everything was absolutely fine. He showed us his office and a waiting room, neither of which contained any people. When pressed, he admitted that it might be bad when Irkutsk had thousands of patients with full-blown AIDS and no medication. (Russia, refusing to admit that it had a problem, still hadn't taken measures to procure anywhere near enough HIV medication for all the people who would soon need it.) But Tanya and Vika started shifting in their seats, and difficult questions dissolved in translation.

Poor, HIV-positive ex-drug users themselves, the Red Cross outreach workers were unconcerned with diplomacy. We rattled through town in the needle exchange van, with its macrocephalous, syringe-wielding infants, into a neighborhood called "the third village," the drug dealing spot. We parked in a courtyard. Some of the windows in the surrounding buildings were smashed in, while others still wore lace curtains. There was snow on the ground, and there were plenty of birch trees; the whiteness made the scene look almost innocent.

People started coming over right away. Intent-looking men in anoraks smoked cigarettes as they dropped used needles into the plastic bag hanging on the fender of the van, took new ones, and answered questionnaires. Two tiny old ladies in fur-collared coats and knit hats exchanged syringes for their drug-addicted sons or daughters. We met a drug dealer: a gnarl-faced, sweat-suit-clad, gloveless old woman, an underworld babushka.

The outreach workers provided information about the meager social services available to drug users: rehab programs cost $400 a month, a vast sum for the average Russian, and probably didn't do much good anyway. In a government clinic, rehab meant two weeks of heavy sedation. If your family decided to pursue alternative methods, you might be kidnapped, tied to a tree, and flogged.

I'd been afraid that the presence of four staring American girls would scare people away, that no one would want to talk to us. I'd underestimated the trust inspired by the outreach workers, the warm apathy of a heroin high, and people's limitless desire to talk about their own problems. We struck up a conversation with a girl named Katya, who was nineteen. She had glassy blue eyes, sores on her mouth, and a filthy cloth bandage on her swollen fingers, but she also had round pink cheeks and a little turned-up nose. She was cute, in spite of everything, and even younger than we were. When we ran out of questions, she pressed us for more, laughing and saying, "Come on! Ask me something else!" She had started taking heroin when she was fourteen, after her boyfriend died. She had been hospitalized thirty times, had a baby who was one year old, lived with her parents, and came to the third village morning and night. She had tried to enroll in school but wasn't allowed to because she was on drugs. She told us all this with a vague, sleepy smile, her gaze drifting away.

Later that week, at the HIV support group run by the Red Cross, we sat in a circle and talked, through the language barrier, about living with HIV in America—not that any of us knew personally. I tried to smile supportively—this was a support group, after all. I had never been in a room full of people with HIV before. Their Russianness was so obvious; their HIV, of course, was invisible. In addition to being the only people in the room without HIV, my roommates and I were the only ones who didn't have fur coats. "You'll freeze to death," one of the ladies in the group told us helpfully.

*

I went to elementary school in the heyday of AIDS education, and I was raised to believe that anyone could get HIV at any time. All it took was one moment of bad judgment. But as far as I could tell, people in Irkutsk didn't get HIV by accident; it was more a by-product of long-term self-obliteration. The inhabitants of Irkutsk didn't seem to be particularly interested in staying alive. They smoked incessantly, and drunks stumbled around as early as nine a.m. After four p.m., half the guys on the street were wielding huge beers, and fat old men teetered down the sidewalk arm in arm. Junkies roamed the streets at all hours, and our new Russian friends relaxed only when we drank and smoked with them. At the Internet café where I checked my email, people smoked cigarettes and drank from plastic bottles of beer as they typed. Soldiers with automatic weapons strapped to their backs drank liter after liter of beer as they played video games, the kind where you shoot people. I didn't like sitting next to them.

One day my Czech-speaking roommate came home and told us that while walking down the street, she'd tripped over a guy who had overdosed. His friends were so high that they couldn't dial the ambulance number on their phones, and they asked her to do it. That night we were awoken by screams and crashes above us; our neighbor was beating his wife. When we went out in the morning, there was a used syringe lying in the vestibule. It was so cold that the inside of the metal front door was covered in frost, and the lock was frozen. We tried to warm the lock with our breath, and we hammered on the icy door. You couldn't blame the people of Irkutsk for wanting to get high.

Like Vadim the MSM, the staff at the Irkutsk Red Cross had learned the jargon of the international AIDS movement without fully understanding it, in the way that language learners use new vocabulary words in the wrong context, or with a valence that's slightly off. Vika and company found out that I knew how to sew, and they suggested that I pass the time allotted me by making an "AIDS kvilt." They were unswayed when I explained that an AIDS quilt should be made by people with HIV or their loved ones. (The original had covered a whole field in Washington, DC, the work of thousands of bereaved family members and friends.) Speaking in a tone that suggested that I was the stupidest person in the world, they explained that no one in Irkutsk would ever publicly admit that they had AIDS.

We were put to work making origami tulips to be sent to Moscow and included in an art exhibit meant to raise awareness about HIV. It took us several hours to master the technique, but from then on we made origami tulips more or less full time. For this work, I calculated that we were paid, through our stipends, ten times the salary of the outreach workers, some of whom had to quit because they didn't make enough to live on. This was especially troubling since the outreach workers and their supervisor, a keenly intelligent, open-minded young woman from Yakutsk, were the only people at the Red Cross who seemed to be doing any meaningful work related to HIV.

We visited a college where, using sign language, we tried to teach students how to make tulips. I could explain how to fold tulips, but I couldn't muster enough Russian to explain to the students why, exactly, we were doing it. Then again, I couldn't muster enough English to explain it to myself. Most of the students thought the tulips were an arts and crafts project and that the red AIDS ribbons we gave them were a reward for their artistic accomplishment. They were enthusiastic until we offered them pamphlets on HIV, at which point they recoiled and left without saying goodbye. (We didn't give out condoms—the Red Cross said it couldn't afford it.)

Many of the students asked why four American girls, *dyevushki*, had come all the way to Irkutsk to make paper flowers. In the Soviet Union volunteers had been forced, or they were gung-ho Communists; in cutthroat capitalist Russia, volunteers were suckers. If a Russian could choose between Irkutsk and New York, she'd choose New York every time. I remembered my high school friend Ilya's Russian immigrant father, who had said, upon hearing about my trip, "Why the hell is she going there? Irkutsk is the asshole of the world."

Tanya, our friendly interpreter, was by now busy with her schoolwork and gone half the time, leaving us to rely on my few stock phrases and on sign language as we were dragged from one school to another, an ostentatious burden. The people in the Red Cross office no longer bothered to acknowledge us, referring to us only as *dyevushki*, sharing our bewilderment as to the purpose of our visit.

At last, in our frustration (we were supposed to be saving somebody!), we asked Vika why we had been invited to Irkutsk. She admitted that she didn't know. It had become clear, however, that the Red Cross had received some money in exchange for hosting us.

"Think of it as a paid vacation!" said Vika, laughing in the way that Russians laugh when things are horrible but they refuse to admit it.

I began to have unkind thoughts about some of our hosts. On the street we passed a stoned man whose face was being burned by the cigarette hanging out of his mouth, and Vika giggled. I saw Larisa, a Red Cross staff member, berating a homeless

16

woman who had come to take some of the free clothes in the lobby. Larisa shoved the woman, waving her fist.

"You're a woman, not an animal! Why don't you take a bath? You stink! Get out!" she yelled.

The next day Vika called and told us not to come in, because there was nothing to do. This was a turning point. Every morning for the next week we rose with our alarm clocks, ate our porridge, and got dressed for work, and every morning Vika called and told us not to come in. I read Bulgakov's *The Master and Margarita* and Turgenev's *Fathers and Sons*, discovering that Russian literature has a particularly powerful effect when read in a state of misery, isolation, and severe cold. Although we had begun to hate one another, my roommates and I tested all the beauty tips in a copy of *Allure* that someone had brought. We straightened our hair, curled our eyelashes, watched Russian music videos, and waited for dubbed American movies to come on so we could lip-read.

On World AIDS Day, December 1, our hosts made an exception and let us come to work. In the morning we folded pamphlets and cut stickers. Then we were herded to the movie theater. The film being shown was *Christiane F.*, from 1981. Christiane is a bored Berlin fourteen-year-old who, for reasons that are left unexplained, goes to clubs where they play only David Bowie, becomes a heroin addict, projectile-vomits daily, sells sex in a subway station, is too high to blow out the candles on her birthday cake, and falls in love with a fellow junkie, to whom she brings a piece of cake before discovering that he is prostituting himself to men. As might be guessed from the release date, *Christiane F.* doesn't mention AIDS. The high school students in the theater shrieked with laughter throughout the film. Television cameras

17

shone bright lights in our eyes as they filmed the audience reactions; a little boy, about five, wandered up and down the aisle, looking at his shoes, trying not to notice the people shooting up on the screen above him.

Taking to heart Vika's suggestion about the paid vacation, we decided to be diligent tourists. Mustering the last of our optimism, we followed the blandly cheerful advice of the *Lonely Planet* guide and found ourselves walking along the riverbank, which was populated mainly by stray dogs—for some reason, mostly Corgis. This was where our oldest roommate liked to go jogging, though she was often chased by Corgis, which are herding dogs, and also, sometimes, by men.

The buildings outside the center of town were faded and flaking, their windows broken or boarded over, and as we continued walking, the wooden houses became tin-roofed shacks. Crosswalks and sidewalks grew rare, the streets were strewn with trash, and we had to dash across small highways, weaving between cars and praying we didn't trip. (We now understood why billboards all over town encouraged drivers not to kill pedestrians.) Soviet statues were flanked by raving old women and children with sores on their faces, and the hurried Angara River was lined with the blackened skeletons of industry.

Walking fast, without a word, we reached a church guarded by a gauntlet of women and children who scuttled up to us, asking for money. The church was big and gaudy, striped and gilded, its interior plastered with incense-darkened icons. A voice behind a screen was speaking in Church Slavonic, fast, flat, and hypnotic, a language invented for the sublime. Old women in voluminous shawls crossed themselves over and over, radiant with grief. They pressed their lips against the glass cases of the icons, and church attendants wiped the marks away with rags.

We were standing at the center of the church, listening to the service, when a clucking attendant, another elderly lady, dragged us to one side. A group of monks began a procession from the entrance of the church to the altar. As the monks passed, the old women kissed the hems of their robes, half sobbing. We hurried out, ashamed; this was no place for tourists.

When we'd run out of sights in Irkutsk, we made an excursion to nearby Ulan Ude, a small, frozen town populated mainly by indigenous Buryat people. The town's main attraction was an enormous Lenin head, almost twenty-six feet tall, cast in forty-two tons of dark gray metal, as if the great leader had exploded in space and his head had fallen to earth like a meteor. Too heavy to move, Lenin's head will probably remain in Ulan Ude forever, after all the people are gone, the wooden houses have crumbled, and the rivers have overflowed their banks.

Tanya resurfaced from time to time, taking us to clubs where we met her friends from the Linguistic University. Over shots of vodka and grenadine, Lena, Zhenya, and Olya told us that they wanted only to leave Irkutsk. Their voices pitched high with hope, they listed the languages they spoke, asking us if we knew any French, Spanish, or Italian men and, if so, whether they were nice. They told us about their dreams of getting to St. Petersburg or France or Israel or the United States or anywhere, really. After a few more shots they confessed, in subdued tones, that they'd considered trying to marry an

American. They didn't plan to marry without love, they said, but they refused to accept a life in Russia. If they'd been Americans, they would have said something like "I deserve better." But they were Russian, so they didn't.

At one of our preferred haunts, the Liverpool Pub, we heard a young man sing Beatles covers in Russian and English. Between numbers, he told the audience that he wished he could be a woman, like Whitney Houston.

On our last night in Irkutsk, I ran into Tanya's friend Zhenya at a club. She had made a particular impression on me because of her thoughtful nature and glamorous way of smoking cigarettes. She was also very beautiful, with high Irkutsk cheekbones, a heart-shaped face, and small, puckish features; she always wore a long fur coat that she had bought cheap in China. That night she seemed more hesitant than usual, preoccupied, and I asked her how she was.

"Not very well," she said, "I have problems with my health." I asked her if it was anything serious. "The doctor thinks I have stomach cancer," she answered. I didn't know what to say.

"Oh well," she sighed, taking a drag of her cigarette, "better not to think about it." She told me that she had met a boy the week before and fallen in love with him at first sight. Yesterday he had taken her driving in his car. We discussed whether she should call him, as I tried not to think about her dying.

We left Irkutsk the next morning, seen off by Tanya's tears and professions of love, and spent the next four days in Moscow, at an expensive hotel in the center of the city, gorging ourselves on fresh fruit and vegetables at the breakfast buffet, taking frequent hot showers and baths, lying spread-eagled in queen-size beds, and telling everybody about how horrible our trip had been. The other Americans seemed to have had a pretty good time. When we reported back to the program coordinator, she was appalled. "Why didn't you tell me?" she asked. We had submitted midterm reports explaining the situation, but they had never reached her; the assistant who reviewed them had only passed on "success stories."

A college friend who was living in Moscow took me to Patriarch's Pond, which I'd read about in *The Master and Margarita*, and we watched children skating. I admired the surrounding buildings; old but well kept, they would live for a long time. My friend took me to Gorky's mansion, a gift from Stalin, who had more sympathy for buildings than for people, and to Moscow's Chinatown, which is very old and has nothing to do with China.

Moscow was the most wonderful city I had ever seen.

Chapter 2

Resurrection

Like Russian intellectuals who came before and after him, the late nineteenth-century philosopher Nikolai Fyodorovich Fyodorov had one Big Idea. To the perennial question *What is to be done?* he offered a simple answer: *Conquer death.* In his view, mankind's united fight against this one true enemy would bring an end to all wars between people, self-destruction replaced by self-perfection. Every generation would be resurrected, starting with the one that had died most recently and ending, several thousand years later, with the first man. These earliest ancestors were to be reconstituted from dust gathered from outer space, mankind, with its newfound sense of purpose, having learned how to synthesize bodies and steer the earth rather than being held in thrall to the sun. The legions of newly resurrected ancestors would live in colonies across the galaxy, all ruled by a Russian autocrat.

Fyodorov's ideas intrigued generations of Russian intellectuals. Dostoyevsky wanted details: was the resurrection literal or allegorical? During his ascetic-pacifist phase, Tolstoy was impressed by Fyodorov, though mainly because Fyodorov was a vegetarian who gave away all his money and slept on a humpback trunk, covered with newspapers and using only a book as a pillow. (Tolstoy was still wearing silk underwear under his peasant smock; he envied Fyodorov's consistency.) Fyodorov's special appeal for writers made sense, because he loved books above all else. For him, the preservation and rediscovery of a book was a sacred task, a first step toward universal resurrection. It didn't matter if the book was bad, because, as he put it, "behind a book, a man is hidden."

Fyodorov was in the vanguard of the "immortality myth" that preoccupied twentieth-century Russian writers, philosophers, and scientists alike, in an era when the line between truth and fiction became exceptionally thin. Inspired by utopian fantasies and advances in the life sciences, specialists and quacks sought to prevent death using a variety of methods, including calisthenics, special diets, and the surgical insertion of animal glands; new theories were elaborated in the blossoming genre of science fiction. Aleksandr Bogdanov was a Bolshevik doctor and science fiction writer who believed that sharing the blood of young and old, healthy and sick, could slow aging and cure diseases. In his 1908 hit novel *Red Star*, Martians used blood exchanges to prolong their lives. When he was appointed head of a Moscow institute for blood transfusions in 1926, Bogdanov put his ideas of "physiological collectivism" into practice on Earth. Through blood, youth and health and sex drive would be distributed equally across the Soviet population. (Lenin's sister was one of Bogdanov's patients.) Bogdanov died in 1928, after exchanging a liter of blood with a young man who had tuberculosis.

Some revolutionary-minded Russians believed that death was merely an artifact of bourgeois capitalism. Others believed that Communism would bring relief from toil, another punishment for man's fall. In a 1921 essay called "Idleness as the Highest Truth of Mankind," Malevich argued that if socialism was for the good of man, and man preferred to relax, then socialism ought to maximize leisure. What happened was just the opposite. Employment became obligatory, and anyone who wasn't officially employed was a "parasite." Soviet culture glorified workers and machines, and workers who made themselves into machines; the scale and pace of industry were inhuman.

The Soviet "industrial novels" of the 1920s and '30s were open about the fact that utopia would be achieved only with great suffering. In *Cement*, for example, the hero and heroine leave their little daughter in the children's home so that they can work full time building a cement factory. This is not a decision they regret, even when the child dies of starvation. In Nikolai Ostrovsky's autobiographical novel *How the Steel Was Tempered*, the idealistic hero, Pavel, destroys his health with revolution and labor. While still in his early twenties, Pavel is afflicted with a terrible condition that causes him intense pain, paralysis that spreads gradually across his entire body, and blindness. But like his author, Pavel continues working. Bedridden and blind, he educates young people and dictates a novel glorifying the Bolshevik revolution. Again and again, he pulls himself back from the brink of death. One of his comrades congratulates him: "Well done, Pavel, for not dying. What use would you be to the proletariat dead?"

By the time the Soviet Union dissolved in 1991, dreams of immortality, permanent vacation, and industrial paradise were long forgotten. No one thought any longer of utopia or perfection. They hoped for freedom, and for the resurrection of a functioning society. But even these dreams were too ambitious. Hyperinflation devalued money overnight, and there were food shortages and endless lines. The educational, medical, and legal systems were in shambles. The rates of murder, suicide, and death related to drunkenness, stress, and poverty skyrocketed.

While the Soviet Union had guaranteed a reasonably steady live-lihood for those who followed the rules—not exciting, perhaps, not lucrative, but steady—now there was panic and uncertainty.

Many people—especially the young—looked for comfort or excitement in chemicals. The old friends, cigarettes and alcohol, had become harder to get: sometimes you couldn't buy proper cigarettes, just long uncut cigarette rolls, and people ate squares of "marmalade," wine so old that it had turned into jelly. But drugs had become easily available, carried across newly open bor-ders, sold under the noses of the corrupt, dysfunctional police, or made at home from poppies or chemical precursors. Alcoholism had been the scourge of the Soviet Union and the Russian Empire before it, but easily accessible drugs were a novelty, the vice of a new world. Teenagers boiled marijuana in milk in their parents' kitchens, drinking it from glass bottles. LSD promised a world that was no more insane than the real one and perhaps more enjoyable. Amphetamines offered a sense of purpose and energy. Opiates were liquid utopia, a warm barrier against the chaos outdoors. In any society, people may use drugs for many reasons—curiosity, social pressure, self-medication, family problems—but drug use flourishes in times of social upheaval.

Since Soviet medicine preferred shots to pills, Soviet children got over their fear of needles early. The high is more intense when you inject a drug, and it's more economical, since you don't need as much. People shot up with old-style glass syringes, which could be used over and over, and shared them readily, as if in a parody of Bogdanov's vision of a communal blood supply. In Russia, there were rumors that HIV was transmitted not through dirty needles but through heroin that scheming Central Asians had infected in order to wipe out the Russian people. (This didn't stop Russians from using heroin.) Another popular conspiracy theory was that HIV was invented by American pharmaceutical companies; this stopped people from taking HIV medications when they finally became available. Some drug users knew about HIV but didn't worry about it much. Drug addiction shortens your perspective; if you're in withdrawal, it's hard to think about anything but your next fix.

By the late 1990s, there was a marked increase in HIV rates among army conscripts and pregnant women, two groups that were tested routinely. Post-Soviet governments continued to do little to prevent or treat HIV and AIDS; instead, they threw large numbers of drug users into prison, where HIV spread even faster. (I once heard about forty Russian inmates injecting heroin with a single syringe fashioned out of a ballpoint pen.) Police loitered outside pharmacies, waiting to fill their arrest quotas with drug users who'd come to buy syringes. If they didn't have drugs on them, they might have used needles, or a cotton ball with the trace amounts of drugs needed for a conviction. If not, it was easy enough to bully or torture them into confessing. Drug users were easy prey. They were considered "socially unproductive": dangerous, useless members of society, like the "parasites" prosecuted in the Soviet era. Just as HIV had become treatable, even manageable, the post-Soviet states produced what would soon be the fastest-growing HIV epidemic in the world. Russia and Ukraine were hardest hit.

After returning to New York from Siberia, I got a job at the Open Society Institute, a grant-making organization based in

New York. OSI was founded by George Soros, a Hungarian who escaped the Nazis, made a fortune, and decided to use some of his wealth and influence to try to ease the transition from Communism after the fall of the Soviet Union. My job was in the international public health program, which had started needle exchange programs throughout Eastern Europe and had funded the Red Cross in Irkutsk.

At first, most of my responsibilities were with the palliative care program, which sought to relieve pain, especially for terminally ill patients. Palliative care was a strange field for a twenty-three-year-old: hot with indignation, optimism, and the desire to rescue everyone in need, I was in no mood to accept the reality of death. Still, the job promised to take me back to Russia someday; as depressing as Irkutsk had been, I was hooked. In the meantime, I enjoyed pressing a button and sending thousands of dollars to Georgia, Romania, or Ukraine, learning to recognize the family names (Gomiashvili, Dumitrescu, Savchenko) peculiar to each country. I bought a map of Eurasia and hung it on my cubicle wall, memorizing all the Eastern European capitals and hoping to visit every one.

A few months after I started, I accompanied my bosses to a palliative care conference in Budapest. Most of the attendees were in late middle age or older; they kept asking me if I was somebody's child. I sat in the back of the hall, eating scones and taking minutes. One presenter spoke indignantly about the tremendous discrepancies in per capita morphine consumption in countries around the world. The doctors practiced telling a patient he was dying of lung cancer. It involved many hypotheticals: *What kind of person are you? Are you the kind of person who wants to know the truth, even if it's bad news?* I learned that in palliative care, priority is given to patients who are both conscious and dying, and whose disease progression is defined as apocalyptic. I'd never known that *apocalyptic* was a medical term.

At the cocktail reception after the conference, I waited for a drink beside an almost freakishly tall man, young but not very, thin to the point of emaciation, with a shaved head. His eyelids drooped over bored, off-kilter black eyes. With his beaklike nose, he resembled a dissolute vulture. Inexperienced though I was, it was obvious to me that he was not a *palliateur* or an oncologist: he looked more like a lost member of the Ramones, or Iggy Pop's Eastern European cousin. I introduced myself, just as he plucked the last orange from the bartender's bowl and started eating it, peel and all.

With a heavy Russian accent but an easy drawl, he told me that his name was Alik. He offered me his hand; the skin was soft and loose.

Alik was a doctor and activist who worked to help Eastern European drug users get HIV treatment. He had come to the conference because he was trying to learn more about palliative care for drug users, who were almost always denied pain medication. His interest in palliation was not purely professional: he soon mentioned that he was not only a doctor, but an on-again, off-again drug user.

I told him about Irkutsk; he had been there. I told him about the tulips; he said that his friends, activists from St. Petersburg and Moscow, had trampled them in protest against the Russian government's refusal to take meaningful action against AIDS. I was ashamed to have been associated with the tulips, and eager to enter the ranks of the tulip stompers.

When the reception was over, we adjourned to my hotel room. I wasn't sure if it was a good idea to let this strange man come upstairs, but Alik was more interested in stories than sex. He dazzled me with a long series of unbelievable anecdotes. It turned out that he was from Kiev, though he had spent some years working at a factory in Liverpool, and in Africa working for an international AIDS NGO. While there, he'd gotten a child's HIV-infected blood sprayed in his eye. I wondered whether it was the eye that drifted off to one side, damaged, he told me, when another child at his school had beaten him on the head with a stone. He let me touch the soft spot on his skull, and let me in on a few secrets: Lou Reed had HIV, and one of his AIDS activist friends had slept with Tennessee Williams.

"When did Tennessee Williams die?" I asked, suddenly suspicious.

He changed the subject, turning to his native land.

"My father was in KGB, you know. He was anti-Semite. The most important thing my father taught me is that I am a Jew. My nanny killed man. But at that time in my country, everybody killed man. My granny killed man too . . ."

He waved his hand dismissively, and sniffed.

Before I met Alik, I was just another girl in a cubicle, doing the usual two years before leaving for graduate school, the standard trajectory for administrative assistants at OSI. I had the feeling that I was a mass-produced good. My row of cubicles was almost entirely female, dark-haired and petite. We all wore colorful pashmina shawls to protect us against the air conditioning, and we got our periods at the same time. I had replaced Danielle, another small, dark-haired, Ivy League-educated woman in her mid-twenties, who was moving to Africa to do something more interesting than filing grant reports. It was true that I went home at night and read books about Russia—but how could anyone guess that as I sat at a staff meeting, taking notes?

With Alik's help, I was promoted to a job working on programs that reduced drug-related harm through needle exchange, drug treatment, and other services. Alik and I spoke often on the phone and exchanged frequent emails. Over the next year I learned more about his life, finding the facts in his rushing river of auto-fictionalization.

Exceptional though he was, Alik was in many ways representative of his generation. Born in the mid-1970s to a bohemian mother and an alcoholic sailor-turned-KGB officer, he reached adolescence just as the world collapsed around him. As a teenager, he lived with his grandparents. They had been relatively well off, but inflation made their savings worthless, and they had to sell their belongings to survive.

Alik went to medical school, where he specialized in dermatovenerology, the treatment of diseases of the skin and sexual organs. But he couldn't resist the call of newly open borders. He had always been fascinated by American culture and had learned good English. Now he took a break from medical school and went to Liverpool, where he learned to do a passable imitation of a Liverpool accent. (Another Ukrainian friend rode his bicycle all the way to Berlin, where he spent a few months squatting with musicians and artists.) Alik traveled through Europe; one highlight was the Amsterdam airport, where, he said, you could root through the garbage cans and find drugs jettisoned by departing tourists. He wasn't sure whether he ought to go back to Ukraine, but he did, and finished medical school.

Kiev was exciting, full of change and opportunity, but there were also many people about Alik's age who were dying of over-doses, or jumping off buildings, or crashing their cars, or falling into rivers, or losing their minds. Then people started to die of AIDS. Alik got a job working for an international NGO that was bringing HIV treatment to Ukraine.

The life story of Ostap, a Ukrainian man I met through Alik, is a case study of the drug-addicted children of perestroika. Ostap was from Chernigiv, in northern Ukraine. As a teenager in the mid-1990s, he tried drinking but didn't like it. He smoked pot, but it was hard to find. Then someone offered him some opiates. At that time, an opiate brew made from poppies was available more or less everywhere, and it was extremely cheap.

As Ostap explained it to me, injecting drugs was fashionable in the 1990s. It made you seem like a criminal, and criminals had credibility: they were the only ones who were thriving. Ostap started shooting up.

After he'd been using opiates regularly for some time, he went to the seaside in Bulgaria. He didn't understand why he wasn't sleeping, why he was sweaty and nauseous and throwing up, why his nose was running. When he talked to his friends in Ukraine and complained about his health, they told him not to worry— he wasn't sick, just in withdrawal.

Back in Chernigiv, Ostap often tried to quit drugs. Once, he was "coded." This process, still popular in the post-Soviet world, is a form of "autosuggestion" that involves persuading someone that if he takes drugs or drinks again, he'll die. Sometimes a capsule is implanted in the patient's body; he's told that as long as the capsule is in place, drugs will kill him.

Ostap's parents took him for an implant, but he knew it was just gelatin.

"Where's the guarantee?" he asked. "Let's make a deal—you code me, and if I go and shoot up and nothing happens, give me my money back."

The doctor refused to code him, saying he only treated alcoholics.

Ostap also spent a lot of time in the Chernigiv "nuthouse," as he called it. He committed himself on a regular basis, usually for about two weeks. There you were put in a medically induced stupor that kept you from noticing the agonies of drug withdrawal; by the time you got out, your drug tolerance was far lower, which made it cheaper to get high. The nuthouse charged almost nothing, they'd accept you under any name, and they'd feed you three meals a day for a solid month. If a parent needed a vacation from an addicted child, sending him to the nuthouse for a few weeks was a cost-effective choice.

About 10 percent of the nuthouse beds were paid places, for addicts. According to Ostap, the addicts were always doing something stupid. They'd knock out a psychiatric patient's tooth, take the gold crown, and trade it for moonshine, or steal all the sleeping pills in the dispensary. Once they stole the soldiers' uniforms and boots and traded them for moonshine. In order to elicit confessions, a doctor had all the patients tied to their beds and injected with haloperidol, a powerful antipsychotic.

"How to describe haloperidol?" Ostap said. "You can't drink—you'll miss your mouth. Your head gets stuck when you try to turn it." Haloperidol was used to sedate Soviet dissidents in the 1970s, when they were sent to psychiatric hospitals instead of the Gulag.

During the interrogations, the haloperidol was accompanied by a mysterious oily substance that was heated and injected into the patients' buttocks and shoulder blades, causing a high temperature, shakes, and chills. Then the staff turned over the beds, so that the patients were hanging from their straps, facing the floor. But Ostap wasn't resentful. He said the addicts left the doctors no choice.

The nuthouse figures prominently in artistic depictions of the post-Soviet 1990s. The Russian word *nevmenyaemost* comes up, too: it indicates the state of derangement in which a person can no longer be held responsible for his crimes. Such was the zeitgeist.

It took a life-threatening illness to make Ostap kick heroin. In 2002 he noticed that when he shot up in his legs, he couldn't even feel the needle. He saw a neurologist, who prescribed ointment; he saw five more neurologists before someone did an X-ray and found that his spine was fractured. He had tuberculosis of the bone and a malignant tumor under his jaw—lymphoma. This, it was discovered, was probably because he had HIV, as well as hepatitis C, another blood-borne virus widespread among injecting drug users. The doctors knew how to treat his cancer, and he even found a surgeon willing to operate on his back, but no one knew anything about treating HIV. He got chemotherapy for six months, lost his hair, and swelled up like a balloon. He was bedridden for four months; it took him another month to stand.

But he did. Like that of Pavel, the hero of *How the Steel Was Tempered*, Ostap's body was almost destroyed by the hard times in which he lived; like Pavel, Ostap returned from the brink of death.

He hadn't talked to anyone but his parents and his doctors during his treatment; all his friends were users, and he was afraid he'd relapse if he saw them. Then he got a phone call from some ex-user AIDS activists he'd met during a stint in rehab in Odessa. They asked Ostap to help open a branch of their organization in Chernigiv. He wanted to, but his parents were afraid of what would happen if their neighbors found out about his illness. So he packed his belongings into a single black plastic bag and moved to Kiev, to work with the activists.

Ostap told me that of his group of thirty or forty friends from high school, only three or four survived into their thirties. The rest died from overdoses, from injection-related diseases like sepsis, or from HIV-related illnesses like tuberculosis. Those who were still alive were in prison.

In the summer of 2006, I attended the International AIDS Conference, the biggest health and development conference in the world. It was held in Toronto, in a conference building the size of a town, with glass walls and endless escalators. It reminded me of the interplanetary market in *Star Wars*: groups from every part of the galaxy moving in pods, a din of competing languages and cultures. There were sex worker activists in high ponytails and tight T-shirts with clever, obscene slogans. There were the Eastern Europeans, with their bad teeth and mullets. There were Indian *hijras* in bright saris, including the famous Laxmi,

35

who'd won the admiration of Salman Rushdie, and Thai and
Indonesian activists dressed warmly against the air conditioning.
Most of all there were Africans, many of them in colorful outfits
made of waxed cotton printed with AIDS ribbons or anti-AIDS
slogans. In the "Global Village," you could buy handicrafts like
African-print handbags made by HIV-positive rape survivors in
Rwanda, embroidered blouses made by HIV-positive Mexican
women, colorful jewelry made by South African AIDS orphans,
or, my personal favorite, a piece of African beadwork imploring
DON'T SHARE NEEDLE INJECTION.

The AIDS Conference wasn't always so inclusive; it started
as a strictly scientific event. In 1989 activists from the American
group AIDS Coalition to Unleash Power, or ACT UP, pushed
their way into the conference, carrying their SILENCE = DEATH
posters. ACT UP was famous for its direct actions in the United
States, where members were often arrested during acts of civil
disobedience. Over the years ACT UP members infiltrated the
New York Stock Exchange, chaining themselves to the VIP balcony to protest the price of the only AIDS drug approved for
use; marched to the White House carrying the casket of a dead
ACT UP leader; and put an enormous condom over Senator
Jesse Helms's house in Arlington, Virginia. At the 1989 AIDS
Conference, ACT UP members seized the microphone and presented scientists with a report on the failures of AIDS research.
From then on the conference included people with HIV, and scientists and pharmaceutical companies made a show, at least, of
consulting with them about research and drug trials.

The research and activism bore fruit, and the world's first
effective HIV treatment was introduced in 1996. People who
had been about to die recovered suddenly. For a long time things

had moved in only one direction, flesh melting off bodies, skin disfigured by Kaposi's sarcoma, legs growing too weak to hold the weight of a body, eyes losing the power of sight. And then, suddenly, people started making the journey backward. People who had been in wheelchairs could walk again. The lesions healed, the weight was gained back, and the sick were well again, more or less. (The drugs have many unpleasant side effects.) It's been called the Lazarus effect.

Perhaps because they have witnessed this triumph over death, achieved through the hard work of humankind, AIDS activist slogans have a Fyodorovian optimism: END AIDS NOW! END AIDS BY 2016! Demands often revolve, like Fyodorov's theories, around the word *universal*, one of many indicators that such activists are the heirs to the utopian ideas of the nineteenth and twentieth centuries. Providing universal access to medications that have already been invented is a lot easier than collecting ancestral dust from outer space. And yet it's unlikely that any of these demands will be met in the next century, let alone in the next decades. AIDS drugs exist, and energetic activism has succeeded in driving down their prices and getting rich governments to contribute to AIDS treatment efforts, but still no one will pay for them to be delivered to every single person with HIV, for the remainder of these people's lives.

By the time I arrived at my first AIDS Conference, the international AIDS bureaucracy—what Eastern Europeans, with their usual cynicism, call the "AIDS business"—was bloated and pious. Bureaucrats agreed on everything that was vague and euphonious—human rights, equality, universal access, a fight against all kinds of "stigma and discrimination"—and yet national governments continued not to pay for medicine or prevention programs, and to punish drug users and sex workers and gays. Angry activists, some of them veterans and some of them younger people inspired by the example of the first generation of AIDS activists, seemed almost quaint in their anger. During one session I attended, in a cold, sepulchral room, representatives of pharmaceutical companies were speaking when, in their matching T-shirts, ACT UP members filed onto the stage, chanting about price reductions for an AIDS drug. They were right, of course, that the drug ought to be cheaper, and ACT UP did win important victories from time to time. But storming the stage was no longer a shocking disruption, as it had been in the 1980s. Now it was a scheduled event, part of the agenda. As the protesters shouted, the speakers sat patiently, looking irritated. They were used to this process. The audience, too, looked unimpressed, though the protest was more interesting than the session had been. It ended soon enough, just as everyone had known it would. In the 1980s ACT UP had turned anger into action, harnessing it to accelerate research and change policies. But by the time I arrived on the scene, anger had been assigned its place in the bureaucracy.

My most important task at the AIDS Conference was to help Sasha, an HIV-positive Russian AIDS activist in her late twenties, to write a keynote speech. Sasha was attractive without being beautiful, with a straight nose, crooked teeth stained by tobacco, golden-brown hair cut into an awkward mullet, and large, expressive green eyes. Just out of rehab, she had the edginess of a person unaccustomed to sobriety.

Sasha had been diagnosed with HIV when she was only twenty-two, after sharing needles with her boyfriend. The staff at the clinic gathered around her, staring at her, as she later told a journalist, as if she were some mysterious beast. The doctor said, "That's it, girl, you're HIV positive, go where you like." She didn't find out about HIV treatment until three years later.

Hospitalized with HIV-related complications, Sasha found that no one was helping the young, dying AIDS patients around her. She and some other HIV-positive activists started an organization to provide palliative care in St. Petersburg's infectious disease hospitals. Drawing on her training as a psychologist, she helped teach Russian doctors and nurses how to talk to their patients about death—although there was no reason they had to die, from a medical perspective. HIV drugs were easily in reach for the oil-rich Russian government. And yet Russia didn't care to exercise its power to conquer death. Committees of doctors decided who was eligible for state-sponsored treatment and who wasn't—who would be resurrected, and who would be left to die. HIV treatment cost $12,000 a year, more than almost anyone in Russia could afford. In 2004 there were five hundred people receiving government-funded HIV treatment, and a million on the waiting list.

Sasha was always dressed in the same uniform: jeans, Converse sneakers, and the T-shirt of her organization, Front AIDS. The logo had a man waving a red banner that formed an AIDS ribbon. Under FrontAIDS was written a slogan, in Russian: WE WILL LIVE—THAT IS OUR POLICY!

FrontAIDS was a radical protest group formed by Sasha and her fellow activists, some of them anarchists or eco-activists (the sorts of people who would later form Pussy Riot). Like their American counterparts, FrontAIDS held disruptive actions with a high risk of punishment. For them, too, silence equaled death. No one would rescue them; they would survive only if they were ready to fight. Once, demanding treatment for HIV-positive prisoners, they handcuffed themselves to the Ministry of Justice in Moscow, chanting "A prison sentence is not a death sentence." In St. Petersburg, activists carried empty red coffins to City Hall. Just behind a large statue of Lenin pointing the way to the future, the activists draped the facade of the building in a banner that said OUR DEATHS, YOUR SHAME. FrontAIDS activists were conscious inheritors of the ACT UP legacy, but they were also the heirs to the 1917 revolution.

Many of the FrontAIDS activists protested with masks on; public exposure as HIV-positive people and as drug users could lead to firing, ostracism, and police harassment. But Sasha decided that masks only made it easier for the public to treat HIV-positive people as frightening and alien. In 2005 she agreed to have her face and her story used for an anti-AIDS campaign, making her one of the first Russians to publicly admit to having the virus.

In Toronto, the conference sponsors had paid for a nice hotel room for Sasha. She was letting two other AIDS activists stay with her: a Russian man, Aleksandr, and an American who had been living in Russia for many years and was the kind of earnest, hard-working expat woman who, I found, often propped up NGOs in countries without much history of civic engagement. They all slept in Sasha's king-size bed. Aleksandr, a tall, obese, bearded man in his late twenties, had traded his FrontAIDS shirt for an African dashiki that squeezed his pasty flesh.

Sasha had trouble concentrating on her speech and kept asking me to buy her what she called, charmingly, "energetic drinks," picking them based on whether they matched her outfit. She told me everything she wanted to say, and I wrote a speech; but it was full of big words and complicated clauses, and when she tried to read it out loud, she stumbled.

"I'm sure it sounds very nice, Sophie," she said. "But it's not my language. I need it to be simpler." I took out all the big words and shortened every sentence. Her speech was a success.

One afternoon we went swimming together on the roof of her hotel. My bathing suit was a little too big and kept slipping down, making it hard to swim. I watched her do fast laps across the pool, her long, powerful blond limbs hardly splashing as they moved through the water. She laughed with happiness and told me she had once been an athlete, a *sportsmenka*. But that was in another life.

Chapter 3

City of Gardens, City of Ravines

Not long after the AIDS Conference, Alik moved back to
Kiev. He started using drugs heavily again and indulging what
he called, with his usual ironic self-awareness, his "Jesus complex": he always had to feel he was saving or being saved. This
required a constant state of danger, and relationships with fellow drug users-turned-activists offered the perfect conditions.
He'd tell me about the latest "patient" he'd taken to the hospital
or allowed to sleep on his couch, or about his latest overdose and
the brave, tragic girl who'd saved him by giving him mouth-to-
mouth resuscitation, the kiss of life. Sometimes, after we got off
the phone, I'd have to go and lock myself in the office bathroom,
trying not to vomit with anxiety. One of my co-workers wrote a
guide on how to revive an overdose victim; I studied it carefully,
like the good student I'd always been.

I visited Kiev for the first time in May 2007, for a workshop
I'd organized on health programs for women drug users. In New
York, a graduate student had been giving me Russian lessons
once a week, but I hadn't made much progress. (Both Russian
and Ukrainian are spoken in Kiev.) I made Alik promise to
pick me up at the airport. I hardly slept on the plane, afraid he
wouldn't show up, that he'd get the day wrong or forget, which
wouldn't have been a surprise. But when I entered the arrival
hall at Boryspil, Kiev's dinky international airport, there he was
in a cheap black suit, damp with sweat. He'd been swallowed up

again by post-Soviet space; you could almost see his life expectancy declining. Still, I was happy to see him.

We drove along the smooth, narrow highway to the city, past walls of trees broken only by the occasional Ukrainian theme restaurant or hotel. There were a couple of lonely bus stops, and I wondered what sort of people waited at them: were they living in huts, in the forest? But soon we were passing cheap high-rises and shopping centers, and then we crossed the Dnieper River. Kiev's Right Bank came into view, with its white-walled, golden-domed churches nestled in a bed of trees, and the "Mother-Motherland" statue, a colossal stainless steel woman standing high on a hill, holding a sword and a shield, a memorial to the Second World War. In the 1950s there had been an idea to build a Lenin and a Stalin side by side, each 650 feet tall, but Kiev got the Mother instead. Her shield bears the Soviet coat of arms.

After Ukraine became independent, there was talk of pulling the Motherland statue down and melting her. Soviet ideology would be reduced to a neutral element, made into something better suited to the new world of Ukrainian freedom. But the statue was so enormous that its removal would have been prohibitively expensive. Besides, it stood for victory in the Second World War, still one of the most cherished memories of many Ukrainian citizens. The Motherland statue stayed, gazing toward Moscow: the Soviet past was too valuable and too vast to be forgotten.

Meanwhile, the resurrected symbols of the prerevolutionary Ukrainian nationalist past, of the short-lived rebellions against Russian imperial power, began to crowd forward. The new Ukraine adopted an old blue and yellow flag, a trident, and the anthem "Ukraine Has Not Yet Died." These emblems were part

44

of Ukraine's new national identity, its idea of itself. Language, too, became a way of asserting Ukraine's distinction, its difference from Russia. The Ukrainian language had been subordinated to Russian in imperial Russia and then in the Soviet Union, confined to villages and grandmothers, folklore and nationalist rebellion, and excluded, for the most part, from the spheres of government, education, or high literature. As a result, Ukraine had always been a bilingual country. Now Ukrainian became Ukraine's national language, the linguistic boundary serving to reinforce the new national borders.

A sudden change of languages and symbols, with government institutions switching to Ukrainian almost overnight, was nothing new for Ukraine. One of Alik's favorite writers was Bulgakov, who came, like Alik, from a family of Russian-speaking intellectuals and began his professional life as a doctor. But Bulgakov's career was disrupted by the First World War, the 1917 Revolution, and the Russian Civil War. Bulgakov seems to have fought on the side of the White Guard, the forces defending the monarchist system against the socialist revolutionaries and, in Ukraine, against the Ukrainian separatists led by Symon Petliura. Bulgakov's novel *White Guard* is set in Kiev in the winter of 1918–19, as the German-backed Hetman Pavlo Skoropadsky, who had been supported by the Whites, abandons the city, and Petliura's Ukrainian peasant army moves in. The Turbin family, a stand-in for the Bulgakov family, is trying to defend its cozy, Tolstoy-reading nineteenth-century home from the apocalyptic snowstorm raging outside. But the doors fly open and the windows break. The educated, Russian-speaking city is invaded by Ukrainian-speaking peasants and Cossacks from the wild steppe. Though Bulgakov was not an impartial observer,

45

White Guard offers a fairly accurate picture of Ukraine's social and linguistic divides: city dwellers and the upper classes spoke mostly Russian, while Ukrainian was spoken in the countryside.

In 1919 Petliura was driven from Ukraine by the Bolsheviks. Shaken by the failure of the Ukrainian peasants to support the revolution, and despite Marxism's opposition to nationalism, Lenin and Stalin developed a policy that allowed limited self-government for the various "nationalities" (Ukrainian, Belarusian, Kazakh, Jewish, and so on) of the Soviet Union. The logic behind the policy was dialectical: by making room for nationalism, the Bolsheviks would hasten its extinction. Every Soviet citizen had to choose a nationality—not always easy in a multiethnic, multilingual empire—and a complicated system of local governance was organized. Soviet policy included the use of national languages in public life. In Ukraine, the 1920s saw a wave of Soviet-mandated "Ukrainization," a sudden switch to the newly standardized Ukrainian language in government and schools, on street signs, and in newspapers, not unlike what Ukraine would experience again in the 1990s.

But Russian soon regained its old dominance, becoming the language of the centralized Soviet government. Ukrainian-speaking intellectuals and the Ukrainian Soviet Socialist Republic's top political leaders were annihilated in Stalin's purges, accused of "bourgeois nationalism." Some were accused of "terminological wrecking," the attempt to create a Ukrainian language that would isolate Ukraine from the rest of the Soviet Union and bring it closer to the hated Poland and other Western enemies. For Stalin, even word choice could be a form of political sabotage.

*

Bulgakov disliked the Ukrainian language, which he found silly and inconvenient, but he passionately loved his native city. As Alik and I drove into Kiev that first day, I understood why. Kiev was precipitous and green, a garden city, with a center full of brightly painted Art Deco-style buildings, buxom caryatids, squat gargoyles, and lavish churches. Its glamour was more than a thousand years old, the glow of a distant but powerful star. In the Middle Ages, Kiev was one of the biggest cities in Europe, capital of Kievan Rus, the first state to unite the Slavic tribes. It was traditionally known as "the mother of Russian cities," "the Jerusalem of the Russian lands." But it was sacked by the Mongol Horde in the thirteenth century, and the Slavic Jerusalem never quite regained its former glory. In his 1923 essay "The City of Kiev," Bulgakov describes Kiev as a "quiet backwater," lovable for its peaceful atmosphere, modest scale, and friendly, unpretentious inhabitants—who are compared, inevitably, with the pushier, sharper-toothed Muscovites, notorious for their grandiosity.

My favorite part of Kiev was Alik's neighborhood, Podil, a low-lying area that skirted the northern end of the old hill city and was once the center of Jewish life in Kiev. In the first full bloom of spring, Kontraktova Square, the heart of Podil, was wide, leisurely, and green, full of young people chatting, eating ice cream, drinking beer, and playing guitars. Alik, who knew all the local lore, showed me a painted statue of Samson opening the jaws of a very small and unfrightening lion. Samson's poorly molded arms looked like tubes of cookie dough, but he was meant to protect Kiev.

Bulgakov's Podil looked very much like Alik's Podil, which was, to a great extent, a reconstruction. The Bolsheviks blew up churches and cathedrals and replaced them with state buildings, or humiliated religious spaces by turning them into museums of atheism. This was more than just destruction. In tenth-century Kievan Rus, when a pagan temple was torn down, a Christian equivalent had to be built on the same site, squeezing out the pagan gods. After the end of the Soviet Union, Ukraine rebuilt the churches that had been destroyed. Their whitewashed or pale blue walls were made for shadows; their sites had housed many generations of gods. But reconstruction is easier than resurrection. No one could bring back Kiev's Jews, who were massacred in 1941, during the German occupation, at Babi Yar ravine, a few miles west of Podil.

Above Podil, overlooking the Dnieper River, stood a statue of Prince Vladimir, the illegitimate son of Sviatoslav I and his housekeeper, Malusha, who was said to have visions of the future. Vladimir converted to Christianity in 987, supposedly because it allowed the consumption of alcohol and pork but more likely because he married an Orthodox Christian Byzantine princess. He baptized the people of Kiev en masse in 988 and had his wooden idol, Perun, the golden-mustached god of thunder and lightning, bound to a horse's tail and dragged to the river, beaten with sticks, and drowned.

Vladimir figures prominently in *White Guard*; Bulgakov grew up close to the monument, on the steep, winding street named Andrew's Slope for the Baroque Church of St. Andrew at its upper end. A few blocks past St. Andrew's stand the majestic Byzantine-style Cathedral of St. Sophia and an equestrian statue of Bohdan Khmelnytsky, the Cossack hetman who signed a treaty with Muscovy in 1654. When the Polish-Lithuanian Commonwealth controlled the land that is now Ukraine, the Catholic Polish nobility used Orthodox

East Slavic peasants as serfs and Jews as tax collectors, causing intense resentment toward Poles, Catholics, and Jews alike.
Khmelnytsky led an uprising against the Poles, allying with the
Russians. In the original mid-nineteenth-century design for the
statue, Khmelnytsky was trampling his enemies: a Polish noble-
man, a Jesuit, and a Jew.

In the climactic scene in *White Guard*, whirling masses crowd
into the Cathedral of St. Sophia for a service. As the church bells
peal in a terrible cacophony, a black sea of worshippers follows
the church procession onto the frosty square. Blind Ukrainian
minstrels sing about the end of the world; pickpockets steal, and
beggars plead for change. There are rumors that Petliura, leader
of the anti-Bolshevik Ukrainian People's Republic, has arrived.
Petliura's troops, including a Cossack company, march into the
square, waving blue and yellow flags as the crowd cheers. Little
boys climb up Bohdan Khmelnytsky's ankles and soldiers try to
knock off his inscription, which celebrates a "united, indivisible
Russia," but bayonets are no match for granite. Petliura is
nowhere to be found. After his defeat, he became a Soviet villain;
when Ukraine became independent, he was a hero again, with a
street in central Kiev named after him.

Prince Vladimir and Bohdan Khmelnytsky are among the
only nineteenth-century statues that survive in Kiev. The
Bolsheviks began their tenure by deposing the icons of the old
world. For example, the 1911 assassination of Pyotr Stolypin,
the tsar's reformist minister of internal affairs, wasn't enough;
when the revolution came, the people built a gallows around
his statue, hanging him in effigy and then smashing him to bits.
This was revenge for all the revolutionary terrorists hanged
from "Stolypin's necktie." Prince Vladimir was spared because

Kievan Rus was the shared heritage of both Ukraine and Russia; Bohdan Khmelnytsky lasted because of his role as an anti-Polish revolutionary leader and agent of Russian-Ukrainian friendship. After 1991 surviving heroes had to be translated into Ukrainian. Vladimir became Volodymyr; Bogdan Khmelnitsky became Bohdan Khmelnytsky.

When I explored Kiev for the first time, the city's streets were punctuated by monuments to the great men of Ukraine's past: round-edged metal figures holding cities, books, and swords. Not all of the statues were new. A Soviet-era statue of Taras Shevchenko, the nineteenth-century poet-prophet of the Ukrainian nation and the Ukrainian language, stood in Shevchenko Park, across the street from Shevchenko University, which resembled a giant red velvet cake. A statue of Lenin stood at the end of nearby Shevchenko Boulevard. Lenin and Shevchenko made a strange pair. Shevchenko was born a serf, and spent most of his life railing against the Russian slave masters and lamenting Ukraine's lost glory. (He was sent to prison and into exile for pro-Ukrainian agitation.) He wept over the burial mounds of Cossacks, the fierce horsemen of the steppe and the embodiments, for him, of Ukrainian independence.

Shevchenko was, and remains, a savior figure for Ukrainian patriots. He would have hated the Soviet Union. In one of his most famous poems, he asked to be buried above the Dnieper, expressing the hope that someday the roaring river would carry the blood of his enemies (among them, the Russians) out of Ukraine, into the Black Sea. But Soviet policy demanded the canonization of literary heroes of each Soviet "nation," and Shevchenko was Ukraine's designated bard. It helped that he had spent most of his life in poverty: Soviet critics dubbed him a "Red Christ," "apostle of day laborers and hired hands." In 1939, on the 125th anniversary of his birth, a spate of publications celebrated Shevchenko as a revolutionary opponent of social injustice and a devoted student of Russian revolutionary thinkers.

Maidan Nezalezhnosti, Independence Square, has been Kiev's center since the nineteenth century, when it became home to Ukraine's parliament. In those days it was called Parliament Square. In 1919 it was renamed Soviet Square, and in 1977 it became the Square of the October Revolution. A large Lenin was erected, only to be pulled down again in 1991. Lenins were tolerated in post-Soviet Ukraine, but they had to know their place.

Maidan was the site of a 1990 pro-reform student hunger strike that spread through the country. In 2001 it saw protests against then-president Leonid Kuchma, who was implicated in the murder of Georgiy Gongadze, an investigative journalist who had been decapitated and dumped in the woods. In 2004 Maidan was the site of the Orange Revolution, when hundreds of thousands of orange-clad citizens protested the blatant voter fraud—including state-sanctioned bullying, coercion, and violence—used to elect Viktor Yanukovych as president.

Yanukovych was poorly educated and terrible at public speaking; as a young man he had been convicted for theft and assault. He wasn't promising presidential material. But he was a highly placed member of the Donetsk business "clan," in eastern Ukraine, and Kuchma's camp put him forward to compete with the cosmopolitan Viktor Yushchenko, a liberal, Western-leaning politician who was married to a former US State Department employee. Before the election Yushchenko was poisoned, apparently during a meeting with the head of Kuchma's security services. Though he recovered, his face was disfigured by the lesions caused by dioxin—an ingredient in Agent Orange.

The Orange Revolution protests, which combined a surge of public outrage with political and financial support from Western governments and renegade Ukrainian oligarchs, resulted in the fair election of Yushchenko. While previous Ukrainian presidents had played the West and Russia against each other, trying to extract the maximum benefit from each, Yushchenko chose to side with the West from the start. He declared his hope that Ukraine could help spread democracy throughout the post-Soviet world. Putin was displeased; under Kuchma, Ukraine had drifted back into Russia's orbit, and Yanukovych would have been easier for Russia to manipulate. The West was thrilled, feeling that this was another step toward the peaceful democratization of the entire world, the expansion of Western influence, and the dwindling of Russian power. Western aid poured in, and Ukrainian NGOs flourished; this was how I ended up working with Ukrainian AIDS organizations.

Yushchenko proved a better international figurehead than leader. His prime minister, Yulia Tymoshenko, was a Russian-speaking oligarch from Dnipropetrovsk, in south-central Ukraine. She was canny enough to polish up her Ukrainian and do her hair in phony wheat-gold braids, modeling her image on the Berehynia, a dangerous female water spirit rebranded as a mother goddess. Tymoshenko's economic reforms met with mixed results, and she became involved in a bitter feud with fellow oligarch-turned-politician Petro Poroshenko, who was known as the Chocolate King because he'd made his fortune in the candy business. Just a year after the Orange Revolution, Yushchenko dismissed Yulia Tymoshenko, who became his political opponent.

Yushchenko's anti-Russian liberal rhetoric and promotion of Ukrainian linguistic and national identity were unpopular in Ukraine's east and south and in Crimea, regions with closer ties to Russia and less affinity with Ukrainian nationalism. People in these regions hadn't appreciated the resurrection of prerevolutionary Ukrainian nationalist symbols, either; Ukraine's new national idea seemed designed to exclude them. In 2006 Yanukovych, who'd tried to steal the presidential election just two years earlier, became Yushchenko's prime minister. Ukraine's political, legal, medical, and educational systems were still miserably corrupt, and optimism was starting to ebb. But when I visited in 2007, Ukraine still felt like a relatively free country, a place where something good might happen.

After my workshop was done, Alik took me to drink tall, slim half-liter glasses of beer at Olzhin Dvir, a bar at the upper edge of a cliff-side park that plunged several hundred feet down, with a rickety flight of wooden steps that seemed to lead into a forest. Alik told me there was a neighborhood at the bottom of the steps, a corrupt real estate developer's fantasia, a cluster of retro pastel buildings where no one could afford to live. When he took me to see it, we were the only people on the empty streets, which were littered with bits of rebar and haunted by stray dogs.

From Kiev, I was flying to Warsaw for a harm reduction conference. Alik wasn't going, but his new girlfriend Valya was. She lived not far from the airport, and he proposed that we all sleep at her place the night before our early-morning flight.

Valya's tidy little apartment was in a *khrushchevka*, one of the big, anonymous apartment buildings that Khrushchev built in the 1960s to alleviate the Soviet housing crisis. Alik and I arrived and took off our shoes, as is the custom in Ukrainian and Russian homes. Valya invited us into the kitchen, putting out some Armenian cognac and a box of cheap, too-sweet Ukrainian chocolates that would serve as *zakuski*, the snacks that follow a shot. As we drank and ate, Alik and Valya spoke Russian, and I did my best to follow. Then Alik and I switched to English. Valya didn't seem to care what we were saying; she exuded the single-minded purpose common among people who are addicted to drugs.

Valya and Alik were in a serene mood, because they had some heroin. They decided it was time to get high. Valya had trouble with her veins, which were scarred by years of injecting, so Alik—who was a doctor, after all—injected her, then injected himself. The process was surprisingly innocuous, almost clinical, completed in a calm, businesslike way. I thought about the research papers I had been reading in my cubicle in New York, about how being injected with drugs by someone else increases HIV risk, statistically speaking, and about how women who inject drugs are more likely to have a sexual partner who injects drugs. I knew that this scene illustrated the scientific findings that I read about in my research and used in public health work. And yet this was a story about two characters, not a population, and it couldn't be expressed in statistics. Alik and Valya were two people trying to help other Ukrainians and also themselves, bound together in a relationship of mutual self-destruction. They were like the underworld equivalent of President Yushchenko and his ex-prime minister Yulia Tymoshenko: reformers gone astray, disfigured and overtheatrical. And I was the confused, well-meaning American observer.

Valya was nodding off on the couch, looking in my general direction. Suddenly she sat up, her eyes widening.

"Why aren't you wearing any slippers?" she asked. She had noticed that I was barefoot. In Ukraine, as in Russia, walking on cold floors is believed to lead directly, almost inevitably, to illness.

Valya pulled herself up and tottered over to the entryway, where she found a pair of fluffy pink slippers embroidered with cartoon cats. She handed them to me, watched me put them on, and then sat back down and resumed her nod. Alik found a blanket and put me to bed on the couch, tucking me in. Alik never nodded out.

Kiev's lilacs blossom in May, which is generally considered the city's most beautiful month. As Bulgakov wrote in *White Guard*, in spring "the snow melts, the green Ukrainian grass appears, running in braids across the land . . . . There is no longer even a trace of blood." After the Bolshevik revolution, during the May Day celebrations, "agittrams" and "agitcars" rolled around the city with mobile moving picture shows. In the military parade, there were "living paintings" of the French Revolution, the Paris Commune, and the February and October Revolutions. History creaked through the streets, and winter's bare branches and gray skies were distant memories.

On my last afternoon in Kiev, I passed a woman in plastic leopard-print high heels, holding a sprig of lilac in one hand

and a liter of Amstel Light in the other. She stuck in my mind long after I left; she seemed to embody Kiev as I had encountered it, a blossoming city scarred with the ravines of a violent past, facing an uncertain future, chemical reassurance always close at hand.

Chapter 4

Men's Day

Wyndi, an American consultant in her thirties, was brave and perverse, big-boned and outgoing, with well-toned arms and an exotic mixture of southern charm and radical feminism. An expert on pregnant women and drug use, she was my companion on my second trip to Ukraine, in February 2008.

Our flight was crowded with Hasidic Jews; Uman, in central Ukraine, is a pilgrimage destination, site of the burial place of Rabbi Nachman, founder of the Breslov Hasidic movement. (On their entry forms, pilgrims list the rabbi as their host.) Rabbi Nachman was rumored to be the Messiah. When he fell ill with tuberculosis, he was convinced that God was punishing him for writing a mystical book. He had the two manuscripts of the book burned, in an attempt to bargain for his life. No one knows what the book contained: the rabbi who copied it said, "There is no way of communicating the exaltedness of this book. If it had survived, everyone would have seen the greatness of the Rebbe."

Aerosvit, the now-defunct Ukrainian airline, offered a good opportunity to readapt to the manners of Eastern Europe. The flight attendants denied us blankets, pillows, and even English; I was proud of myself for speaking to them in Russian. My language skills had improved since my last trip. Fantasizing about passing for a person who was not American, I sat alone, half-hypnotized by a sleeping pill, in the exit row, where it was so cold that I had to wear my coat and gloves. When we arrived at the Kiev airport, I wandered into the men's bathroom, in a daze. I thought I saw a syringe in the toilet, then realized it was only a waterlogged cigarette.

Wyndi and I visited a needle exchange point at an AIDS Center in a run-down neighborhood far from the city center. The tiny office consisted of a vestibule stacked with boxes of syringes and a room, perhaps four by eight feet, with space for only about five people at a time. We were there for a meeting with Nikita, a very tall bald man with an alarming gleam in his blue eyes. He took up a lot of space.

Wyndi and I sat on the couch and watched Nikita make us tea. He announced proudly that he'd stolen the mugs in which he served it.

Nikita was gregarious and flirty, and it was obvious that he liked women. Above his head was an oil painting: a naked woman in black garters was getting it from behind from one guy while a second man sucked on her nipple.

Nikita found it odd and rather funny that we were so interested in women drug users.

"The only thing I know about women," he blustered, "is how to get them pregnant!"

Once he was done laughing at his own joke, he ran across the courtyard to summon his gynecologist friend, Irina. While we waited for her to arrive, Nikita told us that he helped women drug users get abortions if they didn't want to have their babies.

"These children have no future," he explained earnestly. He was probably sincere, but he sounded like a bad actor.

After the Soviet Union dissolved, US policy makers hoped that Ukrainian independence would prevent Russia from regaining its imperial power. Ukraine became the third-largest recipient of US aid, after Israel and Egypt. The European Union, the United Nations, and private foundations like OSI also made grants in Ukraine. In a floundering economy, with a social welfare system that barely functioned, NGOs became an important career opportunity, and a means of survival. Educated, English-speaking Ukrainians vied for well-paid positions at international organizations with offices in Ukraine, while others opened their own NGOs. Running an NGO meant having a job (albeit a precarious one, since grants were almost always short term) and having the means to help others, too. In the 1980s, as I later learned, Nikita had worked as a *fartsovshchik*, trading souvenirs for jeans, records, tapes, and other foreign goods that he then sold. (Denim and vinyl inspired particular lust in Soviet people. Alik joked that he once had sex with a girl just to listen to her U2 records.) In the 2000s Nikita had taken on the safer and more dignified work of an NGO employee.

One of the purposes of our trip was to visit programs and decide whether to fund them. It was only natural that NGO employees put on the best performances they could, complete with props, extras, and set pieces. Many NGO staffers were willing to say whatever grant makers wanted to hear.

Nikita's performance was rather perfunctory. He began our conversation by telling us that what we were about to see was a real, radical harm reduction project—he wouldn't be staging any circuses for our benefit. In this we could not doubt him; we spent about two hours in the center and saw only one client, an older man who seemed to know Nikita well but who fled at the sight of us. Nikita explained that the fleeing man had recently approached him, said that he had stopped using, and asked for help starting HIV treatment. Unfortunately, Nikita explained in a tone of resigned regret, the man was lying. Since he was still using, he wouldn't be able to get HIV treatment.

I was furious: we were supposed to be fighting for the right of drug users to receive HIV treatment. Apparently Nikita hadn't gotten the memo.

Irina the gynecologist arrived. She was small and matter-of-fact, with cropped hair. She and Nikita were extremely chummy; she seemed ready to jump into his lap at any moment, right there under the oil painting.

Irina explained that all Ukrainian women received a cash payment of 8,000 hryvnia (then about $2,000, a large sum for a poor Ukrainian) for every child they bore, and that some drug users had babies so that they could use the money for drugs. We had often heard this story, and I was never sure whether it was true. In general, Irina said, many women, whether or not they were drug users, avoided gynecologists because of the intense stigma of premarital sex. Many women even avoided prenatal care unless there was an emergency. In Irina's opinion, the average Ukrainian ob-gyn was simply intolerable.

I was having trouble concentrating. In addition to the oil painting, the room held a small library, with translations of Jane Austen, and several framed pictures of Nikita posing against blue backgrounds, alone or with women. I didn't see a single condom, educational poster, or pamphlet.

Wyndi asked for the bathroom, and Nikita led her there by the hand. When they came back, he said that they'd found someone jerking off; he found this very funny. And what did Nikita do in his office, I wondered, with his oil painting and Jane Austen?

When Nikita showed us his unopened boxes of needles and unassembled sharps containers, I noticed the lone piece of HIV information in the room: a sticker on the closet that said EXTREME SEX and showed two nearly identical scenes. On the left, a stick figure woman was bent over a table that was covered with empty cocktail glasses. Two men with erect penises as long as their arms were lined up behind her.

NO! said the sticker.

On the right was the same picture. This time the men were wearing condoms.

YES! said the sticker.

From the AIDS Center, we went to visit a syringe exchange point located near a pharmacy that sold drugs illegally. Two energetic outreachers worked there: a man and a woman, both former users. Two clients were there when we arrived, but they ran off at the sight of us. Here was the eternal problem of "site visits": you scared the natives. This was another reason that NGOs often had to plan their performances in advance. They had to show the grant makers they were working, but it was impossible to work with the grant makers hanging around.

The outreach workers told us that the pharmacy allowed them to stand outside on the condition that they didn't go into the pharmacy or bother anyone. They hung their box of syringes on a tree so that only the male outreach worker, who was exceptionally tall, could get at them; otherwise, they said, people stole them. It was like hiding your food from bears on a camping trip.

It was too cold to stay out for long, and soon we left to meet up with Alik at Kontraktova Square. Sober for a few months, Alik was more thoughtful than the last time I'd seen him, slower moving, more vulnerable and less grandiose. His skin was clearer and smoother, his hair was neat, and he was wearing a beautiful pinstripe suit in gray flannel.

Alik and Nikita had known each other for a long time. Nikita seemed to occupy a secondary position in the pride; as soon as he saw Alik, he became subdued, almost deferential.

We went to a Georgian restaurant and had delicious *khachapuri*, sizzling cheese-filled bread.

"Unlike some people," Nikita told us as we ate, "I don't want to leave Ukraine just because things aren't going so well. But I don't want to live in shit either, so I decided to start shoveling it out."

Horribly behind schedule, we took a taxi to another organization of potential grantees, a program for poor, HIV-positive mothers. (Not all of them were drug users; some had been infected by sex partners, often by boyfriends or husbands who used drugs.) There we discovered, to our horror, that Anna, the unbelievably diligent manager of the project, had kept a group of clients waiting for hours to meet with us. We were being treated like monarchs on a tour of our realm.

The two young clients, one fashionably dressed and one with only half a mouthful of teeth, spoke passionately about how the program had transformed their lives. If they were acting— and I didn't think they were—they had a special talent. A third woman was a former client who now worked at the program; she was serene, thoughtful, and well spoken. They talked about the unbearably long waits at government clinics, where those who couldn't pay were always last in line. Sometimes, they said, they had to leave to feed their children before they had seen a doctor. Corruption was endemic among health care providers, and because of the $2,000 baby payments, doctors were especially impatient with new mothers who didn't offer bribes; they were rich, after all, if only temporarily. Doctors demanded payment for milk formula that was supposed to be provided free to all HIV-positive mothers. Poor women had little to bargain with, and their poverty could be a death sentence.

Our next stop was Odessa, the port city founded by Catherine the Great and developed by the Duc de Richelieu, a refugee of the French Revolution. Odessa became one of the most cosmopolitan cities in the Russian Empire, and this diversity is still reflected in the city's street names: French Boulevard, Albanian Street, Jewish Street. Odessa was a center of Jewish culture, but the great majority of its Jews were killed during the Second World War. Most of those who survived eventually emigrated, often to New York. Now Odessa, which remains a predominantly Russian-speaking city, feels hollow, trading on the ghosts of the past. Because it's a port, Odessa developed an exceptionally severe drug problem in the 1990s and a corresponding HIV epidemic. The city became notorious for its street children, who lived in the sewers and started injecting drugs before they'd hit puberty.

While we were waiting for our flight, a short, rotund man with white hair and snaggleteeth came up to us, all smiles, and said in a southern accent, "I *thought* I heard Americans!"

I pretended not to hear him, New York style, but Wyndi gave in to her southern instincts and chatted with him. He told us

63

proudly that he was from suburban Maryland and worked for Lockheed Martin.

"Are you ladies here for business or pleasure?" he asked.

Wyndi told him that we were there for work. "Are you in Ukraine for business?" she asked politely.

"Personal business," he chirped. "I'm here to meet a young lady."

A fat little boy, about eight or nine, ran up to him.

"Daddy! Daddy!" he cried. Snaggleteeth excused himself.

On the plane, I listened to him talking to his female companion, a middle-aged Ukrainian woman who spoke excellent English.

"I think I'll tell her you're my translator, just so she doesn't get *confused*," he was saying.

The flight was full of American men. These were the bride-buyers, hoping to find a good old-fashioned wife in the rubble of Communism. The kind of woman who still knew how to be a woman, as the bride-buyers liked to say; the kind who hadn't been ruined by feminism, who still knew that the customer came first. Some of the Odessa beauties the businessmen met online were genuinely desperate to get out of Ukraine; others were con artists.

We were greeted at the Odessa airport by a local harm reduction NGO worker named Natalia, and by a large number of stray dogs. We drove to Hotel Valentina, where Natalia and her NGO had helped us organize a training session on harm reduction for women, for potential grantees from Ukraine and Russia.

Natalia bragged that Deep Purple, one of the bands most beloved in the former Soviet Union, had stayed at Hotel Valentina. A short walk from the discotheques and theme restaurants of Odessa's famous Arcadia beach, the hotel was a summer resort. The windows were duct-taped, but that wasn't enough to keep out the icy air.

Wyndi said that the hotel reminded her of a summer camp, then revised her opinion: it was more like the hotel in *The Shining*. We ate in the giant dining room alone, confronted by an array of Slavic "salads": processed meat and mayonnaise with a sprinkling of vegetables.

The dogs of Odessa sang their wild song all night, and the wind blew a loose piece of metal against the side of the hotel. Every time it hit, it sounded like a gunshot. I hardly slept.

When our training started, the Russian participants complained loudly and frequently that Ukrainians didn't know how to heat a building properly; the Ukrainians grimaced. The Russians seemed to be unaware that as far as gas was concerned, Ukraine was at Russia's mercy. The post-Soviet Ukrainian economy remained dependent on huge subsidies on Russian gas (though Russia also needed Ukrainian cooperation, since its gas flowed through Ukraine to Europe), and Russia used this to manipulate Ukrainian politics. When things got really bad between the two countries, Russia threatened to cut off the gas to Ukraine entirely. This would mean economic disaster and perhaps death by freezing, depending on the season. It wouldn't have been the first time Moscow had cut off Ukraine's means of survival: in the 1930s, during the collectivization of agriculture, millions of Ukrainians starved to death, although they lived on the most fertile land in Europe.

The tactless Russian participants also made jokes about the Ukrainian language, which they found deeply comical, almost comprehensible but not quite, like ludicrously bad Russian. The polite Ukrainians smiled irritably; they had long ago grown tired of being cast as lovable hillbillies. I too was implicated in Russia's linguistic imperialism. With only enough money for one training, we had decided to hold it in Russian, since (we assumed) all the Ukrainians spoke Russian, while the Russians didn't speak Ukrainian. We had simultaneous translation for the English-speaking organizers, and another level of translation would have turned the training into a Tower of Babel. But our choice of language replicated the old Russian-Ukrainian power imbalance. Some of the participants from western Ukraine, where Russian never fully took hold, weren't comfortable speaking Russian, although they understood it. They were reduced to the position of silent observers.

In the van to the airport on our way back to Kiev, Olga, one of our future grantees, told us that today was a very important holiday—Men's Day, the corollary of Women's Day, March 8, a very big deal in the former Soviet Union. "Men's Day" was a war holiday when women congratulated men, and men went to the sauna or the bar and congratulated each other. Technically it was Defenders of the Fatherland Day, previously known as Red Army Day, commemorating the establishment of the Red Army. (There were a number of women in the Red Army, so it wasn't really fair that the holiday should have morphed into an occasion when women give men even more care and attention than usual.) Men's Day remained a national holiday in post-Soviet

Russia, but not in independent Ukraine. Still, Ukrainians kept celebrating: it was a great excuse to get drunk.

Alik invited me to come out to a club with him and watch a boxing match. I imagined two burly Ukrainians in a disco, beating each other to death without gloves.

The club, Khlib, was supposedly the coolest underground spot in Kiev: a grimy, strobe-lit basement with Turkish toilets. We were let in for free by Vasya, Alik's childhood friend from around the way. Vasya was even taller than Alik, with an enormous paunch acquired, Alik said, after he had stopped being addicted to speed. Vasya seized my wrist and stamped it with glow-in-the-dark ink, then steered me through the club by my shoulders. He and Alik were drinking methamphetamine dissolved in Coke. How ironic, I thought, and how perfectly post-Soviet.

I was waiting for the boxing match to start, but it never did—there were just a lot of greasy teenage ravers, leaning against the walls and staring at each other. I was a little ashamed for Alik and Vasya. Unable to part with their youth in the deranged 1990s, they were the only grown men in a club for disaffected teens.

We went to a pub to watch the match, which was being broadcast at four a.m. from Madison Square Garden. A Russian was fighting a Ukrainian.

Part II

Living Together

Chapter 5

Buckwheat and Rye

In September 2008, after receiving a grant from the US government, I moved to Kiev to study Russian and collect oral histories about women's rights and AIDS activism in Ukraine. My new apartment was on Bohdan Khmelnytsky Street, next to the Opera and a few blocks from Khreshchatyk Street, Kiev's main strip, and Maidan. Known in Soviet times as Lenin Street, Bohdan Khmelnytsky Street escaped bombing during the Second World War; it was still lined with beautiful old apartment buildings and theaters in the Parisian style.

I was renting the apartment from an elderly Ukrainian brother and sister, classical musicians who had emigrated to Canada decades earlier. Rather than having the place renovated, they'd left it just as it had been circa 1975, complete with mass-produced armoires and credenzas in ersatz wood, scratchy Ukrainian rugs covering the walls and floors, and curling posters advertising performances at the Opera. The apartment was a time capsule. Soviet-produced classical music records sat near a baby grand piano that was terribly out of tune, its keys yellow and cracked. The kitchen had the white-and-orange-polka-dotted tea set found in every Soviet apartment, matching white and orange plastic furniture, forks and knives stamped with their price in kopecks (legacy of a planned economy), a line for drying laundry, and an old blue and white plastic radio with only one knob, for adjusting the volume. When the radio was made, there hadn't been much reason to change the station.

My elderly neighbor, too, was a relic of the past. She'd lurk at the door of her apartment across the hall, ready for attack, her thin hair in disarray and a look of wild disgruntlement in her eyes. She knew my landlords and seemed to feel responsible for me. When she saw me going out, she berated me if I wasn't wearing a hat and scarf—a typical preoccupation of old Slavic women. Once, after she caught hold of me on the landing and shook me by the shoulders, bellowing, "YOU'LL CATCH COLD," I had to remind her that it was summertime. It was easy to forget the season in the chilly, windowless stairwell, with its chipped marble steps and single bare lightbulb.

My neighbor spoke only Ukrainian, simply increasing her volume when I answered her in Russian. When she came to my door one day to impart some dire warning, it took a while for me to understand that she was telling me to fill up bottles of water, because the water would be shut off the next day. (Water shut-offs were a regular feature of Kiev life; in the summer, the hot water was shut off for weeks at a time, neighborhood by neighborhood. If you didn't like cold showers and were too decadent to heat water on the stove for a bath, you had to make appointments to shower at the apartment of a friend who lived in another area.)

"YOU WON'T BE ABLE TO DRINK TEA!" my neighbor howled. She was red in the face, like the Queen of Hearts.

Outside my building, another epoch reigned. The city was full of sushi bars, strip clubs, casinos, and advertisements for "dating" agencies. As I sat at my kitchen table late at night, drinking tea from a polka-dotted cup or Crimean wine from a Soviet wineglass, I listened to the sound of cars pulling up and leaving, high heels clicking on the pavement, men barking and women laughing. Across the street was a club called Avalon, popular among foreigners trolling for Ukrainian women, and just below my apartment was a Hard Rock Café knockoff, a favorite haunt of moneyed men and their female companions. I'd been there once, before I moved to Kiev, with an Italian I knew through work. Claudio was pleasant and amusing but was also, as I came to understand, a classic "sexpat," among the most common species of foreigner in Kiev.

One of many people who'd left Berlusconi's Italy in search of opportunity, Claudio was making the most of his position as an attractive, well-paid single man in Kiev. He once showed me the address book in his phone. There were hundreds of women's names, each with a little note about the woman's appearance and how and where he'd met her—how else could he keep track of all the Oksanas and Svetas and Alyonas? Often there was also a note about what he had given her. Depending on how much he liked a woman and how sorry he felt for her, he might pay for her taxi home, pay her university fee for the semester, or pay her month's rent. (To be fair, he also gave money every day to the old woman who sat begging outside his apartment building.)

Though he'd lived in Kiev for years, like many expats Claudio still knew hardly a word of Russian or Ukrainian, mustering just enough to give a taxi driver an address or order a meal in a restaurant. His predilections were betrayed by his language: he spoke the diminutive-riddled Russian of flirty young women. This had a grotesque and comical effect, as if he were ordering dinner in baby talk.

Female expats like me were a rarity in Ukraine, which had little to offer a foreign woman. Until very recently it had been hard to buy Western groceries or clothes or get a good Internet connection in Kiev, and Ukraine had still been in the throes of postindependence violence. Most 1990s expats had been businessmen (often very shady ones) trying to profit from the transition, buy something up, sell something off, get rich quick, and have plenty of sex along the way. Sometimes Ukrainian women were not only a diversion, but a source of income. Ukraine is one of the world's most important hair markets, a rare country full of desperately poor blondes. A Ukrainian friend (not a blonde) once told me about going to the party of an Indian expat hair dealer. He took her into his bedroom and opened his drawers: they were full of piles and piles of beautiful blond hair.

Local attitudes, too, were off-putting for Western women. At twenty-six, by Ukrainian standards I was already well on my way to spinsterhood. A friend in her late twenties went to the gynecologist and asked for an IUD; the gynecologist refused, telling her she ought to get pregnant instead. When another friend, also in her late twenties, was hospitalized with appendicitis, she had to be examined by an elderly male gynecologist. (In Ukraine, as in Russia, women even had to get a gynecologist's certificate to use public swimming pools.)

"How old are you?" the gynecologist asked my feverish, exhausted friend. "Are you married? Have you had a baby yet?" She said no, but he kept asking, as if hoping that eventually he'd receive a different response. The nurse explained that having children was the only reason to live.

And yet Ukrainian marriage seemed less than appealing. In many cases, women were the ones supporting the family as well as raising the children and doing the housework; they often seemed to be punished rather than rewarded for their efforts. If a woman reported being abused by her husband, the police might ask if she'd forgotten to make dinner that night.

During my first months in Kiev, I took Russian classes at a small private language school a few blocks from my apartment, near the Golden Gates, which had failed to hold back the Mongol Horde in the thirteenth century but were rebuilt in 1982, to commemorate Kiev's fifteen hundredth anniversary. The director of the school, Andrei, was fond of war and obscenities, and partial to the many baby-faced US Air Force cadets who were sent to his school to learn Russian. He liked to teach new students the word *nedoperepitsya*, a miracle of prefixes (the word contains three) that means "to drink more than you should, but less than you'd planned."

My Russian teacher, Lena, was a small, plump woman with fluffy blond hair. She always whispered, for some reason, and opened her eyes very wide as she spoke. Extraordinarily kind, she was more like an eccentric aunt than a teacher: she once brought in a recording of birdcalls and told me we could practice Russian by identifying them.

A doting mother to her young son, Lena was obsessed with home remedies. She told me about the virtues of cupping and mustard wraps and hot potato inhalers and compresses made from cottage cheese, though she warned me that the cottage cheese cure hadn't been tested on children and ought only to be used on adults, for safety reasons. She tried to convince me that if you put magnets in your shoes and in your drinking water, you'd never become sick, and that you could treat a sinus infection by reducing urine in a spoon, mixing it with honey, and putting it up your nose. (It had to be a child's urine.) She told me that if you made preserves when you had your period, the jar might be cloudy, and that when your liver is angry, everything smells too strong. Slavs are obsessed with their livers, complaining about liveraches the way Americans complain of headaches.

Lena took me on excursions, showing me the city. On Theophany, January 6, she took me to watch Orthodox believers carry a cross onto the frozen Dnieper; the really brave ones jumped through a hole in the ice. Lena whispered that the water from the river was holy now, and that we'd better take some. In the nineteenth century, Kievans carved crosses from river ice dyed red with beets. A priest would bless the water, and the people would pray to exorcise the devil from the Dnieper, hanging crucifixes on their doors and windows so that the devil, driven out of the river, wouldn't try to move in.

We went to Petrivka, a market in the northern part of the city. It had a huge section of used books and magazines, as well as a flea market where old women sold their silverware, pots and pans, knickknacks, even old bras—whatever they had. Lena haggled over an edition of Shakespeare for her son and perused a table of year-old periodicals.

"New news is nice," she said sagely, "but old news is good enough for me."

Lena wasn't a babushka, but she understood the babushka soul, honoring its ancient wisdom. (*Babushka* means "grandmother" but is used in Russian, as in English, to describe any elderly woman with a certain folksy look.) Babushkas hated it when you ate too fast, when you ate too little, when you looked too thin. Babushkas loved romance novels, puzzle books, and women's magazines. Babushkas knew about cannibalism; as children, during the famines, some of them had barely escaped being eaten by their neighbors. Babushkas might or might not know how to cook a boot or give an abortion with herbs, and they believed that birth control gave you a mustache. Babushkas could be caught licking their granddaughters in the middle of the night, trying to remove the evil eye.

Babushkas knew how to grow things, and they sold fruit and vegetables and raw chickens and little plastic cups of forest nuts and berries on every street corner. They foraged when they had to: a friend told me that in the spring, harvesters sometimes found "snowdrops," the corpses of people, usually babushkas, who'd come to the fields to steal corn for their pigs and had frozen to death or been killed by wild boars. The boars were the worst, because they'd start to eat you before you were dead.

Every Monday night, Kiev's babushkas gathered with their few remaining male counterparts and danced to old waltzes played on the accordion. When the weather was warm, they danced on the island between the right and left banks of the city; when it was colder, they gathered in the metro station down the street from my apartment, and I often saw them. I wondered when a babushka stopped being a woman and became a babushka, and whether babushkas were an endangered species. Would they die out, products of a lost way of life? Or would Lena, too, become sturdy and square, with a flowered kerchief over coarse gray hair, swollen ankles dripping with flesh-colored stockings?

*

Babushkas had plenty of free time and a shared outrage over their miserable pensions, high food prices, and bad medical care and housing; they were an important political force. Leonid Chernovetsky, a lawyer who made his fortune in banking, had been elected mayor of Kiev in 2006, in part because of his tremendous appeal to the babushka bloc. He serenaded the babushkas with Soviet tearjerkers, gazing soulfully into their eyes. He offered to auction off kisses; already in his fifties, he still had plump pink lips. He knew how to tell babushkas what they wanted to hear: that they were the true heroes of Ukraine, that the citizens of Kiev should kiss the hems of their garments, that he loved them almost as much as he loved Jesus Christ. (He was an evangelical Christian.) Before the election he gave every babushka in the city rice, buckwheat, and sugar in plastic bags printed with his face. He promised that next time it would be pineapples and caviar, that he would buy their apartments and send them to live in beautiful new homes where they would never be alone. (Apartments in central Kiev were very valuable, so people were always trying to trick babushkas into moving out of them.)

Chernovetsky was nicknamed Cosmos; *cosmonaut* is a slang term for someone fond of dissociative drugs like ketamine and PCP. On one occasion, the mayor crawled under his desk in the middle of a television interview. When he emerged, he explained that he'd been asking God for advice, and that God had said the interview was over. His increasingly erratic and authoritarian behavior prompted calls for a psychiatric examination. In response, he jogged and did pull-ups and laps for news cameras, posing in his little bathing suit, puffing up his chest and flexing his muscles. He was like Putin on acid. The babushkas loved him.

*

One day in late winter, Alik took me to visit his eighty-nine-year-old grandmother, Lyudmila, in her apartment near the Botanical Garden, not far from where I lived. She had prepared a big spread of pickles and little cakes, along with tea. As we ate, she told us that on her birthday, two weeks earlier, a friend had called and sung her an old love song over the phone. He was the last man alive from her class at the medical institute. As a young man, he'd won prizes for singing; at ninety, his voice was still true. He died that night, on her birthday. She smiled serenely and sang us the song, in a sweet, wavering soprano.

Technically, Lyudmila was a babushka. But she had none of the stubborn folkways of the classic babushka, no scent of the village. She never would have fallen for Cosmos's romancing. Lyudmila was the product of the revolutionary intelligentsia—of a world that seemed, in some ways, even more distant than the world of cottage cheese cures and the evil eye.

Lyudmila was born in 1920, the child of two idealists from families of modest means. They had moved to a small town southeast of Kiev to become village teachers, enlightening the people. Some of Lyudmila's ancestors were peasants; her family was part of the gradual movement, in the second half of the nineteenth century, of common people into the intelligentsia. Her mother came from a big Jewish family in Podil, and Lyudmila made frequent visits to the capital city.

Taking advantage of the Soviet Union's emancipatory policies toward women, Lyudmila went to medical school. When war broke out, she and her fellow medical students dug trenches around Kiev. After the medical school was evacuated, teachers and students marched to Kharkiv, in eastern Ukraine. Lyudmila finished her studies early and was sent to the western front to serve as a doctor in a rifle regiment. Her new husband, a Jewish man from Krasnoyarsk, in Russia, was assigned to the same regiment.

Lyudmila's first official duty was to act as medical supervisor at the execution of two deserters. As Alik put it, "They didn't know who the fuck Hitler was—they just wanted to go home." But most of her time was spent rescuing the wounded. Over the course of the war, she saved the lives of about a hundred soldiers and officers.

Lyudmila's husband was killed in 1943, just a few months after Lyudmila gave birth to a son who was sent to live in a village with her parents, outside the combat zone. In Kiev, most of Lyudmila's large Jewish family had been killed at the Babi Yar ravine, along with 150,000 other Jews, Roma, Ukrainian nationalists, and Soviet prisoners of war. Posters had been plastered around Kiev ordering all of Kiev's Jews to Babi Yar with their documents, money, valuables, warm clothing, and linen. When they'd finished shooting, the Germans blew up the walls of the ravine, burying the corpses along with any wounded.

Before he died, Lyudmila's husband gave her a Walther, a little German gun, telling her, "If anything happens—you know who we are." He meant that they were Jews, and that it would be better to commit suicide than to be captured by the Germans. Lyudmila carried her Walther with her through the war and after, when she moved into a tiny, dirty room on ruined Khreshchatyk Street, which would soon be rebuilt by German prisoners of war.

There wasn't much to eat in the city, so Lyudmila's son stayed with her parents and their kitchen garden, in the country. Only twenty-three, Lyudmila went on with her life, working as a surgeon. She dressed in fashionable foreign clothes, brought by soldiers, that she found at the Jewish bazaar, and she made new friends, going to dances and the theater. With an acute shortage of men and much anxiety about the responsibilities women had assumed during the war, female veterans were often treated viciously. Lyudmila was accused of being a PPZh—a *pokhodno-polevaya zhena*, a camp wife, a comfort woman, a whore. She brushed off the accusations and, according to Alik, acquired not one but two lovers, one of them a Party official with a limousine and an apartment with five rooms.

One day a beautiful man named Georgiy came into Lyudmila's ward with his pregnant wife, who died in childbirth. Georgiy came from a long line of engineers, architects, and artistic types. He and Lyudmila fell in love, got married, and had a daughter, Alik's mother. Lyudmila outlived her husband and her son, who drank himself to death. She survived the transition from Communism, and she helped raise Alik. She lived to be ninety-three, but she never became a babushka.

Lena was a better guide to Kiev than a Russian tutor. Alik suggested a new teacher: Vakhtang, a Georgian-Ukrainian philosophy professor and his friend of many years.

Vakhtang was darkly handsome, with taste that ran to purple fedoras and velvet jackets. In addition to German philosophy, his interests included his band, in which he sang and played the guitar, and frequent trips to Spain. (He came from an affluent family.) His wife, Marta, was equally good-looking; it was said that in their prime they had been the most beautiful couple in Podil.

Several times a week, I went to Vakhtang's office in Podil for my lesson. I don't know what Alik had told him about me, but

Vakhtang had decided to teach me Russian by having me read short stories that were almost always about sex, death, or drugs. The first one we read, I think, was Bulgakov's "Morphine," about a doctor who becomes addicted to morphine during a winter posting in a remote village, missing the 1917 Revolution entirely. ("If I hadn't been spoiled by a medical education, I would say that a person can only work properly after a shot of morphine.") After I'd read a story, I'd paraphrase it to Vakhtang in Russian as he sat in silence, fixing me with his stern gaze. I don't remember him smiling even once. His was a terrifying and therefore highly effective pedagogical method. I will never forget trying to paraphrase Ivan Bunin's story "Antigone," blushing as I searched for the words to explain that the master of the house had seduced his maid in the drawing room. Bunin had implied it with subtle artistry; I had to rely on simple verbs.

"And then—and then—they sleep together," I stammered.

"Do they *sleep* together?" Vakhtang said coldly. "Do they lie down? Do they go to bed?"

"No," I said. Vakhtang introduced me to several words that, while equally inoffensive, were more technically correct.

We read some of Isaac Babel's stories about the Jewish criminals of Odessa, and Vakhtang told me to try to find the parts that were in incorrect Russian—the Jewish thieves had their own way of speaking. I was delighted by these irregularities, which I found miraculously familiar, their syntax more comprehensible than that of Russian literary language; Yiddish-inflected Russian followed some of the same patterns as Yiddish-inflected English, familiar to a child of New York City. I discovered the joy of reading in Russian (correct or otherwise) for the first time. Every narrative surprise was thrilling, because it was so hard won.

By the time summer arrived, I had learned to speak Russian, though my Russian was speckled with Ukrainian words I'd picked up from signs and from the speech of those around me. Many Ukrainians mixed the Russian and Ukrainian languages, whether unwittingly or on purpose. This mix was called *surzhyk*, which is the name for a low-grade blend of wheat and rye flour. Since prerevolutionary times, *surzhyk* had been associated with Ukrainian-speaking peasants trying to make their way in the Russian-speaking city, and with poorly educated people who spoke the language of the streets rather than the language of books. *Surzhyk* therefore carried a stigma, as it does today.

In *White Guard*, Bulgakov writes about a wolfish bandit who speaks "a frightening and incorrect language, a mix of Russian and Ukrainian words—a language familiar to inhabitants of the City who had spent time in Podil, on the banks of the Dnieper, where in summertime the wharf's winches whistle and spin, and shabby men unload watermelons from barges." Some of Bulgakov's characters speak *surzhyk* when they are trying to accommodate the Ukrainian speakers who are seizing political power; in this context, *surzhyk* is a language of compromise, or cowardice. When Nikolka Turbin, in *White Guard*, sees his brother-in-law, Talberg, studying a Ukrainian grammar book, he knows for certain that Talberg is a man without principles. Sure enough, Talberg abandons Turbin's sister and flees with the Germans. In post-Soviet Ukraine, *surzhyk*—especially in the media—was seen by some patriots as a betrayal of the purity of the Ukrainian language, and therefore of Ukraine itself. Meanwhile, Russians considered *surzhyk* the risible half-language of southern hicks. Even speaking good Russian with a Ukrainian accent marked a person as provincial in Moscow or St. Petersburg. Soon enough I would be scolded by Russian acquaintances for speaking with a Ukrainian accent, or for using Ukrainian words by accident.

Some Ukrainians scolded me for studying Russian rather than Ukrainian—we were in Ukraine, after all. Language policy was one of Ukraine's most fraught political issues. In 1989 Ukraine passed a law making Ukrainian the only official state language. Government institutions suddenly switched to Ukrainian, which caused problems: many Ukrainian citizens weren't even fluent in everyday Ukrainian, let alone familiar with the Ukrainian versions of the specialized terms of their fields. Sergei, a doctor I knew at the Ukrainian Network of People Living with HIV/AIDS, told me about scrambling to learn Ukrainian medical terminology after spending years learning it in Russian. Street signs were changed to Ukrainian. To save money, this was often done by simply altering the existing signs, since many place names differed only by a couple of letters; in some of Kiev's metro stations, you can still see the places where the Russian letters used to be. As an act of resistance, especially in Russian-speaking regions, people defaced the signs so that the spelling was Russian again. Some Russian speakers—especially in the predominantly Russian-speaking east and south and in Crimea—were angry at the sudden change of language. They felt, not without reason, that they were being pushed out of the new Ukraine.

In the 1990s and 2000s there were multiple attempts to "Ukrainize" the media and advertising. Some of the angriest popular debates took place around the dubbing of imported shows like the American soap opera *Santa Barbara*, which was hugely popular in the former Soviet Union. People in Russian-speaking Crimea, in particular, were furious when the show was dubbed into Ukrainian, which they couldn't understand. Eventually the Crimean parliament decided to switch *Santa Barbara* back to Russian, in hopes of "avoiding the kindling of anti-Ukrainian actions." At the same time, Ukrainian television dubbing became famous for its high quality, with clever insertion of Ukrainian cultural references. One of my Ukrainian friends, raised in a Russian-speaking household, told me that he learned Ukrainian by watching *Alf*.

Partly in response to the new Ukrainization rules, television shows started practicing "nonreciprocal bilingualism." A talk show host might speak Ukrainian, as mandated, while guests would speak whichever language they preferred. Some talk shows had one host who spoke only Ukrainian and another who spoke only Russian. This reflected common practice in Ukraine's public sphere and on the street. People would switch between Russian and Ukrainian depending on the circumstances. For instance, Russian speakers might switch to Ukrainian in markets, hoping to get better prices by emphasizing their kinship with the Ukrainian-speaking country people who'd come to sell produce and meat there.

I myself often engaged in nonreciprocal bilingualism in shops. A salesperson would speak to me in Ukrainian; I would answer in Russian, because my knowledge of Ukrainian was only passive; the person would continue speaking Ukrainian. Many Russian visitors to Ukraine considered this a form of rudeness, an uncouth nationalism; in fact, it was a compromise that worked well for most of the population. My friend Yulia M.'s father spoke Russian as his primary language, while her mother spoke Ukrainian; through decades of happy marriage, they mixed the two languages, as many Ukrainians did.

Though political debates about language policy could be explosive, in daily practice most Ukrainians were easygoing and practical about language choice. Ukraine's bilingualism made it an easier place to learn Russian than Russia itself. Russians are more prescriptive about language use, less tolerant of mistakes, and less able—or, I think, willing—to understand the Russian of a nonnative speaker. Ukrainians, being accustomed to a mixture of languages and a range of dialects, pay less attention to mistakes, and figure out what you mean much more quickly. This was something I loved about Ukraine; to me, it seemed a mark of pluralism, of cosmopolitanism.

Occasionally, I'd encounter a nationalist zealot who would refuse even to listen to Russian. I met very few of these, but every encounter was memorable. One guy in a bar demanded that we speak English rather than Russian, and then lectured me about how the only way to stop Russia was to blow it up. In a hotel in Lviv, in nationally minded western Ukraine, a hotel receptionist refused to speak to me until Alik intervened and explained that I was speaking Russian because I was American. Suddenly the receptionist smiled sweetly, and we finished our conversation in Russian. She didn't speak English.

At the same time, I knew that I was missing out on a certain side of Kiev life. My friend Orysia, a Cleveland-born child of the Ukrainian diaspora, was another grant-funded student in Kiev. She had her very own Ukrainian babushkas, who had taught her to eat honeycomb and to drink birch juice for her health—but with caution, because too much birch juice would make your liver angry. Orysia had grown up speaking Ukrainian and learned Russian only as an adult. She was quiet when we hung out with my friends, who spoke mostly Russian; but she was embraced (often literally) by Ukrainian speakers, who saw her as a long-lost daughter who'd finally come home. One summer in Podil, we went to buy fruit from her favorite corner babushka. Orysia's conversation with the babushka in Ukrainian about which berries were the tastiest had the tenderness and intimacy of a conversation between an actual grandmother and grand-daughter. Russian was the language of urban life, of industry, of empire; Ukrainian was the language of grandmothers, of home.

Chapter 6

Carpathian Cowboys

Apart from Alik, my closest friend in Kiev was Alina, who'd
known Alik for many years. Around 2000 Alina had won a
green card lottery and moved to America, without speaking
English. Charming, clever, and highly adaptable, the child of a
Ukrainian mother and an Azeri absentee dad, she'd moved up
quickly: from a trailer park in Pennsylvania to a job selling glass
animals and Russian dolls in Brooklyn, and then to graphic
design at a Manhattan department store. During a visit to New
York in 2006, Alik brought me to meet her at a boardwalk café
in Brighton Beach, New York's biggest Russian neighborhood.

"Who is this Natasha Rostova?" Alina asked him scornfully in
Russian. She was comparing me to the sweet, starry-eyed young
heroine of *War and Peace*. For most people, this would have
been a compliment, but Alina was skeptical of youthful idealism and easy dazzlement. She was pleased, if also embarrassed,
when I understood her jab and answered back. We became close
friends, hanging out at her apartment in Brooklyn and watching
Russian television. Alina moved back to Kiev not long before I
arrived; she was helping to raise her brother's small daughter,
who looked exactly like her.

Alina introduced me to her old friend Igor, who was from
Rakhiv, a small town in the Carpathian Mountains. Igor had an
endless store of tall tales about western Ukraine. One night in a
bar, he told me about a friend in Lviv who could summon rain or

snow and had made himself immune to all drugs. This friend had
also, Igor claimed, been honored by the Pope, who was not at all
opposed to Ukrainian witchcraft. But the most magical place of
all was Rakhiv, where the mountains were so high that you could
walk through the clouds, and where the Hutsuls, the "Carpathian
cowboys," as Igor called them, lived above the law, literally: Rakhiv
is the highest city in Ukraine. Once it got warm, we headed west.

As we drove away from Kiev, we seemed to retreat from moder-
nity: the landscape became steeper and greener, and we saw
more and more livestock on the side of the road. Igor's Russian
became more Ukrainian gradually, almost imperceptibly, so that
by the time we reached Transcarpathia, he was speaking pure
Ukrainian, without any Russian words mixed in. By then we
were in Rakhiv, passing old men in carts drawn by horses with
red-tasseled bridles. The rivers surged through the hills on rocky
beds, past trees that had just come into blossom.

Rakhiv was half rustic and half modern, a village of concrete
houses with tin roofs and Limp Bizkit graffiti. We wandered
through an abandoned Soviet carton factory, built, according to
the date on its facade, in 1950. The building had no roof and was
surrounded by apple trees. In a field on a hill, we passed a metal
skeleton—probably a train car—sitting in the grass, with white
flowers growing from what had once been a floor. This was the
way in Rakhiv, as in much of Ukraine: nature's lushness embracing industrial decay. A rooster couldn't stop crowing, though it
was already midday, and his call mixed with techno blaring from
passing cars. An old woman in a kerchief was shoveling a hole in
the middle of a dirt road. Everyone we passed greeted us with

the same words: "Christ is risen." This, Alina explained, was the post-Easter greeting.

In 1887 Habsburg geographers declared a village near Rakhiv the "geographical center of Europe." Although it was rarely considered a serious contender for the title anymore, the town was still proud of this distinction. Rakhiv was certainly a crossroads. Many of its inhabitants spoke three or more languages (Igor spoke five); its small population was Ukrainian, Hungarian, Romanian, Russian, Hutsul, Rusyn.

Igor struggled to explain who the Rusyn were, though he was himself half Rusyn. "Some people say they're Ukrainian, some people don't," he shrugged. When the term *Ukrainian* came into wide use in western Ukraine in the early twentieth century, the Rusyns of Transcarpathia chose to stick to their earlier name. Sometimes they're considered a distinct ethnic group, sometimes a subset of Ukrainians. In the mountain air Ukrainianness became particularly fragile, crumbling at the touch.

Today we often think of ethno-national identity as something that has always existed, something close to race: a man is Ukrainian, as were his ancestors before him. In fact, for most of history, identity had to do with familial, tribal, imperial, or religious loyalties, and communities existed on a much smaller scale. What mattered was your village, your extended family, your local dialect, your faith. The ethno-national identities that we take for granted today were largely the product of nineteenth-century nationalist movements that created "imagined communities," a sense of blood relation between people who had never met and who had dramatically different ways of life.

Language became a convenient mark of ethnicity, easier to classify than other components of ethnic identity, like folklore,

customs, cuisine, or dress. The languages of church and empire—
Latin, French, German, Church Slavonic, Russian—were used
across huge territories, lingua francas for educated elites; but
before the advent of politically motivated efforts to standardize
and promote the languages of the common people, there was a
spectrum of dialects across the land, much as Igor's speech shaded
from Russian into Ukrainian over the course of our car ride. People
in eastern Ukraine spoke a version of Ukrainian that was closer to
Russian than the dialect spoken in western Ukraine, which incorporated elements of Belarusian, Polish, Slovakian, or Hungarian,
depending on the location. Even late into the twentieth century,
people could disagree about which language they were speaking.
The scholar Laada Bilaniuk writes about a Ukrainian linguist
who, on a train in the early 1990s, praised a fellow passenger for
her "beautiful, pure Ukrainian language"—to which this fellow
traveler replied that she was speaking Belarusian. Transcarpathia,
where Rakhiv is located, was the last region of today's Ukraine
to adopt a modern ethno-national consciousness, and some residents remain reluctant to join the national mainstream.

In the center of Rakhiv, a handsome metal Hutsul, a
"Carpathian cowboy," burst out of a boulder, in his fedora and
embroidered blouse and vest, a sack slung over his shoulder,
an ax in his hand. The inscription on the brand-new monument announced, "We know who we are." Following the custom
of the region, by which people referred to their dialect as "our
language" rather than giving it a name, the monument didn't
need to specify the man's tribe. We know who we are, said the
Hutsuls. We don't need you to tell us. Russians, Hungarians,
Austrians, and Ukrainians passed through, but the Hutsuls
(who, like the Rusyn, are sometimes, but not always, considered

a subethnicity of Ukrainians) were there to stay. The Hutsul houses in Rakhiv were decorated with mirrors on the outside walls, to ward off misfortune.

We went to meet Igor's friend Vanya at a café, where we had Ukrainian beer, Parliament Lights, and dried fish. Vanya had an elfin quality, with a crooked nose and a maniacal grin. Like everyone else in Rakhiv, regardless of age or sex, he was wearing a tracksuit—a *sportivnyi kostyum*, as it's called in Russian. Young women paired their tracksuits with high heels; old men wore them with fedoras. Only babushkas were immune, wearing a more traditional costume of flowered head scarves, galoshes, and men's blazers.

As we walked along the ridge of a mist-covered mountain, passing flocks of black and white sheep, Igor told us that Vanya had robbed a Prague bank and a Warsaw jewelry store. Both times he'd done it on impulse, and both times he'd been caught, but the Warsaw jail had gotten fed up with his misbehavior and sent him back to Ukraine. It occurred to me that this unlikely tale was less fact than metaphor: the people of Rakhiv were such shape-shifting cosmopolitans that they could slip across any European border and plunder capitals on a whim. When you lived in the geographical center of Europe, high above national boundaries, able to speak any language you pleased, you could do things that were unimaginable for those subject to the ordinary constraints of ethnicity and nationality.

Still, Rakhiv hadn't been impervious to Soviet authority. The local Hutsul chief, Igor said admiringly, had served in the Soviet Army, where he'd killed six Uzbek soldiers who were trying to beat him up. He served twenty-five years in prison, then came back to Rakhiv to be a cowboy.

The mountain people weren't immune to nostalgia for socialism, either.

"Life is too uncertain now that the Union is gone," Igor's father complained over shots of vodka and a Hutsul corn dish called *banush*. "Now you choose a path, but you don't know where it will end."

He reminisced about the day Rakhiv's men had gathered to watch porn in 1990, when they'd first gotten international television service.

"It was about Catherine the Great!" he chuckled. "Or maybe Rasputin."

We drove to Igor's grandmother's house near the Hungarian, Slovakian, and Romanian borders. Her village made Rakhiv, a small mountain town where no building was more than five stories high, look like an ultramodern metropolis. She and her daughter drew water from a well and used an outhouse.

"She doesn't speak our language?" she inquired in her Rusyn dialect, pointing a trembling, bony finger at me. I did not. Even Alina had trouble understanding her.

We went to the family cemetery to pay our respects. "Did they say anything?" Igor's grandmother asked when we got back. Alina and I spent the night in a huge, sagging bed that dated from the days of the Austro-Hungarian Empire. The region was full of ghosts, but not the frightening kind.

Being in the geographical center of Europe—and more importantly, on the EU's poorly policed eastern border—meant that smuggling and counterfeiting thrived in Ukraine's western regions. The Romanian border was lined with people selling

94

fruits and vegetables, live chickens and ducks, cheap clothing, and all kinds of other goods, often from shipping containers that had been made into roadside shops. People in this area were rumored to make and sell fake French wine, fake Scotch, fake Marlboros, and fake Ecstasy, smuggling goods, both real and fake, into the EU, where they were sold on the black market. Smugglers dug tunnels beneath the borders; one even had a small train. Others used hang gliders to drop contraband onto EU territory.

In green fields of yellow flowers, we saw brand-new half-built brick and concrete castles, many of them with turrets and other Gothic ornamentation. There were balconies without railings, windows without glass, doorways without doors, and few signs of ongoing construction. Igor joked that the local smuggler princes built their castles mostly to compete with their neighbors; they'd dig an expensive swimming pool in a bean field and replace it with a tennis court the next year. They built them for their daughters, he laughed: the better the daughter, the bigger the castle. Finishing the mansions was beside the point.

Lviv, the unofficial capital of western Ukraine, has been reinvented many times. Lviv was part of Poland from the fourteenth to the eighteenth centuries, then part of the Austro-Hungarian Empire, where it was called Lemberg. (The city retains a threadbare Habsburg glamour, with graying Gothic crypts and wood-paneled Austrian coffeehouses.) In the nineteenth century Lemberg was mostly Polish, German, and Jewish, though the surrounding countryside was full of peasants who called themselves Ruthenians, and who were learning to call themselves Ukrainians. Because the Austro-Hungarian Empire was less hostile than the Russian Empire was to the use of the Ukrainian language and promotion of Ukrainian ethno-national identity, Lemberg became a base for Ukrainian-language publishing and for Ukrainian educational and cultural organizations. After World War I Lemberg became Lwów, a Polish city in which only one-sixth of the inhabitants were Ukrainian.

During the Second World War the city went to the Soviets and then the Germans, becoming part of the Soviet Union after the war ended. It was renamed Lvov, the Russian version of Lwów. Lvov's Jews had been killed in concentration camps, mass shootings, or pogroms, and its Poles and Germans had been driven out, deported, or killed. Ukrainians from the countryside helped fill the empty spaces in the city. It was only as part of the Soviet Union that Lviv became the quintessentially Ukrainian city, the bastion of Ukrainian identity, that it is today. When Ukraine became independent, Russian Lvov officially became Ukrainian Lviv. The city had never been Russified, and it remains the only major Ukrainian city where the public sphere is predominantly Ukrainian-speaking.

On our first night in Lviv, we visited a discotheque behind a McDonald's. It was classic post-Soviet entertainment: flashing neon and black lights, dancers flapping listlessly to anonymous Euro-techno. Though the music was too loud for conversation, we did our best to chat with a six-foot-tall woman in fringed white knee boots, and with her pudgy companion, a man in a white Andy Warhol wig and matching sunglasses. He was smoking a cigar and wore a huge onyx ring on his middle finger.

The next day, Lviv's "City Day," men in chain mail, armor, and red velvet cloaks rode horses through the street, waving banners. Hutsuls in colorful folk costumes played violins and danced.

Mimes did tricks on unicycles, women in princess dresses walked on stilts, and huge Cossack puppets strode down the cobbled street. People in camouflage rode by on a tank, waving a flag: Ukrainian nationalists.

Lviv had a somewhat unwarranted association with the interwar and World War II-era Ukrainian Insurgent Army (UPA) and Organization of Ukrainian Nationalists (OUN), which were based in the forests and villages of western Ukraine and fought for decades against the Soviets and Germans, killing many thousands of Poles and Jews as well. OUN and UPA pursued a violent, authoritarian, ultranationalist ideology based on the dream of a Ukrainian state cleansed of outsiders, and they briefly allied themselves with the Nazis against the Soviets, before the Nazis turned on them. The Soviets worked hard to purge their lands of OUN and UPA, killing more than 150,000 western Ukrainians, deporting 200,000, and incarcerating some 110,000—far more than had actually fought with the nationalist guerrillas. After 1991, OUN and UPA became tragic heroes of the new Ukrainian history. Orange Revolution president Yushchenko awarded two of their most famous leaders, Stepan Bandera and Roman Shukhevych, the posthumous title "Hero of Ukraine" in 2007.

In Lviv, entrepreneurs with a sense of humor decided to capitalize on their city's reputation as a hotbed of Ukrainian nationalism. They opened Kryivka, a Ukrainian nationalist theme bar in the cellar of a Habsburg building that was once the Venetian embassy.

The restaurant's entrance was through an unmarked archway off the main square. Halfway down a flight of stone stairs, we gave the "password" to a man in a soldier's uniform.

97

"Glory to Ukraine!" he said. He was holding a vintage machine gun.

"Glory to heroes," we replied. He poured us shots of honey liqueur from a metal flask. The slogans "Glory to Ukraine," "Glory to heroes," and "Death to enemies" had been popular with Ukrainian nationalists in the first half of the twentieth century.

We passed through a tunnel into the bar, which was meant to look like a Ukrainian hideout during the Second World War. The walls were decorated with vintage weapons and old photos of Ukrainian guerrillas. Kryivka was part of a chain that included a restaurant honoring Lviv native Leopold von Sacher-Masoch, where sexy waitresses promised discount cards for anyone who'd consent to a lashing, and a "Jewish" restaurant that had no prices on the menu because patrons were expected to bargain. But Kryivka was by far the most popular, visited by almost every tourist to the city.

Somewhat ironically, many of Kryivka's visitors were Russian tourists looking for a thrill. For people raised on the Soviet vilification of Ukrainian guerrillas, Kryivka was like a haunted house. Its chief function was to confirm that you were safe; Russia had killed off the *real* Ukrainian guerrillas long ago. Ukrainian nationalism was reduced to kitsch, play-acting by the "Little Russians," as Ukrainians were called in the Russian Empire.

When a Russian lifestyle TV show filmed a segment on Kryivka, the program's cheerful host explained that the restaurant was run by "Ukrainian nationalists who don't like Russians." Armed men were shown dragging a man in a Red Army hat—the kind ubiquitous in post-Soviet tourist markets—through the restaurant, then throwing him into the "dungeon."

"Of course, this is all just a tourist attraction!" the host reassured his viewers.

After receiving the "password," the obliging doorman told the television personality, in a mix of Ukrainian and Russian, that the liqueur he had poured was poison for *moskali*—the derisive Ukrainian term for Russians. When the *moskal* ordered his meal in Russian, a jovial old soldier strode in, shooting his pistol offhandedly and saying, in Ukrainian, "We've received information that there's a *moskal* in our midst. Does anyone know where he is?"

The *moskal*, who was dressed in a hipster's red plaid shirt, said gamely, in Russian, "I don't know!"

The soldier tested him on his Ukrainian pronunciation, to laughter from the other guests.

"If you sing a Ukrainian song, you'll live," the soldier said as he threw the host into the dungeon. "If not—we'll shoot you!" The *moskal* produced a few lines of a Ukrainian folk song, and returned to the dinner table.

Chapter 7

The People's Music

On a sunny spring day, Alik and I walked down one of Kiev's grandest streets, with its billowing fin de siècle facades, through an archway, past a shoe repair stand, and into a yard, a classic Kiev *dvor*, covered in bright graffiti. We were on our way to visit Zakhar, a youngish artist who had started a new underground gallery in an old garage. The gallery probably would have been called Garage if that hadn't already been the name of a chic new gallery in Moscow, an oligarch-funded project located in a bus garage built by the avant-garde architect Konstantin Melnikov in 1927. Zakhar's was a regular garage. There were no oligarchs involved, just a moderately rich lady who'd agreed to let Zakhar use the space.

Zakhar was in his late twenties, athletic but gaunt, with high cheekbones, sunken blue eyes, a Roman nose that had been broken more than once, and a large collection of scars. He wore neon-green plastic sunglasses, a shiny thrift shop blazer with shoulder pads, swim trunks, and the cheap slip-on plastic sandals favored by middle-aged Ukrainian women. A few other languid art-hipster types were lounging around in similar attire.

Alik introduced us in Russian. As he looked me over, Zakhar reminded Alik in Ukrainian that he didn't much like the Russian language. Alik told him that I, "Sopha," only spoke Russian; Zakhar found this explanation acceptable, and showed us around.

The central piece in the garage was a new work of Zakhar's, of which he was very proud. He had stolen a dumpster, spray-painted it gold, and lined the inside with blue bathroom tiles. The result was strangely beautiful. We took turns having our pictures taken inside the dumpster, sitting on a little tiled stool. We looked at some of the other art, in which the male member played a prominent role. One work was a video of someone watching porn on a cell phone while standing in an art gallery.

Zakhar took us back outside, to a rusted blue car. "What do you think of my car?" he asked. "I like to sit in it and think things over. Everything works but the engine."

He sat down in it and demonstrated. "Onward!" he shouted, pointing into the future like Lenin.

I found Zakhar fascinating, but hard to talk to. I tried to make a joke about garage rock, but he had never heard of it; I tried to explain about New York artist lofts but couldn't make an impression. I wasn't sure whether the problem was the language barrier or the cultural distance. Still, we got along. He and his friends fed me homemade jam and gave me knowing looks, then invited me and Alik to a psychiatric hospital to look at a room where they'd been asked to paint a mural. But Alik had another engagement, and I wasn't ready to go to the mental hospital unaccompanied.

A few days later Zakhar took me to the Botanical Garden, where he explained that he was deeply depressed because someone had broken into his garage and stolen his dumpster and his bicycle. (They didn't bother with his car.) He suspected that his enemies were to blame, but he wasn't sure which ones.

"Do you like *plavlenyi* cheese?" he asked, cheering up.

"What is that?"

"It's the cheapest and worst kind of cheese. We always used to eat it in the Soviet Union. It's delicious! I'll give you some as a gift." He took a damp, foil-wrapped square from his backpack, along with a liter of Ukrainian beer. I took the beer but declined the cheese.

Zakhar told me that he'd grown up partly in an *internat*, a Soviet boarding school, because his mom wanted to "party," as he put it. She took him home on Sundays. When I met him, he was living sometimes with his girlfriend, Alla, a Russian who had inherited an apartment in Moscow and lived on its rent in Kiev, and sometimes with his mother. Zakhar bragged that he'd never read a book. I think this was an exaggeration, but he certainly wasn't one for book learning. His specialty was a knowledge of social categories and types, a watchfulness obscured by his expert performance of the role of the post-Soviet madman who can't be held responsible for his actions. With the help of large quantities of fortified wine, Zakhar said what he wasn't allowed to say, stripped in public, and provoked friends, enemies, and strangers until they were ready to assault him. He was a genuine iconoclast: when some rich people built a tacky statue of the Little Prince near his garage, Zakhar smashed it with a hammer. In retaliation, the rich people hired toughs to break his legs.

Several years after we met, I discovered Zakhar's prototype: Pyotr Mamonov, front man of the 1980s experimental Russian rock band Zvuki Mu. Maybe Zakhar knew his fate as soon as he looked in the mirror: Mamonov, too, has a Roman nose, high cheekbones, fair hair, deep-set eyes, and a slender, broad-shouldered build. In videos from the 1980s, he stands rigidly onstage, staring into the distance, twitching like he's been possessed, or at least electrocuted. Like Zakhar, Mamonov was heavily scarred by attacks and accidents. During a fight in St. Petersburg's Hermitage Gardens in the 1960s, somebody stabbed him with a sharpened file and broke his ribcage, putting him in a coma and leaving a scar above his heart. On walks in the park, he'd run into walls at full speed just to see how people would react.

One onlooker described Mamonov's performance style as "Russian folk hallucination," and it was clear that, regardless of any resemblance to Western punk or New Wave musicians, he was doing something distinctly Russian. Driving audiences insane in Moscow and Leningrad, Kharkiv, Vladivostok, and Tashkent, he was the violent, alcoholic patron saint of Russia's musical "Red Wave." Gorbachev's dry laws almost killed him, as he resorted to drinking first cologne, then solvent. But, in the 1990s, after he'd been picked up by Brian Eno, he converted to Orthodox Christianity and moved to a village. In Pavel Lungin's 2006 film *The Island,* he plays a man who shot his friend in the Second World War and ends up living as a monk on a remote island in northern Russia, trying to expiate his sins. In real life, Mamonov spent most of his time farming, and lost his front teeth. When *The Island* aired on Russian television, its ratings rivaled those of President Putin's New Year speech. After the film received the blessing of the Orthodox Church, the lame, the blind, the orphaned, and the wretched started showing up in Mamonov's village, hoping to be healed.

In 2009 Zakhar hadn't found God or attracted any pilgrims, but as a lifelong Kiev scenester, he knew pretty much everyone in town. One night he introduced me to another famous Kiev character. Topor, whose name means "ax" in Russian, was a self-described "charismatic Moldovan," an accordionist, a singer, and leader of a street band called Toporkestra. Tall and slender, with long, thick black hair, a black beard, large black eyes, and pale skin, Topor looked a lot like Jesus, or at least like an Orthodox priest; crazy people and drunks often approached him for help. He had a similar allure for old women and little children.

Topor told us that he had been hired to play at the birthday party of the grandson of a "gypsy baron" outside Kiev, and invited us to come along. We got in his car, along with a pair of college students we'd acquired while standing on the street.

"But Sophie, you have to say you're Zakhar's wife," Topor warned as he drove, "or else the gypsies might try to steal you."

We drove along the highway that led to the airport and pulled off onto a rutted dirt road. The gypsy baron's village was full of cheap suburban palaces with ornate woodwork and bare concrete steps, more finished versions of the smuggler castles Igor had pointed out to me on the western Ukrainian border. We were greeted with great enthusiasm by our hosts, who brought us into a vestibule with a door on either side. On the left was a dining room, with the men of the family seated around a long wooden table. On the right was a living room, where the women of the family sat quietly. Topor introduced me and Zakhar as man and wife, and our hosts invited us all into the dining room to sit with the men.

Topor sang a few Balkan songs, accompanying himself on his battered red accordion, and then the men started to sing, in order of age. First was the birthday boy, who was only about nine years old but sang very beautifully, in Romani, the language of the Roma, who are usually called "gypsies" in Russian and Ukrainian. They worked their way up through the family, from the adolescents to young adults to the middle-aged, until the grandfather of the family sang most beautifully of all. The songs were interspersed with toasts; the women kept bringing in more food and drink, swift and silent.

"I don't think you're really married to that guy," said the Roma man nearest to me, gesturing toward Zakhar.

Zakhar had become drunk and was beginning to yell. I defended our marriage only halfheartedly.

"If you're married, then why don't you have a ring?" my neighbour asked. I told him that in my country we didn't wear wedding rings.

He laughed and pulled his chair closer to me.

"Let's get married," he said. Although he was very good looking, I explained that this was impossible.

"I think we should get married." He smiled and leaned closer.

The baron was already paying Topor, who seemed to have noticed my plight and become aware that it was only a matter of time until Zakhar took off his clothes and got a beating. (At a Roma wedding in Moldova, he had once behaved so badly that he'd been locked in the cellar for the night.) We went outside, along with all the men. Topor played another song and then hustled us into the van. In my youth and ignorance, I felt that I'd had an encounter with the wild, soulful gypsies, just barely escaping a bridenapping. In retrospect, I realize that the man who asked to marry me had only been teasing; with my drinking and carousing and transparently unmarried state, I was presenting myself as a woman who could be acquired without commitment.

Topor had no Roma roots, but for Ukrainian purposes he was close enough. Apart from Balkan and Roma music, he played Ukrainian folk songs, ironic covers of Soviet pop, "chansons" of the Russian underworld, and Jewish wedding tunes. His music united the nations in a big, fun party: the Soviet Union reimagined as a drunken dance marathon. Toporkestra performed, in some configuration, pretty much every day. There were many evenings spent at the houses of friends who lived in the center of town, including mine; more than once I woke up to find my living room floor strewn with musicians. Toporkestra played in parks, in underground passages, in fountains both drained and full, on beaches and piers and boats and trains, in bars and nightclubs and restaurants. Most of all they played on the street, often inciting surreal dance parties: vivacious young people, withered babushkas, drunks with swollen faces, little children.

Toporkestra's musicians always had *vyshyvanky*, traditional embroidered Ukrainian blouses, in their kits, to be thrown on whenever there was a need to perform Ukrainian identity. This situational, almost cynical use of the *vyshyvanka* as a declaration of national pride was nothing new. In the nineteenth century the Russian Empire's "Ukrainophile" intelligentsia was forbidden any kind of real organization, whether political or cultural. This meant that the only legal way for them to express their Ukrainian identity was through their choice of language, music, dance, food, hairstyle, and clothing. Fusing Ukrainian peasant and Cossack elements, the intelligentsia devised a private subculture, one that did not correspond to any single existing culture but rather constituted an imaginary space, reserved, for most people, for festive occasions—holiday Ukrainianness, you might call it.

"Going to the people" in their *vyshyvanky*, looking to discover the pure folk culture of the Ukrainian village, young nineteenth-century "Ukrainophiles" expected to blend in, but they didn't fool anyone. Some older peasants believed that the tsar had punished former landlords for their oppression of the peasants by forcing them to wear "ordinary clothes"; others believed that the gentlemen in peasant costume were spies. They didn't appreciate the playacting, especially when gentlemen in peasant garb came into the fields to imagine how it felt to be oppressed by a landlord—who might very well be the gentleman's father, the one who had paid for his *vyshyvanka*. Celebrating one's Ukrainian identity was, for the most part, the luxury of those who had money and education.

At the end of the summer, Topor invited me to come with his band to the "mushroom festival" in Vorokhta, a small Hutsul town in the Carpathians.

"Is it a hippie thing?" I asked, thinking of the wrong kind of mushroom.

"No," he laughed, "it's mushroom-picking season. People will listen to the music, get drunk, and then pick mushrooms."

This seemed, if anything, stranger to me than a magic mushroom festival, but I was aware of the Slavic passion for mushroom picking. I met Topor and the rest of the band, along with a number of other musician friends, at the train station the next evening. There were accordions and clarinets and trumpets and violins and a trombone and a tuba and a group of female a cappella folksingers who called themselves the Daughters of Sound. We drank and sang for most of the overnight trip, despite the frequent protests of the lady conductor. In the *tambur*, the space at the end of the train car where you were allowed to smoke, I fell in love with a golden-haired guitar player, Kotik.

The mushroom festival, which was held in a field at the foot of a smallish mountain, had many features that I would soon recognize as typical for Ukrainian folk festivals. It had been organized in honor of the 850th anniversary of the founding of Vorokhta and was advertised as a "festival of contemporary culture of daily life." In fact, it was an open-air display of ethno-nationalist kitsch, with a strange dose of hippie contemporaneity. Women in western Ukrainian folk costume—colorful fur-lined embroidered vests, embroidered blouses, and headscarves—served traditional Ukrainian dishes, Crimean wine, and *medovukha*, a potent honey liqueur. Beaded jewelry, embroidered shirts and dresses, woven belts and headbands, woolen socks and shawls, and woodwork were also for sale. People sat on the grass and played the *trembita*, a very long Hutsul horn, or formed the inevitable hippie drum circles. There was traditional music, or something like it, and Ukrainian rock, and folk dancing, and a fire dance to Ukrainian bagpipes. (This was more like the sort of mushroom festival I had imagined.)

Just as Soviet policy anointed a poet for each "nationality," with Taras Shevchenko serving as Ukraine's national bard, the USSR promoted standardized, sanitized versions of the folk culture of every Soviet national group. Each had a codified folklore, folk costume, folk dance, traditional cuisine, and folk music, displayed in national museums and trotted out for national events. According to the original logic of Soviet policy, the display of respect for national identities would enable the eventual disappearance of these identities, as they were replaced by an all-embracing socialist one. This helped explain why the Soviet versions of national folk culture felt so lifeless and artificial. National movements among stateless peoples of Eastern Europe often started with elite interest in folklore; institutionalizing folklore was a way of defanging it. Soviet official folklore was brittle kitsch—dead culture, but not the heroic kind of dead, like

Shevchenko's Cossack ghosts and burial mounds. Instead, it was a culture of cheap synthetic peasant blouses, tacky ethnic souvenirs, and mediocre renditions of played-out folk songs. Many Soviet people rejected it, preferring popular, or underground, or foreign cultural products.

So it was ironic that Ukraine employed this kind of Soviet-approved folklore as a signifier of its post-Soviet identity. In the early 1990s Ukraine hosted music festivals that rejected the Russian language and promoted folkloric and nationalist music. Such festivals were (and are) supposedly intended to dissociate Ukrainian culture from the Soviet and Russian experience and to develop a sense of a unique Ukrainian cultural heritage. And yet post-Soviet Ukrainian folklore wasn't so different from the Soviet version, just as Ukraine's government consisted largely of Soviet institutions repackaged with the iconography of Ukrainian nationalism.

Ukrainian-language musicians such as Oleh Skrypka, frontman of the popular rock band V. V., and Haidamaky, a rock group with a singer who wore a Cossack costume, performed on Maidan during 2004's Orange Revolution. (Haidamaky took their name from the Cossacks who rebelled against the Polish nobility in the eighteenth century, stars of Shevchenko's bloody epic poem "Haidamaky.") Skrypka started the annual music festival Kraina Mriy, "Country of Dreams," where Toporkestra performed. Though it encouraged the mixing of old and new, Kraina Mriy was a festival where Ukrainian was favored over Russian; almost everyone there was in Ukrainian folk costume. It was a holiday when people participated in a group performance of pastoral, pre-Soviet Ukrainian identity, much as Ukrainophile intellectuals had done in the nineteenth century.

Once, at Kraina Mriy, I commented on the legions of people in standard-issue *vyshyvanky*, comparing them to an army.

"No," a musician friend said laconically, "it's like a children's home."

"Do you want to come to the *brynza* festival in Rakhiv with me?" Kotik the dreamy blond guitar player asked when it came time to leave the Vorokhta mushroom festival and go back to Kiev. *Brynza* is a type of sheep cheese, similar to feta. I wondered if I would spend the rest of my life celebrating food products. It didn't seem like a bad way to live.

We waited by the side of the road for someone called Seryozha the Gypsy, who pulled up in a car that was filled to the roof with shoeboxes. Seryozha was small and strong, with a shaved head, a round, open face, and eyes like sparkling brown marbles; the gold fronts on his teeth served as his gypsy bona fides. He was a Moldovan Roma singer, piano player, and accordionist who made a living by buying cheap Chinese shoes in Odessa and selling them in western Ukrainian markets. This was safe work by the standards of his Moldovan musician friends, some of whom had resorted to selling their organs.

Kotik and I squeezed in beside Seryozha's shoes. He gave us a lift to the bus station, where we met Kotik's DJ friend, who'd arranged the gig at the *brynza* festival.

After a long bus trip through the mountains we arrived in Rakhiv, which I'd first visited a few months earlier. The geographical center of Europe was swarming with tourists sampling Hutsul delicacies, buying Hutsul textiles, and, of course, eating *brynza.*

111

Kotik and his friend were performing at Rakhiv's lone night-club, which I'd visited with Igor and Alina. Tonight it was packed with young people who kept breaking into circle dances and lifting each other up on chairs, as if we were at a Jewish wedding rather than a small-town discotheque.

Five hours of frantic joy peaked with "Hava Nagila," a song that I had heard only at bar mitzvahs. I'd never imagined that it could provoke such frenzy; I'd always associated it with shuffling horas, middle-aged parents, and cheap canapés. The way the people danced to it in Rakhiv made it seem alive again, evoking the mystical Judaism that once flourished in Ukraine, and the klezmer musicians who'd been stars of the Eastern European wedding circuit.

This unfamiliar liveliness was a testament to the intimacy of Jewish and Ukrainian culture. It was also painfully ironic: Ukraine was once full of Jews, and many Ukrainians didn't like them much. As the historian Amir Weiner puts it, over the centuries "the Ukrainian countryside gained an almost mythical reputation for anti-Jewish violence." Only the music remained.

One of the closest friends I made through Toporkestra was Mitya Gerasimov, a conservatory-trained clarinetist from Kazan, Russia. Mitya was Jewish, and he wanted to play klezmer music. There wasn't any klezmer scene in Kazan, so he went first to St. Petersburg and Moscow and then to Ukraine, where he started playing with Topor.

If he'd been born a century earlier, Mitya could have been a great silent film actor; he could keep up his end of a conversation with facial expressions alone. Woeful and well read, he had sad eyes and a dry sense of humor. He stuttered when he spoke but never when he sang; he was absent-minded and a little awkward, prone to doing things like losing an envelope full of money on the street, but his clarinet playing was nimble and tender, with an absolutely pure tone, like a ray of sunlight dancing through forest cover.

Mitya's grandmother was from Kiev. On the anniversary of the Babi Yar massacre, he wrote:

On the 29th of September 1941, a Monday, they started shooting the Jews in Kiev. My grandmother wasn't yet 17 when her whole family was killed at Babi Yar. She and her sister were saved—by a miracle, they were able to leave the city before the Germans came.

My grandmother served in the war, she wanted to have revenge for her relatives, or to be killed. After the war she ended up in Kazan. She was never able to return to Kiev. After many years she went to Odessa to visit relatives. The train stood for a couple of hours in Kiev, but she didn't even get out.

Grandma sometimes asks me about Kiev: where I hung out, what I saw. She asked about Babi Yar, what's there now. I first went there five years ago. I thought I'd see some kind of memorial. I searched the park for a long time, looking for some kind of marker, asking passersby. On a clear autumn day mothers were walking with strollers, with little dogs, teenagers were sitting on benches drinking beer. In the end I found a menorah monument and put flowers on it. I also stumbled on a plaque in memory of the Roma who were shot there. For some reason they removed it later ....

Since childhood, I've heard from my grandmother about Kiev, about what a beautiful city it was, how she loved it. Even now she remembers Vladimir Hill, and the Lavra, where she went to listen to the choir, and Khreshchatyk. And how she and her brother caught fish in the Dnieper and cooked fish soup with sorrel. When I was little, she sang me Ukrainian songs. Her first language was Yiddish, then Ukrainian—she learned Russian during the war. In childhood I laughed at her accent, and then it turned out that everyone in Ukraine talks that way. When I suddenly, unexpectedly, moved to Kiev, my aunt in Israel, my grandmother's niece, said, "Well, Mitya has closed the circle!"

I also love Kiev. When I think about Babi Yar, I understand that it wasn't so long ago. In my grandmother's youth.

After the war, Soviet Jews were prevented from commemorating their particular losses: where they wanted to put Jewish stars, only Soviet stars were allowed. Jewish mourning was considered a kind of Jewish separatism, especially after the state of Israel was established in 1948. Soviet authorities dissolved the suffering of the Jews into the suffering of the Soviet Union. At one point the Soviets made plans to build a marketplace on the site of the Babi Yar massacre; when a monument was finished, in 1976, it made no reference to Jews, mentioning only that 140,000 citizens of Kiev had been killed by the fascists. The small menorah Mitya searched for was a post-Soviet innovation. Even today many mass graves of Jews are marked only as places where "Soviet citizens" lost their lives. Jewish cemeteries and other landmarks lie in disrepair.

*

After a couple of years playing with Toporkestra, Mitya left to start his own group. As he imagined it, the music that had evaporated into the atmosphere after the destruction of Ukraine's Jewish community would condense into sound again, as he and his bandmates gave new life to the klezmer tradition. He called his group Pushkin Klezmer Band because, he said, echoing an old Russian truism, "Pushkin is our everything." The name was a clever choice. On one hand, it evoked the long struggle of the Russian Empire's Jews to establish their homes on the metaphorical Pushkin Street, as historian Yuri Slezkine calls it—to establish themselves as Russians rather than mere Jews, as inheritors of the great current of Russian culture rather than as interlopers and intermediaries. At the same time, the juxtaposition of Pushkin and klezmer was a joke; the klezmer revival could have happened only after the end of the Soviet Union, where Judaism was a nearly taboo topic and Prishkin was a secular saint. In the Soviet Union Mitya could never, for example, have brought his band to the huge Rosh Hashanah celebration in Uman, burial place of Rabbi Nachman, dancing through the night on an actual Pushkin Street, with Hasidic men from all over the world.

One of the great moments of Pushkin Klezmer Band was when, with Seryozha the Gypsy, they performed the song "Tutti Frutti" at a Jewish-Muslim friendship conference in Kiev. (Don't ask me why they were having a Jewish-Muslim friendship conference in Kiev.) "Tutti Frutti" is a contemporary Balkan Roma song about having a dance party, drinking Tutti Frutti-flavored Fanta and then smashing the bottles. It was one of Seryozha's top hits, and his voice was perfectly suited to it: plaintive, a bit hoarse, slanting easily up and down the notes. Like many Roma songs, "Tutti Frutti" made you dance almost against your will. It had been agreed in advance that there would be no dancing at the event, for religious reasons. But when the conference attendees heard "Tutti Frutti," they couldn't resist. The most hard-core Orthodox Jews went back to their rooms, and everyone else had a dance party.

Chapter 8

The Last Jew in Stalindorf

In college, I became close friends with a Russian girl named Anya Meksin. During our sophomore year, I spent Thanksgiving with her family in Columbus, Ohio, where I was impressed to see the whole Meksin clan taking shots of whiskey with their turkey. Over the years, I also grew close with Anya's older sister Leeza, an artist. Anya had been only seven in 1989, when she and her family emigrated from Moscow. Leeza was five years older, and she retained a trace of an accent. Anya and Leeza often talked about Russia and about being Russian; I was fascinated by their stories.

In 1989 emigration from the Soviet Union was only half-permitted. Jews (or people who pretended to be Jews in order to emigrate) told authorities they were going to Israel, gave up their Soviet passports, and then went to Western Europe and applied for visas to a third country. The Meksins sold or gave away their possessions, including a precious library that they had been building for generations, and bought tickets to Austria with a loan from the Hebrew Immigrant Aid Society.

From Austria they took a train to Rome. During a two-week stay at a Roman monastery, Leeza and Anya saw a crucifix and a bidet for the first time. *So this is the West,* Leeza thought with bemusement; she hadn't wanted to leave Moscow in the first place.

The family spent several off-season months in the seaside town of Santa Marinella as they applied for American refugee status, dressing up for periodic interviews in Rome. Leeza and

Anya sold Russian souvenirs: nesting dolls, Lenin pins, wooden spoons, and embroidered linens. Even as they gave away all of their possessions, the Meksins had packed their bags full of tchotchkes, knowing they could generate precious income. The Italian ladies at the Santa Marinella market called Leeza "little gypsy girl," and though they said it with condescension, she was happy to be mistaken for anything other than what she was—a little Jewish girl. In Moscow, the Meksins had received letters saying things like "Get out, Yids," and had once had their mailbox set on fire. Leeza's parents, both scientists, had made little professional progress, being Jews without Party membership.

Anya's memories of Russia were of the hazy, poetic early childhood variety. We both loved animals, and I was enchanted by a story she told me in college about sitting in a green field outside Moscow, watching a bunny eat a strawberry. I later found a gruesome parallel in a childhood memory of another Russian immigrant friend, Marina, who'd been sent to visit her relatives in the countryside near Chernobyl after the nuclear disaster. She spent the summer playing in the woods and fields, where she found berries the size of melons and bits of plastic that glowed in the dark. These fragmentary memories, lyrical and appalling, were glimpses of an alternate universe, tantalizingly close but completely inaccessible. No matter how much time I spent in Russia or Ukraine, no matter how well I learned to speak Russian, I could never go to the Soviet Union, because the Soviet Union no longer existed.

Years later, when I reminded Anya of the story about the bunny and the strawberry, she'd forgotten it, as if she had transferred some portion of her Soviet childhood to me, giving me possession of a tiny relic of a vanished world.

*

During my first summer in Ukraine, Anya and Leeza came to meet me. Anya was in film school, and I'd gotten us a grant from my old employer, the Open Society Institute, to film a documentary about women and drugs in Ukraine, focusing on programs I'd worked with in Poltava, Odessa, and Dnipropetrovsk.

Though they were charmed by my interest in Russian, the Meksin parents hadn't been pleased by Anya and Leeza's decision to come with me to the old country; they'd had good reasons for leaving it, after all, and it hadn't been easy to get out. But they shared what advice they could, urging Anya and Leeza to bring cartons of American cigarettes and ballpoint pens as gifts for new acquaintances. When I explained that capitalism had brought unlimited cigarettes and ballpoint pens to Ukraine, they packed I LOVE NY T-shirts and souvenir magnets instead.

Before we started work, we spent a few days in Kiev, having fun. We met up with Toporkestra, who were playing on Khreshchatyk Street, in front of McDonald's, and Leeza banged joyously on their signature big red drum. That night Topor took us to a wedding in a wooded part of Kiev, near a lake where we went skinny-dipping, the musicians still playing their instruments in the water. Zakhar showed up in his worst form, drunk and belligerent, abusing his equally drunk sidekick, a diminutive artist named Tolik. In the car on the way back from the lake, as we drove along the highway, Zakhar pummeled poor Tolik, then tried to climb out the window onto the roof. This was too much for the Meksins, who were afraid the car would crash. They were perplexed by my fascination with post-Soviet punk delirium. To them, it seemed like *nostalgie de la boue*, unsavory and unreasonable. This world was something to be escaped, not explored. They were refugees, and I was a tourist.

*

In Poltava, not far from Gogol's birthplace, we filmed at a harm reduction organization called Light of Hope, run by an exceptionally talented man, exactly my age, named Maxim. Maxim had been a heavy drug user as a teenager. Like many drug users, he had been tortured by the police, who put a hood over his head and cut off his oxygen, attached electric circuits to his ears, and shocked him. (The police often cleared cases by torturing drug users into making false confessions.) When Maxim told me about his experience, I was horrified, of course, and also overwhelmed by a sense of cognitive dissonance; I knew him as a happy giant, blond, fresh-faced, and robust. Anya's childhood was a dream world, mysterious and vague; Maxim's adolescence was a dystopian nightmare.

Maxim had eventually joined Narcotics Anonymous; when I met him, he didn't even drink coffee. He ran one of the most successful and effective harm reduction organizations in Ukraine and was a master networker, fund-raiser, and lobbyist; he later went on to win a position in the local government. Light of Hope rescued the lost, giving them a new society, a kind of home. Clients would sit in the center for hours, drinking tea, chatting, playing checkers. Nearly every client we spoke to said that the organization had saved his or her life.

One of Light of Hope's tasks was to greet people who'd just been released from prison. Many of them were drug users, likely to relapse as soon as they got out; Light of Hope tried to meet them right away and help them establish a new, sober life. One sunny afternoon we accompanied two Light of Hope social workers meeting a prisoner who would be released that day. The timing was never exact, so we loitered outside the local prison, eating ice cream bars and trying to film B-roll when the guards weren't looking. This led to repeated scoldings and threats to confiscate the camera.

Finally we spotted the man we'd come to pick up. What was it like to walk through a door and be free again? As we drove him to his mother's house, his eyes shone and he squirmed with excitement, staring out the window with a hungry look. It was a sultry day, and we passed a river where people were swimming.

"Girls! Girls in bathing suits!" he cried. "I haven't seen a girl in so long! They're all so beautiful!"

He asked us to stop so he could buy a cup of cold kvas, a malted, faintly alcoholic beverage beloved of the Slavs. He bought some from a barrel wagon painted with the word KVAS in yellow letters against a sky-blue background. We filmed him as he took his first sip in freedom; he looked delirious with happiness.

There were those, of course, who couldn't be saved, even by someone as gifted and resolute as Maxim. We followed an outreach worker named Galya to the TB hospital for a meeting with Sveta, an old friend from her drug-using days. (Sveta was HIV positive, making her highly susceptible to TB.) When we asked Galya what we ought to bring as a gift, she suggested a carton of cigarettes and some underpants. We bought the smallest pair in the shop, but when we saw Sveta, we knew they would be far too big. Sveta, who was no more than thirty, had dyed red hair and white, almost transparent skin; she had once been known for her extreme beauty. Now, in the last stages of tuberculosis, she was still lovely, but she looked like she was disappearing. For the first time I understood the nineteenth-century romance of consumption, the exquisite quality of a person who stands between the worlds of the living and the dead.

*

In Odessa we went with a social worker to meet a Roma woman, Anna, who was being released after three years in prison. As she came through the gates, Anna wept and shouted and clutched the skinny social worker in her muscular arms. The social worker greeted her kindly, embarrassed by her exuberance, and presented her with a bright yellow sequined shirt and a pair of stretch jeans studded with rhinestones—a new outfit for a new life. Crowing with happiness, Anna found a relatively deserted corner and changed right there, on the street, with our cameras rolling. She showed us her lacy green underwear, which, she explained, she had bought in prison with some of the money she earned sewing.

On the bus Anna cried some more, gulping in the scenery. We passed corner stores selling sausage, beer, and vodka; a green cemetery; a gray hospital; and kiosks selling spangled stretch tops and racy underwear. Everything was bigger, newer, and stranger than when she had gone inside, Anna said. The world had changed in her absence. She took out a stack of pictures of her little daughter, showing them to us, holding them up for the camera to record and admire. The child had been in prison with her mother until she turned three, according to Ukrainian prison policy, and had then been sent to the children's home; that had been about a year ago.

Our first stop was not the kvas cart but the social services office, where Anna would try to do the paperwork to get her daughter back. With just enough money for bus fare to her hometown, Luhansk, she had to retrieve her daughter that day; she had no way of staying in Odessa for even one night.

"When can I have her?" Anna asked the bureaucrat who met us. Anna spoke too loudly and stood too close, shifting her weight from left to right, like a boxer getting ready for a match.

She was short but sturdy and strong, even after years of a prisoner's diet and four hours of sleep a night. She had served several years for robbery and assault.

"Don't ask me! Fill out the paperwork, and then we can tell you," the bureaucrat said curtly. She had thick calves and hair permed into brittle, ash-blond question marks.

"How long can you make me wait for my own baby? Fuck!" Anna yelled.

The social worker sighed and the bureaucrat retreated, glaring.

"Bitch," Anna muttered under her breath.

"Please, wait here and don't say anything else. I'll go and find out what's going on," said the social worker, patting Anna on the shoulder.

"I should beat that bitch's face," Anna growled as we sat with her on the bench in the hallway, waiting. She bit her nails and pushed her damp hair from her forehead, slouched and slapped her knees.

When the social worker returned, she explained that Anna could have her daughter back only when she could show proof of legal employment. Legal employment was hard for anyone to find in Ukraine, but for a Roma ex-convict it was especially unlikely. There was no way Anna could take her daughter home that day. We left the social services office.

On the stiflingly hot bus to the children's home, Anna saw an olive-skinned young woman with black hair pulled into a demure bun, her large purse pressed to her chest in spite of the heat. Anna shouted across the bus in Romani, calling out in recognition. The young woman obviously understood and looked up reflexively, but then she looked back down at her lap, pretending not to understand. She didn't want to be exposed in front of a busload of people; nobody trusted a gypsy. But when Anna called out again, her voice hot with solicitude, the woman smiled reluctantly, nodded, and said a word or two in Romani. Satisfied, Anna turned back to us and continued telling us about her daughter.

By the time we arrived, we were all drenched in sweat, despite the Black Sea breeze that ruffled our hair. As we hurried down the street, afraid we would miss visiting hours, the social worker warned Anna to let her do the talking this time.

To my surprise, the children's home was beautiful, new, and obviously well funded, with an enormous, fantastical playground, a swimming pool, and deck chairs where children lay in the sun napping. It had been the gift of a Ukrainian oligarch.

We explained ourselves to the management and sat on a bench by the gates, waiting for Anna's daughter. Finally she arrived, tiny, with nut-brown hair carefully braided and tied with colorful ribbons.

Anna took her in her arms, crying with happiness, kissing her all over her face and shoulders, untying her hair, smoothing it impatiently and tying it back again. She clutched her to her breasts, asking over and over, "Do you remember me? Do you remember me, darling?"

The girl nodded, looking a little confused, and said yes.

After only half an hour, the visit ended. Anna's duaghter went back into the children's home, and we took Anna to the bus station. We filmed her vowing to return.

As we filmed, we had to answer a lot of questions ourselves. Three American women, no husbands, no children: we were a curiosity.

"So, you travel all over the world? You have no home, no husband?" one man asked me in Poltava. "Are you like . . . a sailor?" He looked awestruck. *Sailor* seemed like a nicer word than *tourist*, especially in its Russian feminine form, *moryachka*. I said yes.

The curiosity intensified when Leeza told people she was a lesbian. Although Ukraine wasn't known for its tolerant attitude toward homosexuality, the reaction was almost entirely positive. Men blushed, and women congratulated her.

Leeza had recently broken up with her girlfriend and was eager to get back in the game. This wasn't easy in Ukraine. After many attempts, I got the address of a Dnipropetrovsk gay bar from a friend of a friend in Kiev. We put on our high heels and makeup, glad for a break from our sweaty filming clothes, and took a taxi to the dark alley where the club was located.

The stout, crop-haired woman at the door raised her eyebrows and smirked. "Do you know where you are?" she asked, ready to laugh at us.

"The gay bar?" Anya said timidly.

"That's right," she answered, surprised.

In the center of the club, a young woman danced alone, wearing a leopard-print spandex body suit with cutouts that displayed a pendulous rhinestone belly button ring. Men were better represented. Some sat quietly at tables, but most were dancing in line in front of a mirrored wall, absorbed in elaborate solo performances. They vogued, undulated, and thrust. After a few minutes, the woman in the leopard-print body suit strutted through the line, taking a position closer to the mirror; she looked like a pop star performing with her backup dancers. Leeza (who didn't find love that night) hypothesized that she was not a lesbian but a stripper on her night off, seeking refuge in the one place where she could avoid male advances.

In Dnipropetrovsk, we were filming at Virtus, an organization run by Olga Belyaeva, the woman who'd taught me about Men's Day. We went with her outreach worker—a man named Sasha, whose mission in life was teaching sex workers karate—to a brothel, or "office," in a pleasant new house on the outskirts of town. When I went in with the camera, a sex worker named Snezhana came out of her room smiling, with rumpled black hair, heavy blue eye shadow, black underwear, and a zebra-print bathrobe.

She put on her clothes and a wig, went downstairs, and started taking calls from the four phones on the kitchen table. She spoke to a prospective client in a conspiratorial tone, with a coy smile that made her voice sound friendly. "Two-fifty an hour, honey, but 500 for anal .... Yes, we have very small, thin girls with large chests."

Snezhana told me that she had been sex-trafficked to Europe and found it to be not a bad experience, on the whole. Europe was a nice place.

While Anya was waiting for me outside, the man who drove the harm reduction outreach bus told her how much he wanted to be part of Russia again.

In our spare time, we were investigating Anya and Leeza's family origins. On our last day in Dnipropetrovsk, we wanted to find the village where Anya and Leeza's grandmother had grown up before evacuating to Uzbekistan on the eve of the German invasion. All we had was a handwritten list of half-remembered names.

It was a bright day, leafy and forgiving, the kind that made Ukraine look more like France. Leeza went from car to car on a crowded street, asking drivers if they knew the town—once Stalindorf, now Zhovtnevoe. When they didn't recognize the name, she explained that it had once been full of Jews. Before the war.

Finally, one driver called a Jewish friend for directions. He got them, and agreed to take us. "But there are no Jews there anymore," he warned us, as if afraid we'd blame him for our disappointment.

"Are you girls Jewish?" he inquired cheerfully as we set out.

By now this was a familiar question. Before we'd even stowed our baggage in the trunk, our taxi driver at the Kiev airport had asked Anya and Leeza, who were blessed with strong features and dark beauty, whether they were Jewish. They bristled, waiting for signs of the anti-Semitism that had helped drive their family out of the Soviet Union.

"Why do you ask?" Anya said suspiciously.

The driver looked back at her in the windshield mirror, smiling fondly. "You recognize your own," he said. "I had two Jewish grandmothers—I'll give you a discount!"

"It shouldn't be something you even notice," Anya huffed when we got out of the taxi. "It shouldn't be a topic of discussion." Having never been to Boryspil airport before, or to Ukraine, for that matter, she was not impressed by our discount.

Two weeks later in Dnipropetrovsk, Anya and Leeza were used to it, and simply nodded. The driver informed us, predictably, that he had a Jewish grandmother.

As we drove toward the town once known as Stalindorf, our partly Jewish driver regaled us with all the war history he knew, then provided an analysis of the relative faults and merits of every ethnic group in Ukraine, alive or dead. We stared out the window at the flat yellow fields of rapeseed and the bright, equally flat blue sky.

Arriving in Stalindorf at last, we stopped at the central store. Leeza and I went inside to buy Cokes. When we emerged, we found Anya talking to a grinning, swaying man.

"I *know* the last Jew in town!" he was exclaiming happily. "I'll *take* you to him!"

The man, whose name was Yury, led us down a muddy path, through a field of flowers, past a garden gate, and to the door of a dilapidated blue house. A surly old woman met us at the door and waved us toward the bedroom, then stamped back to the kitchen.

The last Jew in Stalindorf was lying in bed in his underwear. He wore thick bifocals and looked grumpy. On the table beside him were a fluorescent lamp and an insulin syringe.

"Excuse me, but I cannot get up," he said. "I am old and sick."

We explained our mission, and he searched for Anya and Leeza's grandmother's name in an ancient red address book sitting next to his bed. He didn't know her but was happy to reminisce.

His real name was Abram, but he was called Mikhail— his Jewish name exchanged for a Russian one. He spoke of his classmates, about his mother and sister, about the beauty of the landscape and the richness of the land. From time to time he confirmed a name in his address book, peering down his nose and leafing through the brittle pages. He came from a family of farmers who had been sent to the region by the tsar, along with hundreds of other Jews; Stalindorf had once

been the center of a Jewish region. Once upon a time the Jews and
the Ukrainians and the Russians there had gotten along, more or
less. Then Stalin starved them, and they had to eat prairie dogs,
and then the Germans approached and Mikhail's family fled.
Like Anya and Leeza's grandmother, they had received an early
warning through army connections; most of the town's Jews had
not been so fortunate.

At fifteen, Mikhail had driven the family's cows all the way
to Kazakhstan, eating more prairie dogs and wading through
rivers along the way. His sister was killed by a bomb as she
walked beside him; his father, a soldier, was killed in the war,
and he and his mother returned alone to their village. Even in
peacetime, when the crops had grown back, they continued to
eat prairie dogs, having grown fond of the taste. Now the
prairie dogs were gone, and Mikhail's legs were so swollen that
he could no longer walk.

He picked up his cell phone and called his wife in the kitchen
to ask her if it was time for his injection. This was our cue to
leave.

What had happened to the Jews who hadn't escaped in time?
They were in the *balka*. We had already learned that in Ukraine
the word *balka*, which literally means "ravine" or "gully," functioned as an effective synonym for "place where Jews were killed."
With Yury as our guide, we headed there.

Fluffy, well-defined clouds drifted across the bright sky, and
the faded grass was punctuated by trees the color of sage. We
crossed a river and passed a pond. Birds swept over and into the
clear water, their calls the only sound in the air. Plump gray rab-
bits appeared now and then, diving back into the grass as the car
approached.

The land was perfectly flat, an endless procession of fields, until we reached the *balka*, which was now a small rise in the earth. We all got out and studied the plaque commemorating the deaths of "Soviet citizens" killed by the fascists. We thought about all the dead bodies lying in the burial mound beneath our feet.

By the time we were done taking pictures and looking around, I was worried that we were going to miss our train. Yury said he knew a shortcut, and guided our car into the margin of a field of sunflowers. Mud spattered the sides of the car and the front and back windows. It had become apparent that Yury was very drunk.

The tires spun uselessly, spraying mud everywhere. We got out, taking off our shoes. Ankle deep in mud, we pushed together as the driver tried to start the car. It didn't move. Yury giggled.

The driver got out. "Can one of you girls drive?" he asked. "I'll push."

"I can," Leeza answered. She got into the driver's seat, wiping the globs of earth from her feet and calves. As we pushed from behind, she stepped on the gas. And that was how we escaped from Stalindorf.

Chapter 9

The Kingdom of the Dead

Ever since we'd met, Kotik the golden-haired guitarist had been telling me about the Crimean cape of Meganom. Once a Soviet military base, Meganom had remained undeveloped, without houses, resorts, public beaches, or roads, unlike the rest of Crimea, which was packed with tourists. Kotik was a hippie at heart, and Meganom was his imaginative home, the dream of paradise around which he organized his existence.

In 2010, in the pounding heat of the Kiev summer, we gathered our supplies. Kotik bought a plastic bottle full of cold draft beer just before the train pulled off, and we alternated between drinking it and pressing the bottle against our skin. Everyone on the train was sweaty, smiling, and nearly naked, the compartments were crammed with beach toys and equipment, and half the passengers were children dizzy with excitement about their holiday. Through the windows, the golden summer light melted the edges of Ukraine's extravagant summer greenery.

Just after dawn, our train crossed a thread of land into the small southern peninsula of Kherson Oblast. In the morning mist, the narrow green strip of wetland looked like it could disappear at any moment, a figment of the tide's imagination. To reach Crimea, the train crossed a bridge; the only place where Crimea is connected to Ukraine by land is at the isthmus of Perekop, at the northwestern part of the peninsula. On a map, the area between Crimea and Ukraine looks almost like lace, an intricate pattern of lakes, bays, capes, inlets, islands, and isthmuses. This is the Sivash, also known as the "Rotten Sea," a system of shallow, salty lagoons. It is only nine feet deep and has an unpleasant sulfur smell, noticeable even from the train.

Crimea's flat central steppes swell with kurgans, the burial mounds of the ancient Scythians, a group of Iranian nomads who were accomplished archers and one of the first peoples to master mounted warfare. The Russian poet Osip Mandelstam referred to these burial mounds in a 1916 poem:

> Not believing in the miracle of resurrection,
> We strolled in the cemetery.
> —You know, the earth everywhere
> reminds me of those hills
> where Russia suddenly comes to an end
> above the deaf black sea.

The ghosts of the Scythians mingle with those of the Cimmerians, Sarmatians, Greeks, Persians, Romans, Goths, Alans, Bulgars, Huns, Byzantines, Genoese, Ottomans, Khazars, Kipchaks, and Tatars. The Crimean Tatar khans sleep in the sunlit cemetery of their sixteenth-century palace in Bakhchisarai; their short, narrow sarcophagi are topped with stone turbans and Arabic inscriptions, reminders of the time when the Ottomans ruled Crimea. Flowers are sculpted in the stone and sprout from the earth that has collected on top of the graves. The cemetery is the warmest part of the palace, which is mostly part drafty and dim, restored with cheap paint and synthetic fabrics.

In the mountains three kilometers to the east, the ghosts of the Crimean Karaites—Jews who did not accept the Talmud—haunt the ruined "Jewish Fortress," a medieval structure that was inhabited, for a time, by Karaite and Krymchak Jews. The Karaites sometimes claimed that they had been brought there from Persia at the time of the first Exile. Only a few buildings in the Jewish Fortress have survived intact; most have been reduced to caves whose openings form dark frames for views of green valleys in the distance.

The most ancient ghosts in Crimea belong to Homer. The Cimmerians are described in the *Odyssey* as people who live "beyond the Ocean River's bounds," in a realm "shrouded by mist and cloud":

> The eye of the Sun can never
> Flash his rays through the dark and bring them light,
> Not when he climbs the starry skies or when he wheels
> Back down from the heights to touch the earth once
> more—
> An endless, deadly night overhangs those wretched men.

Following the unconfirmed claims of Herodotus, who claimed that the Cimmerians lived north of the Black Sea, people in Crimea will often tell you that Crimea is Homer's Cimmeria. They use this as evidence of Crimea's mythical qualities, its links to ancient civilization and the roots of Western literature. It doesn't seem to bother them that their sunny paradise was known as the dark entrance to the "joyless kingdom of the dead." Crimea, land of ghosts, is the place where Odysseus goes, on Circe's command, to consult with the shade of the blind seer Tiresias. In order to speak to Tiresias, Odysseus has to summon all the ghosts of the dead:

> Brides and unwed youths and old men who had suffered much
> and girls with their tender hearts freshly scarred by sorrow
> and great armies of battle dead, stabbed by bronze spears,
> men of war still wrapped in bloody armor—thousands
> swarming around the trench from every side

In 1944 the Russian-British journalist Alexander Werth visited Crimea, where he found a picture-postcard landscape defaced by war. The smell of flowers mingled with the stench of dead men and horses left to decay along the road. In Khersones, the old Greek settlement, German corpses floated in the sea around the lighthouse. On the beach, a skeleton still wore the remains of a *telnyashka*, the striped shirt of Black Sea sailors.

Kotik and I got off the train in Feodosia, which was founded by Greek colonists in the sixth century BC, destroyed by the Huns in the fourth century AD, and conquered by the Mongols in the thirteenth century. The Genoese soon bought the city, which was called Caffa, from the Mongols, making it one of the most important trade hubs on the Black Sea, and one of Europe's largest slave markets. Caffa fell to the Ottomans in 1475, was recaptured by Zaporizhian Cossacks in 1615, and became part of the Russian Empire with the 1783 annexation of Crimea by Catherine the Great's lover, Prince Potemkin. Catherine renamed it Feodosia, as part of her "Greek Project," through which she hoped to collaborate with the Austro-Hungarian Empire to partition the Ottoman Empire and restore the dominance of Orthodox Christianity in Crimea and its environs.

In 1787, just before the beginning of yet another war with the Ottomans, Potemkin, now "Prince of Tauris," organized a six-month trip through Crimea. Traveling down the Dnieper River with an entourage of seven galleys, each with its own orchestra, and eighty ships built to look like Roman galleons, Catherine toured through the recently conquered lands of southern Ukraine, which had been renamed Novorossiya, "New Russia." Catherine, her foreign guests, and her court were treated to an elaborate "spectacle of happiness." Peasants, Cossacks, and townspeople greeted her from villages decked in flowers. There were elaborate fireworks, and there was even a reception by the "Amazons" of the Greek Battalion of Balaklava, one hundred soldiers' wives on horseback, armed and in brightly colored costumes.

Kotik and I went straight into the Black Sea, which was just a few yards from the train station. After our swim, we headed for the center of town, where he bought me a copy of *Crimson Sails*, a novella by the early-twentieth-century Russian writer Aleksandr Grin. Though Grin was a social revolutionary, *Crimson Sails* is a romantic half-fairy tale about a beautiful girl who dreams of being rescued from her poverty by a prince who will arrive in a ship with crimson sails. Grin spent some of his last years in Feodosia, which, like his writing, seems to exist outside time.

135

After buying supplies—buckwheat, canned goods, kerosene for the camping stove—we took a *marshrutka*, a taxi-bus, to Solnechnaya Dolina, "Sunny Valley." At a crossroads, we saw a man in his sixties sitting in a broken wooden chair, his shirt open and his red belly on display. His eyes were rheumy, his chin and jowls heavy and covered in large moles, but his backdrop was exquisite: a white wall beneath a canopy of dark green trees that burst from the gray cliff above. He held a cardboard sign advertising rooms for rent, and told us that he was the one who'd built the mansion that sat high on the cliff above us. It looked almost like a church; he said it had a swimming pool, a tennis court, and a garage for twenty cars. Like many Crimeans, he made most of his money during the tourist season. All over the peninsula, dusty roads were lined with women in summer dresses holding signs advertising apartments for rent.

We walked for hours down rocky roads and through prickly fields given color by Queen Anne's lace, purple loosestrife, and yellow mustard. We passed grazing chestnut cows and dim, half-built concrete structures in the copper-colored fields. The buildings looked like grim playhouses, not big enough to live in.

These were the houses of the returned Tatars. During the Crimean War, the Tatars, Turkic Muslims whose ancestors had pillaged Russian and Ukrainian land, were considered potential collaborators with the Turks, and the Russians removed them from Crimea's southern shore. Tatar communities were raided, and many Tatars were arrested. Thousands of Crimean Tatars fled to the Ottoman Empire.

During the Second World War, some Crimean Tatars collaborated with the Nazis. Stalin found this sufficient reason to round up all the Crimean Tatars and deport them to Uzbekistan;

a large proportion died during the trip. The Uzbeks were kind to the newcomers, and the Ferghana Valley boasted a fertile, mild climate. Nevertheless, the Crimean Tatars rejected Uzbekistan as a permanent home. In exile they crafted a collective narrative of expulsion from their homeland, Crimea; the story took on a mythical quality, resembling the expulsion from Eden. The Tatars' connection to Crimea became an essential part of their identity, and the constant retelling of the story of exile meant that even young people "remembered" the experience. Return to the homeland became the guiding desire of the exiled Crimean Tatars.

In 1967 the Presidium of the Supreme Soviet issued a decree that lifted the charges of treason that had been leveled against the entire Crimean Tatar population in 1944. Thousands of Crimean Tatars returned to Crimea, only to be denied permission to reside there; almost all of them were redeported. In 1989 the Crimean Tatars again returned to Crimea en masse, this time to stay for good. Their houses had been taken by Russians and Ukrainians, and there were no programs to return their land or property. Without formal assistance in repatriating, and with minimal financial resources of their own, the Crimean Tatars resorted to a strategy of extralegal land reclamation. They squatted in unoccupied apartments and houses, coming into conflict with the mafia or with others who claimed rights to the space.

The Tatars also built primitive settlements, many without running water or electricity, on empty plots of land. (Some of these plots, which were usually empty because they were undesirable, were given to the Tatars by the government.) This seizure of real estate was accompanied by highly emotional performances and threats. When facing difficulties in

137

trying to register as residents, Tatars screamed and cried until bureaucrats gave in. When the authorities or others tried to evict them from their land or property, the Tatars threatened self-immolation, the ultimate performance of their belief that a second exile from Crimea would be a fate worse than death. These threats were given weight by the 1978 self-immolation of Musa Mamut, a Crimean Tatar who had returned to Crimea and bought a house, only to be refused residency, sentenced to prison time, and threatened with deportation. As he lay in the hospital for five days before dying, he spoke about his self-immolation as an act of protest against the treatment of Crimean Tatars as a group.

Meanwhile, Russians and Ukrainians had their own story about the Crimean Tatars' relationship to the Crimean peninsula. They called the Tatars "heathens," "uncivilized" and "warlike," evoking old stereotypes about the Turks. They argued that the Crimean Tatars did not deserve pity because they had been Nazi collaborators and because they had been exiled to a very pleasant place, much better than the desolate lands to which other exiles were sent.

It was getting dark when we reached the white lighthouse at the eastern end of Meganom. (In the Soviet Union, I later learned, the one perk of the lighthouse keeper's lonely, boring job was access to large volumes of alcoholic chemicals.) We picked our way down a steep, pebble-strewn path to the seaside. It was dark, and we were too exhausted to walk any further looking for a campsite, so we slept in the first flat area we found. It was already occupied by some nerdy Moldovan hippies who were busy with their panpipes, but they were hospitable and agreed to lend us the cave next to their campsite.

It was an exquisite cave, spacious and clean, with the water lapping at one end. We enjoyed two days there, recovering from our journey. Eventually, though, We had to get away from the Moldovans: one morning I looked out of our cave and saw one of them standing on a rock and playing his *drimba*, or mouth harp, wearing nothing but a bandanna and a plaid shirt, his penis flapping in time with his twanging. Meganom was the redoubt of hippies from Ukraine, Russia, Moldova, and Belarus, and most of them were nudists, living a dream of primitive civilization, of freedom.

We relocated to a beach colonized by a group that Kotik had met on a previous trip. Like the Moldovans, they were hospitable and naked, but they were more our sort. The group centered around Olga and Sanya, a couple from the Russian city of Belgorod, on the northeastern border of Ukraine. Sanya, who was in his early thirties, was like a friendly lion, with sturdy limbs, a large, firm belly, and huge blond dreadlocks that fell halfway down his back. Olga, his girlfriend, was a few years younger, with a mermaid's long wavy hair, round green eyes, and slender figure. With them were Max, a fast-talking Jewish fabulist from Moscow who made his living mostly as a truck driver, who'd done time in prison and had a scar that started at the right edge of his lips and extended to his jawbone; Aramis, an itinerant charmer from Belarus who had gotten his nickname because of his resemblance to an actor in the Soviet *Three Musketeers*; Dmitry, a dreadlocked construction worker who had been born in Kazakhstan but lived in Russia; and Botanik, a Belarusian computer programmer who was very handsome, but always drunk. I'm not sure why he was called Botanik, which means "botanist" in proper Russian and "nerd" in slang. Maybe because of his smoking habits, maybe because he worked with computers. (Other men's nicknames were more menacing: "Psycho" and "The Fascist," for example.) Botanik had once been a competitive swimmer, and his alcoholism and heavy smoking didn't prevent him from swimming long distances around Meganom, often carrying bottles of beer or cigarettes. I once saw him emerge from the water after a long swim holding his new baby.

The etiology of Teepee Dima's name was clear: he lived in a teepee on the beach. Tall, lean, and angelically beautiful, he had bright blond hair, innocent blue eyes, and piercings that dotted his face like pox. He supported his itinerant lifestyle by doing tattoos, and most of his lithe body was covered in blue shapes and lines. He was probably the most striking example of the Meganomian longing to return to some approximation of primitive life, drum circles, and sex under the stars, just far enough from the fire that you can't be seen. The year we were there, he too had just had a baby, who was spending her first months of life in the water. But he would soon abandon his daughter; he wasn't the sort of person who maintained close ties. He was famous for having thrown away his passport, shocking even his hippiest friends. In ultrabureaucratic post-Soviet space, throwing away your passport was an act of self-erasure that could doom you to near nonpersonhood for months or years. In Dnipropetrovsk, I'd heard about a legendary drug user who lived without a passport for seven years; he was something like a unicorn.

One day I saw Aramis bobbing on an air mattress, a precious commodity, paddling into deeper water. He retrieved a plastic bottle of grain alcohol, which he'd tied to a rock to keep it cold. When he paddled back, he told me the story of his life, as we watched black crabs scrambling in a tide pool. His mother had worked on a commercial fishing boat and would leave him and his half-brother at the Magadan *internat*, the state-sponsored boarding school, for the duration of the fishing season.

I made sounds of commiseration.

"No, it was exciting there! It was fun," Aramis said, with his high-pitched, nervous laugh. "You arrived, and then you left. I couldn't sit in the same place for more than half an hour, though, so we ran away a lot—usually for two or three days."

In order to avoid army service, he'd decided to fake insanity. He went to the psychiatric hospital and sang songs. The head doctor told him she knew he wasn't crazy, but that she'd give him the diagnosis if he wanted. In the end, he was rejected by the army because of his flat feet.

Sanya and Olga, the den parents, were high-functioning, responsible hippies. They spent every summer on Meganom, arriving in June and staying till August, when Olga had to return to her job as a teacher. (She was also writing a dissertation on the poet Marina Tsvetaeva.) They brought with them everything they needed to live in something close to the comfort of home. They built an entire kitchen, with a tarp roof, benches made from carefully piled rocks, a stone pantry that hid food from the sun, and a stove, with the standard white pots with blue or purple flowers painted on their sides. There were even little wooden shelves hanging from bits of string. Their tent was like a sheikh's, lined with colorful cushions and blankets, and with so many mats on the floor that you hardly knew you were sleeping on a bed of stones. There was even a kind of front hall, also lined with cushions, where you could remove your shoes before entering.

I had obeyed Kotik's instructions to bring as little with me as possible, so I was very envious of Olga's large collection of jewelry and her elaborate wardrobe, which she kept folded in neat piles in her tent. Through diligent secondhand shopping in Belgorod, she had managed to assemble a large collection of Indian tunics and light cotton harem pants. Olga was always chic, always kind and friendly, and she was an outstanding cook and housekeeper, maintaining order and cleanliness in the camp. I ate much better on Meganom, without a refrigerator and with only a kerosene stove, than I had in Kiev, where I had lived mainly on salad, yogurt, and frozen dumplings. But even Olga's skill couldn't make fruit keep in the heat. Sometimes we sat and fantasized about ice water, cold beer, fried *chebureki* (large dumplings), and fresh fruit. I became especially obsessed with nectarines, and would buy a bag of them every time we went to the market in nearby Sudak. Olga and Sanya, whose summers were possible only if they counted every penny and who obsessed over tiny differences in the price per kilo of tomatoes, onions, and cucumbers, considered nectarines an insane luxury.

This was only one of many signs that I was an outsider, an improvident alien with no practical skills. Not knowing how to cook or peel potatoes with a knife or build a fire, not being strong enough to carry six liters of water along a precarious mountain slope from the spring, had never been a problem for me in the past; I was a respectable, educated person. But now I was absolutely dependent on Olga, Sanya, Kotik, and the others. I had never been so acutely aware of my lack of the basic skills that have allowed people to keep themselves alive for millennia. I met a six-year-old who could make borscht; her twelve-year-old brother could dive for mussels. Neither could read—but what good was reading when you were hungry for dinner? The children reminded me of deer, slim and agile, with caramel limbs and sun-bleached hair. They almost never cried, probably because no one would have listened. If they did, they would do it in private, going off into some rocky corner, covering their faces and weeping silently, returning to the group when they were finished.

I had two sources of capital on Meganom, apart from my vulgar cash, which seemed to make everyone uncomfortable. The first was my foreignness. I was the first American nearly anyone there had met, and certainly the first American anyone could remember on Meganom. Crimea was one of the Soviet Union's most popular vacation destinations. Young Pioneers went to Crimean summer camps, and the sick went to Crimean sanitariums. Political leaders had summer homes there. But when the borders opened more affluent post-Soviet people started going abroad for vacation—to France, Spain, or Italy, or on packaged tours to Montenegro or Egypt.

It was people with less disposable income who continued going to Crimea for the summer. The family-oriented resorts were so packed with fat grandmothers, screaming children, and harried parents that you could hardly see the stones on the beach. The youth-oriented beaches, like Lisya Bukhta, a place often shuddered about on Meganom, were strewn with campers who were alternately rowdy and half-dead—sometimes completely dead—from alcohol and sunstroke. ("Cyclops was from Lisya Bukhta!" Botanik once announced.) Meganom was full of hippies, people who didn't like crowds or society or the city, which they called "Babylon," Rasta style. But all three categories of Crimean vacationers were less rich and less cosmopolitan than the urban professionals who left Russia, Ukraine, or Belarus for vacation by plane. They were less likely to speak foreign languages or to have consorted with foreigners. It followed, therefore, that on Meganom I was an interesting novelty, and that people enjoyed asking me questions.

Botanik once tried to convince me that New York had *nothing* that Minsk didn't have.

"What about Harlem?" I asked.

"Who wants Harlem, anyway?" he shouted. But for the most part, the conversations were friendly.

My other advantage, probably more important, was my association with Kotik, who could offer music, the most precious currency aside from food. Meganom was littered with African drums and cheap guitars. Rarely did a night pass without someone forming a drum circle, that exasperating requirement of hippiedom. But as at most hippie encampments, the number of instruments far exceeded the number of people who were able to play them. Kotik was a professional guitarist and drummer with a prodigious memory and a large repertoire. He was a kind of bard, able to play long story-songs for hours on end; when he was tired of playing, he had a large store of anecdotes and jokes. He was also bossy, cutting off the bad guitarists and leading the drummers, teaching them rhythms and drawing their attention to their mistakes. To his store of songs I was able to add some American classics, which I could sing with an exotic American accent. I had also learned a very long Gulag story-song about an Odessa gangster who has his enemy killed. It was full of arcane criminal slang; everyone cracked up when they heard me sing it in my accented Russian.

Over the previous months, Kotik had tutored me in his favorite parts of Russian and Soviet culture. He loved to delight me with the cartoons and movies and songs that every single person in the Soviet Union grew up knowing; it was a pleasure for him to read Pushkin's *Tales of Belkin* aloud to someone who had never heard of them, explaining all the unfamiliar words. Like teaching a child, it reminded him of the joy of first discovery.

In Kiev, Kotik had taught me classic Russian 1980s songs— Kino and Zhanna Aguzarova—that everyone knew. Sitting on a mossy rock over the sea one day on Meganom, he also taught me the girl's portion of a sweet duet from a 1970s Soviet children's movie about going to space. The girl describes lilacs blossoming in winter, stars falling together through the sky, and the boy tells her, every time, "Of course I believe you—I saw it all myself." Everyone on Meganom knew the tune and loved it.

It was on Meganom that I was introduced to Russian Rastafarianism and the bizarre spectacle of Russians, Belarusians, and Ukrainians singing songs, in Russian, about Jah and the longing for Africa. But Meganom was also permeated with nostalgia for Soviet culture. This was especially noticeable in the realm of music. The body of culture in the Soviet Union, a partly closed society, was smaller and more homogeneous than most cultures can be today. That means that Soviet songs were still more likely to be the ones that everyone knew, that people sang together in kitchens or around the campfire.

When Kotik rewrote the schmaltzy 1950s classic "Moscow Nights" as "Meganom Nights," the song was a big hit, and everyone sang happily along with the new lyrics:

> On the shore you can't hear even a murmur,
> Here everything has died down till morning.
> If only you knew how precious
> These Meganom nights are to me.

This song, which was traditionally performed with an orchestral accompaniment, was the kind of pop culture despised by the post-Soviet intelligentsia and the "creative class," and beloved of almost everyone else. Corny though it was, it embodied much of what people still remembered fondly about Soviet culture: an inoffensive, literate gentleness, an appreciation of relationships and nature over material goods. For all their globalized countercultural trappings—the dreadlocks, the reggae, the African colors, the tribal tattoos—the people on Meganom seemed to be retrieving the Soviet past, the friendship of peoples. Here there was nothing to buy or sell except the simplest foods, and money was hardly exchanged; people relied on their abilities to cook and build and gather and tell stories or play music or make friends, rather than on more sophisticated forms of capital. Russians, Ukrainians, Belarusians, and Moldovans lived together in peace, all speaking Russian. Crimea was the ideal site for this post-Soviet reunion, since it was the place where so many children, now adults, had spent their happy summer vacations, flocking there from all over the Soviet Union. For post-Soviet people, Crimea was a gigantic madeleine.

Mandelstam wrote about Meganom in a 1917 poem that refers to the *Odyssey*:

> The veil-gray spring of asphodels
> is still far off.
> In the meantime, the sand still whispers,
> the waves boil.
> But here, like Persephone, my soul
> has begun to circle round,
> and the kingdom of the dead can hold
> no charming, sun-tanned hands.
>
> Why then do we entrust
> the urn's grave weight to a boat,
> and celebrate black roses
> on amethyst water?
> My soul strains forward,
> past foggy Meganom,
> and after the funeral, the black sail
> will return from that same cape.
>
> How swiftly the clouds skim over
> the unillumined ridge,
> and the tufted black roses
> flutter beneath the moon's wind.
> The bird of grief and death,
> the enormous flag of memory
> drags itself along, edged in mourning,
> behind the cypress stern.

In the daytime, I liked to put on a snorkeling mask and float, corpselike, in the quiet depths, watching the light flashing on the stones and on schools of fish. Other times we would sit in the shallow water and eat watermelon, if we had it, or examine the stones on the beach. When wet, they looked like abstract expressionist canvases, with irregular stripes and splashes of red, yellow, and white against a gray background, but when they were dry, they became dull and unbeautiful. The boulders that scattered the beach were dotted with thousands of smaller stones, crushed into them by time and water.

Max had brought a green army net that was made to look like seaweed, and we used branches and rocks to make it into a canopy covering one end of our beach. This was named the Watermelon. It became a kind of living room, a place where everyone would lie on their mats and read, chat, drink tea, and eat endless amounts of kasha. After a few nights Kotik and I started sleeping there, too, because it was stuffy in the tent and breezy on the beach, where the air was exactly body temperature and we could watch the stars, the waves rustling at our feet. Sometimes we slipped into the water, illuminated by the milky spill of stars in the clear night sky; as we swam, we left another trail of stars behind us, plankton that lit up with our movement and then was extinguished for the night.

I went back to Crimea with Olga and Sanya that winter, just after New Year's. All three of us slept in one bed in some old lady's spare flat, for about seven dollars a night. When we went to visit Meganom, we saw that the shops and cafés at its outer border were gone—they had been portable. Only a few fences and faded signs reminded us that hundreds of people had been there just a few months earlier, drinking beer and eating greasy *chebureki*. The sea was deep blue and calm, no longer required to perform. The audience was gone, the sets dismantled. The HOLLYWOOD sign that someone had put in the hills looked even more absurd than usual.

Meganom's outer hills were brown and bare, so worn down by time that they looked like rumpled blankets. On the beach we saw little branches covered in icicles, like translucent fir trees. As we hiked out onto the deserted cape, we saw the traces of a vanished civilization: colored threads tied to naked tree branches, a circle of logs surrounding an ashy ring. Boulders had fallen onto our encampment, ruining all of Sanya's hard work, but we could still see the ring of stones that had made a sort of lagoon where the children had liked to swim, and the larger rock that we'd used for diving. Sanya and Olga would go back there the next summer, clear the beach, and build their civilization again.

Part III

Revolution

Chapter 10

Dreaming of Europe

I left Ukraine as soon as I got back from Meganom; my time was up, and I returned to New York to go to graduate school at last. (I also started writing for magazines, usually about Ukraine and Russia.) But in the summer of 2012 I got a short-term job coordinating harm reduction activities during the European Championship soccer tournament, the Eurocup, which was being held jointly in Poland and Ukraine. The guy who'd hired me—an American—disappeared into the casino-brothels of Cambodia just as our project was getting started. (A lot of people who work in harm reduction are current or former users, and these things happen from time to time.) Since my plane ticket was nonrefundable, I decided to go anyway.

In 2009 Viktor Yanukovych, the man who'd tried to steal Ukraine's presidency in 2004, had been elected president. This time he won in a fair vote. His victory testified to Ukraine's disillusionment with the leaders of the Orange Revolution and to the country's regional divides. Yanukovych and his Party of Regions had always maintained substantial support in eastern Ukraine, their economic and political base, as well as in southern Ukraine and Crimea. Yanukovych's ascent was depressing, but not surprising.

Yanukovych, who was nothing if not classy, invited foreign investors to Ukraine to see the chestnut trees in bloom and watch "how women begin to take their clothes off when it gets warm." As the championship approached, there was much anxiety about the moment when thousands of drunk, virile, Euro-spending soccer fans would descend on a country already notorious for its sex trade and HIV epidemic. Femen, Ukraine's "topless feminist" group, soon joined the fray, claiming that the tournament would increase sex tourism and prostitution. As an act of protest, two gorgeous Femen members stripped off their shirts and snatched the Eurocup trophy that was on display in Dnipropetrovsk. Happy tourists took their picture. Here were the beautiful naked ladies they'd been promised!

The Ukrainian passengers on my flight were bubbling with a patriotic enthusiasm I'd never seen before. About half of them were dressed in soccer jerseys; some were obviously members of the Ukrainian diaspora, returning to celebrate Ukraine's moment in the international limelight. As we approached Kiev, flying low over the green fields, a young man shouted, in Russian, "What a land we have!"

I stayed in my old apartment on Bohdan Khmelnytsky Street. After I'd moved out, my elderly landlords had rented it to another foreign student, but my abandoned souvenirs and even my half-used shampoo bottles were in the same places I'd left them. The cold-water tap still didn't work, the babushka next door was still insane, and the shop downstairs was still selling the same hideous, overpriced porcelain statues of muscle-bound Cossacks and Ukrainian maidens in folk costume. The only difference was that a few chunks of plaster had fallen from the ceiling.

But when I walked down to Khreshchatyk Street, Kiev's main strip, I found a semipermanent carnival. One of Yanukovych's first projects as president had been the prosecution of the golden-braided ex-prime minister Yulia Tymoshenko, who'd been convicted of embezzlement and thrown in prison. She was probably guilty of a number of crimes, but so was nearly every other Ukrainian politician; it was clear that Yanukovych had prosecuted her in order to eliminate a rival. At the intersection of Khreshchatyk and Bohdan Khmelnytsky stood a "Free Yulia" encampment, with pictures of Yanukovych defaced with colored spray paint:

SADIST!

DIE, BASTARD!

DOWN WITH THE CRIMINAL BAND!

THE COUNTRY WILL BE RESURRECTED!

A fairground-style board showed Yanukovych being knocked out in a boxing match; you could look through the hole where his opponent's face should have been and have your picture taken. A sculpted pile of shit had the flag of Yanukovych's Party of Regions planted in it, and a pig Yanukovych was ready to be cooked on a spit. A grotesque papier-mâché puppet of Oleg Kalashnikov, a Party of Regions official, wore a sign announcing his betrayal of his country and his people. (Kalashnikov would be assassinated in Kiev three years later.) Alongside this ugliness shone images of the martyred Yulia Tymoshenko. She beamed as she stroked a white tiger cub; she kissed the hands of a weeping old woman in a flowered headscarf; she stared sadly out from behind prison bars. One image showed her as a Slavic Joan of Arc, dressed in armor, with birds perched on her fingertips. The people running the encampment were giving out free T-shirts,

155

which meant that half the bums in the city were dressed as Yulia supporters.

On Khreshchatyk Street, each national group had its own booth serving its national specialties, and the visiting fans moved in national packs. In the Swedish Corner, strapping men of all ages sat on long wooden benches and drank beer, wearing Swedish blue and gold, served by Swedish bartenders and cooks and even policemen; apparently the Swedes didn't trust the Ukrainian police to protect them, which was reasonable. My friend Julia Y., who always knew everything, said the Swedish cops were afraid to leave Khreshchatyk. Julia spoke perfect English, had traveled extensively in Western Europe, and was always making friends with foreigners, who viewed her as a nonthreatening intermediary, not a "real" Ukrainian woman. When she'd invited eight Swedes over to her apartment, they'd congratulated themselves on even making it to Ukraine, an incredibly dangerous and totally incomprehensible country, and discussed the fact that they'd decided not to sleep with locals under any circumstances, because they'd heard that Ukrainian women would poke holes in the condoms and give them AIDS.

Other Swedes of Julia's acquaintance complained that Ukrainian girls weren't interested in them. The Swedish men and Ukrainian women had gathered one night on Trukhaniv Island, on the Dnieper, but it had been a failure. The Ukrainian girls expected the men to make the first move, the only option according to Ukrainian standards of behavior, while the Swedes, products of one of the world's most feminist societies, were waiting for the Ukrainian girls to introduce themselves. The Ukrainian girls were offended, as they were by the indifference of the Dutch, who seemed immune to Ukrainian charms and paraded around in self-sufficient pods, wearing matching mesh shirts. Some fans wandered around carrying sex dolls, as if they wanted to make it absolutely clear that they had no need for human women. But the foreign hooligans, with their painted faces and beer bellies, loved to dance to Toporkestra on the street, hooting and applauding; this was local color that couldn't give you HIV. One day Toporkestra even got to play on the huge stage in the Fan Zone, looking very small above the EURO 2012 banner.

When the foreigners did make the first move, romantically speaking, they were often less than chivalrous. Many of my Ukrainian girlfriends complained that foreigners kept propositioning them on the street or simply groping them; the foreigners seemed to have the impression that all Ukrainian women were up for grabs, a whole country's worth of sex volunteers. Countless soccer fans were beaten with handbags and berated in a language they didn't understand.

The city had added heavily accented English-language announcements on public transportation; they sounded strange to everyone.

"You know," a young man on the trolley said to me, "in the Second World War they made a rule that all the announcements had to be in German. And then Russians made them Russian. And now they're in English." He smiled grimly.

There was indeed a sense that Ukraine was under occupation. One day I saw a Ukrainian folk choir on Maidan waiting for the American commercials on a giant screen to end, so they could start their song. The Ukrainian singers were dwarfed by the monumental American actors. On my way home one night,

I saw a mob of people, many of them dressed in blue and gold Ukraine gear, surrounding a Pepsi truck, shouting and jostling; they were competing for free cans of soda, like children begging foreign soldiers for treats. A man stood on a car nearby, waving a Ukrainian flag in each fist.

Most of the visiting fans didn't know that the previous March, in the southern Ukrainian city of Mykolaiv, a young woman named Oksana Makar had been raped, set on fire, and left to die. Two of her three suspected attackers were released, apparently because of the political connections of their parents. The media protested, and demonstrators gathered in Mykolaiv, Kharkiv, Lviv, and Odessa.

But this wasn't enough to stop the depredations of local officials, who had become accustomed to impunity. In the summer of 2013, in Vradiivka, a small town in the south, it emerged that two local police officers had raped a woman named Iryna Krashkova, beating her nearly to death. The police department had covered up the crime because of the family connections of one of the officers, who seemed to be responsible for raping and murdering at least one other woman. The police had also apparently forced innocent men to confess. (Two died in police custody.) Hundreds of protesters stormed the local police station, demanding that the officers be prosecuted. They smashed windows, broke doors, and set fire to the building. We didn't know it then, but this *bunt*, this insurrection, was a taste of Ukraine's future.

In November 2013, still in graduate school in New York, I started seeing reports about protests in Kiev. President Yanukovych had pulled out of a planned Association Agreement with the European Union, saying he didn't want to break ties with Russia. About two thousand protesters, mostly students, responded to online calls from Mustafa Nayyem, an investigative journalist, and other activists to assemble on Maidan. It didn't seem like a big deal at first—just another example of Yanukovych drawing Ukraine further into Russia's orbit, with another small, futile protest in response.

But on November 24 a rally on European Square, a few steps from Maidan, attracted an estimated fifty thousand people. The protesters waved EU flags, chanted "Ukraine is Europe," and sang the Ukrainian national anthem, "Ukraine Is Not Yet Dead." The country hadn't seen a demonstration this big since the Orange Revolution. A few protesters tried to storm government buildings, and the police used tear gas and batons, but for the most part the protest was nonviolent, and the government behaved in a relatively conciliatory manner. On November 26 Prime Minister Mykola Azarov announced that negotiations on the EU Association Agreement were ongoing and that Ukraine was still committed to "moving our country closer to European standards." The city of Kiev pitched a tent on Maidan, distributing sandwiches and hot drinks to the core group of a few thousand student protesters.

A stage was erected, much like the one where Toporkestra had played during the European soccer championships. Ruslana, a onetime Eurovision winner, sang for the protesters, along with a few other national-minded musical acts. Lithuanian and Polish politicians arrived to make speeches; these were the EU members most eager to see Ukraine reject Russian influence and act as a buffer between Russia and the EU.

On November 29, when it became clear that Ukraine had not signed the Association Agreement and probably never would, about ten thousand protesters assembled in Kiev, and twenty thousand in Lviv. They called for the resignations of President Yanukovych and Prime Minister Azarov.

At a time when many Europeans were having grave doubts about the EU, it was surprising to hear that thousands of Ukrainians wanted so badly to be a part of it. The Association Agreement was part of the EU's Eastern Partnership program, which was meant to bring former Soviet states closer to EU standards. The agreement included provisions related to foreign and security policy, justice and home affairs, "deep and comprehensive free trade," and standards related to the environment, transportation, and education. It wasn't EU membership; it didn't even guarantee Ukrainians visa-free travel to EU countries. So why were Ukrainians so worked up?

In Ukraine, *European* was a vague term used to signify many things that were desirable but hard to attain. Apartments were advertised as having *Evro-remont*, "Euro-renovations": this meant that they were new, clean, modern, and unaffordable for the average Ukrainian. (My crumbling apartment on Bohdan Khmelnytsky Street was the antithesis of Evro-remont.) Those lucky enough to have the money bypassed the dingy, corrupt state health system and paid to go to private clinics like Kiev's EuroLab, which was clean, up-to-date, and more expensive than the state system.

This metaphorical use of *Europe* was obvious in statements collected by journalists during "Euromaidan," as the protests soon came to be called. One protester said, for example, "I'm not part of any political party, but I understand that only by trying to be more European can we end our troubles." *Europe* meant freedom, fairness, and transparency. (This was before the Greek debacle.) It meant rights for minorities and freedom of speech. It meant exciting vacations to beautiful places where the food and wine were better than they were at home, where the air was clean, where the trains were fast and safe. (Never mind that they were so expensive.) It meant an escape from the past, an alternate reality in which Ukraine was never subjugated by the Russian Empire or the Soviet Union but instead became a "normal" European country like Germany or France. Western Ukrainians, in particular, seemed to feel that they were Europeans who had been held hostage for decades, held back from the European destiny that was rightfully theirs. (They had repressed the memory of domination by the Poles and the Austro-Hungarian Empire.)

Yet the EU was not a spiritual condition; it was a vast bureaucracy with difficulties of its own, and it wasn't about to solve Ukraine's economic problems. When Euromaidan started, Ukraine was on the brink of default. Yanukovych was rushing from door to door, trying to cadge money from the EU, Russia, and China. EU Association offered access to EU markets, but it also required the adoption of about 350 EU laws within ten years, as well as legal and judicial reforms. The EU refused Yanukovych's bold request for 160 billion euros to implement the new standards. And EU Association would mean the wrath of Putin.

On November 30 at about four a.m., Berkut, a Ukrainian special police force whose name means "golden eagle," appeared on Maidan and, without provocation, attacked a thousand unarmed student protesters with stun grenades, batons, and tear gas. They chased down bystanders, beating and kicking them. Some pro-testers were detained, and the rest were dispersed. Around nine a.m. Berkut tried to get into St. Michael's Monastery, where protesters, including some of the wounded, had sought refuge.

Videos of the attack flooded the Internet. Even Ukrainians who hadn't cared much about the Association Agreement were outraged to see Berkut attacking unarmed students—women, young people. A government spokeswoman offered a pitiful excuse, saying that the Berkut attacks had been neces-sary because the protesters were making it impossible to put up Maidan's traditional New Year's tree. (In the conspirato-rial tradition of Soviet and post-Soviet politics, some people, including government officials, suggested that the attacks were a provocation intended to make the government look bad.) That afternoon protesters assembled outside St. Michael's and were visited by a number of ambassadors from EU countries. By evening ten thousand people had gathered, with another ten thousand en route from Lviv to Kiev.

The next day, December 1, hundreds of thousands of furious protesters gathered on St. Michael's Square. Many marched down the hill to Maidan, defying the recent ban on demonstrations there. Riot police failed to stop the protesters from seizing Maidan and occupying several government buildings. President Yanukovych threatened to declare a state of emergency. Protesters blocked the entries to city administration buildings and began forming self-defense units; the police dis-appeared from the city center. Several cities in western Ukraine declared general strikes.

Protesters erected a tent city on Maidan and built barricades using any materials available. Maidan started to resemble a never-ending festival, with cauldrons of soup, open fires, a giant stage, and musical performances around the clock. People took turns playing an upright piano painted blue and gold.

An online news station had set up a live feed by then, and my Ukrainophile friends and I started watching it as much as we could. I would sit and work with the Maidan live feed on in the background, and wake up in the middle of the night to check on the protests. Every night I went to sleep with the national anthem in my head, because Ruslana sang it onstage at the top of every hour:

> Souls and bodies we'll lay down, all for our freedom,
> And we'll show that we, brothers, are of the Cossack nation!

Almost everyone I knew in Kiev was taking part in Maidan: Alik, Alina, Mitya, my old russian teacher Vakhtang, and many more. Like so many other Kiev residents, like so many other Ukrainians, they helped with donations of food, clothing, medicine, wood and tires for barricades, and money, or they worked in the soup kitchen, at the medical assistance points, or in the cleanup crew. A hotline was set up to help people find a place to bathe or sleep or get warm. People went to work during the day and to Maidan at night. As I watched the footage and looked at photos in news reports and on social media, every familiar building, every stretch of sidewalk, was transformed. Familiar people had changed, too.

My friend Julia Y. sounded more idealistic than I'd ever known her to be. As a highly educated, cosmopolitan, multilingual twentysomething, she fit the profile of the pro-EU student type, but years of work in Ukrainian business and politics had left her with few illusions. Now she had devoted her formidable energies to helping Maidan, and she found her hope and anxiety to be almost unmanageable.

"Twenty days of constant protests have made me question my ability to count," she wrote to me.

> Or to estimate the number of people I see. Every day people ask each other: how many people were there today? How many were there on the biggest day? I've realized that it's almost impossible to tell for sure. All most of us can imagine is a stadium. It's about 70,000 people, right? But this crowd is much bigger than that. When someone says there were about 100,000 people, it seems too little, because if you support the demonstrations, you want it to be at least a million, or better two. And the worst part is that I can't help but want it to be more, want more than 2,000 people to spend a very cold Monday night in a camp in the middle of a country of 45 million, and I don't want to wonder how many people are enough to make it matter. I'm afraid that whatever I say will sound like one of the clichés I hear from almost every person who's been to Maidan lately—something about being inspired, about the kind and shining eyes of the people there, about helpfulness and politeness, and how striking that is compared to any regular gathering of people in Ukraine—for example, a ride on the metro at rush hour. But I want to talk about how after being there your clothes, hair, and skin smell of fire, the smell you remember from childhood—just plain burning wood. It comes from dozens of metal barrels that protesters

turned into makeshift furnaces right there in the square, to fight below-zero temperatures. This smell is very hard to get rid of. It follows you everywhere, and I can often tell by the smell whether a person elsewhere has been to Maidan.

Even Alik was intoxicated by revolutionary hope, by the masses of people with shining eyes and a common purpose. His familiar humor and punk ethos were mixed with a political ardor I'd never seen in him.

"One of my friends was on a huge speed binge in November; I was worried about him," Alik wrote.

Then the guy he was getting the speed from disappeared, and he redirected his passion into revolution. As I am leftist and antiglobalist, I made the slogan "Fuck the EU, fuck the police." I had been working against certain points in the EU Association Agreement—it would have extended patents and prevented us from registering generic drugs, which are much cheaper. But that's all over. Now it's about standing against the power that still considers us—left and right and liberal, Christian, Jewish, Tatar, Georgian— as its slaves.

Like Alik, Alina was a skeptic, not a joiner. But she too had been swept up in revolutionary euphoria, even as she remained alert to dissonant notes. "All my old friends have been out on Maidan," she wrote.

In two weeks we've changed more than we have in the last twenty-two years. Vakhtang set up a headquarters and he's there all the time, giving everybody instructions, making phone calls, collecting information, building barricades, guarding Maidan at night. They have to make sure there are enough bodies there so the police will be afraid to fight with them. Marta is out all the time too, helping with food. For a while she was in the Trade Union House making hundreds and hundreds of sandwiches for the protesters. Every half hour, they sing the Ukrainian national anthem. It stinks in there. Now she's making soup. So much soup!

Unsatisfied with the quality of the sandwiches being distributed, Marta, Vakhtang's wife, had started what she called the "Euroborscht" project. "We drove into Maidan with the big pots of borscht in the trunk of the car," Alina told me.

We had to go through a cordon—they ask you why you're coming, what you're doing. On Maidan you can't check anything, so everyone just has to trust each other. It's beautiful, but you also think about how vulnerable it makes everybody.

We opened the trunk and started ladling out the soup. It was gone in ten minutes. There was one guy who had been on Maidan for a long time. He said he had been living in Italy for thirteen years, but he'd never seen anything like that there. Tears were rolling down his face. Maidan smells like wood and food being cooked, like you're in another century.

I keep wondering—is this what a revolution feels like? Is this what it was like in 1917? The people took over the palace—City Hall. There are so many people in the streets, they look like waterfalls. It's strange. Surreal. On Maidan there's the revolution, but then I go home and I see mothers pushing their strollers, people going to the store for bread. Just living their lives like usual, like nothing's going on. At first I was a little afraid to participate. What will happen if we lose? Will they come after us? But then I realized—I don't care. Fuck it. You have to be brave.

Pasha Skala, an army veteran, ex-cop, and drug policy reform activist I knew from my harm reduction work, was on Maidan from the second day of protests; he said he'd felt guilty for not being there from the beginning. As he had during the Orange Revolution, he wore the beret of a UN peacekeeper; in 2001–2 he'd served in a UN mission in East Timor. He felt that his most important role on Maidan was talking to the police—"counterpropaganda," as he called it. He'd show them his police ID and explain to them how police worked in "civilized countries," telling them that Yanukovych was a simple criminal, a bandit. But after three years under Yanukovych, Pasha told me, all the "normal" cops were gone. The only ones left were the ones willing to do anything they were told. It wasn't like the Orange Revolution: this time the police were ready to shoot.

Pasha spent many nights on Maidan, holding the square. During the fight of December 1, he talked to a general and negotiated a neutral zone.

"When they saw my beret, they were ready to talk to me," he said. "But by then it was clear that there was no going back. I collected gas canisters and grenades. By then I had a whole backpack full of stuff." By February 20, he'd added a gas mask, handcuffs, and a knife.

Chapter 11

Are You Alive, Brother?

Early on the morning of December 11, with the temperature down to nine degrees Fahrenheit, troops surrounded Maidan and tried to clear its periphery, though not its center. Protesters gathered to hold the square.

"That was the point of no return for me," Vakhtang told me. "We all thought we could sleep that night—we'd been up for days. I went home and had some vodka, worked on a philosophy article, and went to bed. Then, just as I was falling asleep, a friend called and told me to turn on the TV. I saw that Berkut was trying to clear Maidan . . . . I was back there by one-thirty. People were unarmed, holding Berkut back with their bodies. Some people had their ribs broken by the pressure. At first there were only about three thousand people—up to Bohdan Khmelnytsky Street. And then suddenly there were twenty thousand people there. Taxis brought people to Maidan for free and the churches rang their bells, summoning everyone to Maidan. I understood that there would be a violent confrontation."

"When we heard about the first clearing of Maidan—someone called—we ran down right away," said Lena Grozovska, a calm, pleasant woman I knew from the Kiev art scene. "On the street we met people who told us to turn back. There were so many Berkut, but there were also so many others—hipsters, bon vivants, designers, all kinds of people you'd never have expected,

169

locking arms and blocking Berkut. Berkut looked like black caviar, with their helmets. When you looked into their eyes you saw such hate—they were such frightening people. A horde." Euromaidan protesters often called their enemies—first Berkut, then Russia—a "horde," an oblique reference to the Mongol invaders who sacked Kiev in the thirteenth century.

I spent most of that night watching a live feed from the helmet camera of Mustafa Nayyem, the journalist who'd helped organize the first protests on Maidan. Together we climbed over barricades and ran down dark, snowy streets, through huge crowds. I listened as Nayyem talked on the phone, or asked for information, or bumped into people he knew.

In the end, the riot police were ordered not to attack. They cleared the barricades around the square, but the protesters rebuilt them the next day, passing sandbags full of snow along a human chain. "Now our greatest fear is cops with hair dryers," my friend Sasha R. joked.

The police tried to raid occupied City Hall, but the protesters held them off with hoses, firecrackers, and smoke bombs, coating the steps of the building with ice and oil. Catherine Ashton, vice president of the European Commission, made a stern statement criticizing the police raid. Yanukovych kept hedging, promising a "nationwide dialogue" and making moves to punish some of those supposedly responsible for the violence on November 30. Then Putin offered to buy $15 billion of Ukrainian debt and provide a large discount on Russian gas. He called it "an act of brotherly love," insisting that it had nothing to do with Maidan. There was no chance that the EU would match Russia's offer.

*

In the beginning, most of the protesters on Maidan had rejected political slogans or parties, preferring nonpartisan expressions of patriotism. After the disappointments of the Orange Revolution and the depredations of the Yanukovych administration, Ukrainians had little trust in politicians. This time they wanted power to remain in the hands of the people.

But somebody would have to run the country after Yanukovych was gone. Hoping to anoint themselves as potential replacements, three politicians emerged as "opposition leaders," appearing regularly at rallies and meeting with foreign emissaries: Arseniy Yatsenyuk, a seasoned politician and ally of Yulia Tymoshenko; Vitaly Klitschko, a boxer turned liberal politician; and, alarmingly, Oleh Tyahnybok, leader of the radical nationalist party Svoboda.

Svoboda, whose name means "freedom," began as the Social-National Party of Ukraine (SNPU) in the early 1990s. It had its roots in the western Ukrainian ultranationalist ideology of the interwar period and World War II, represented most prominently by the Organization of Ukrainian Nationalists and the Ukrainian Insurgent Army. The SNPU used a modified Wolf's Hook symbol, claiming that it stood for the initials of the phrase "Idea of the Nation." (The Wolf's Hook looks like an N with a vertical stroke through its center, and also like a truncated swastika; the Nazis used it, and it is popular among European radical right groups.) The SNPU was known for forming paramilitary groups and assaulting Communists and other enemies. Though the SNPU had very little popular support, Oleh Tyahnybok, its most charismatic member, was elected to the Ukrainian parliament in 1998.

In 2004 Tyahnybok attempted to bring the SNPU into the mainstream. The SNPU was renamed Svoboda, the Wolf's

Hook replaced by a logo evoking the traditional Ukrainian trident. In that same year, however, Tyahnybok was expelled from President Yushchenko's parliamentary group for making a speech celebrating the Ukrainian Insurgent Army for fighting the Russians, Germans, Jews, "and other scum who wanted to take away our Ukrainian state," and calling on Ukrainian youth to fight the "Russian-Jewish mafia" that was supposedly ruling Ukraine. The next year Tyahnybok signed a letter petitioning President Yushchenko "to stop the criminal activity of organized Jewry" that was supposedly trying to undermine Ukrainian sovereignty. Nevertheless, Svoboda won increasing support in western Ukraine over the next years, in part thanks to a deal Yulia Tymoshenko struck for Russian gas, and her perceived "friendship with the 'Russian tsars' Medvedev and Putin," as Tyahnybok put it. In 2012 Svoboda won significant gains in parliament, thanks to economic anxiety and anger over the Yanukovych administration's rampant corruption and pro-Russian leanings. When the European Parliament expressed concern about Svoboda's racist, anti-Semitic, xenophobic positions, Tyahnybok dismissed their statement as the result of "Moscow agents working through a Bulgarian socialist MP." Though they comprised only a small minority of protesters on Maidan, Svoboda members were in the vanguard.

So was Right Sector, a coalition of nationalist groups that got its name on the night of November 24, when a speaker onstage tried to prevent a police attack from the right side of Maidan by urging the "nationalist boys" to "hold down" the "right sector." Right Sector was relatively diverse, including neo-Nazi groups as well as more moderate nationalists who rejected xenophobia, racism, and anti-Semitism, though they were still homophobic, sexist, and antileftist. (Ultranationalists, who rejected the idea of EU membership, attacked LGBT, feminist, and leftist protesters during the early days of Maidan.) Unlike Svoboda, which pushed for the exclusive use of Ukrainian in official settings, Right Sector had many Russian-speaking members.

Despite their tiny numbers—from several dozen, at the beginning of Maidan, to about five hundred at its conclusion—Right Sector members played a key role in Maidan and its aftermath. One Right Sector group, Tryzub, or "Trident," was a radical nationalist scout group whose emphasis on "military sports" left them exceptionally well prepared for a physical confrontation with law enforcement. The leader of Tryzub and then of Right Sector, Dmytro Yarosh, became a sort of opposition-opposition leader, a gadfly to the Yatsenyuk-Klitschko-Tyahnybok trifecta.

The ultranationalist presence on Maidan provided ready fuel for Russian claims that Maidan protesters were fascists eager to persecute Ukraine's Russian speakers. Western politicians, on the other hand, were overjoyed to see Ukrainians revolting against Russian influence; they had little trouble suppressing concerns about extreme nationalism. Victoria Nuland, a US assistant secretary of state, former adviser to Dick Cheney and ambassador to NATO, baited Russia by handing out cookies to the protesters on Maidan. On December 14 John McCain appeared on the Maidan stage with Klitschko and Tyahnybok. McCain probably didn't know much about Tyahnybok's fascist leanings, but Western officials who were familiar with Svoboda announced that the party was kinder, gentler, and more democratic than they'd thought. Cold warriors lurched up out of their coffins, yelling about freedom, democracy, and the right side of history.

Maidan certainly wasn't a fascist movement, but the wide-spread use of old Ukrainian nationalist symbols, chants, and heroes such as Stepan Bandera, a leader of the Organization of Ukrainian Nationalists, was disconcerting. (The Russians revived the term *Banderite*, which the Soviets had used as a slur against Ukrainian nationalists.) When two hundred thousand people on Maidan shouted "Glory to heroes! Glory to Ukraine!" I felt uneasy. The anxiety became acute when the occasional person shouted "Death to enemies!" as if he thought he was taking part in a bloodier kind of revolution. (One student activist told me that she and her fellow students hated this cry, countering it with chants like "Freedom for the innocent.") Equally discon-certing, the Maidaners started calling their movement "the Birth of a Nation."

I was surprised at how many of my friends and acquaintances defended Svoboda and Right Sector. Laima Geidar, a Russian-speaking lesbian feminist activist, the last person you'd expect to make excuses for Svoboda, later told me, "Even though they're homophobes and fascists and racists and often very unpleasant in their values, Svoboda did some good work and impressed a lot of people."

Vakhtang told me that my anxieties about ultranationalism on Maidan were misplaced. "For Yanukovych," he said, "power was the same as violence. That was the greatest weakness of his administration. It's not true, as some people say, that the base ideology of Maidan was far right—it was essentially liberal, even if it wasn't consciously liberal. It never initiated violence. Maidan was oriented around the defense of rights. In fact, there weren't many political slogans, and it's hard to call it a revolu-tion, because it wasn't at all radical. Maidan isn't right or left, it's civil society. I was originally against Right Sector, because I'm against the radical right. But then I understood that Right Sector isn't very radical. A lot of Right Sector members are Russian speakers. Lots of people started saying they were for Right Sector, because they saw that Right Sector was very active on Maidan."

Mitya, my Russian-Jewish clarinet player friend, insisted that Maidan was not anti-Semitic, at least not particularly, no more than the rest of Ukraine. He told me that Right Sector had organized protection for Kiev's synagogues and that Ukraine's main rabbis had supported the protests. One Right Sector member was an Orthodox Jew from Dnipropetrovsk. Mitya embraced the ironic label "Yid-Banderite," whose humor derived from the fact that Bandera was no friend of the Jews. He believed that chants like "Glory to heroes" had become new when they were resurrected; they stood for something different now, something he was glad to defend.

Mitya's Yiddish teacher, Tanya Batanova, had been writing a dissertation about the Jewish party in the 1918 Ukrainian government, during the brief moment when Yiddish was an official language of Ukraine. Tanya stopped working on her dissertation when Maidan started. As Mitya put it, "The theme of her dissertation became the theme of her life." Tanya wasn't Jewish; she'd learned Yiddish because she liked languages and believed that Yiddish was important for Ukrainian history. "I'm a little idealistic—a bit of a nationalist," she told me, "but I believe that it's good to be able to speak to someone in their own language."

The musicians in Mitya's Pushkin Klezmer Band were all from southern or eastern Ukraine and spoke Russian. When Maidan started, they had been fairly pro-Russian in their political views.

The first time Mitya came to rehearsal wearing a blue and gold Ukraine ribbon, they laughed at him, saying that the Maidan demonstrators were paid (the standard line on Russian television) and that Mitya was an idiot. Though they refused to play on Maidan, he persuaded them to learn a Ukrainian song, as well as the Yiddish revolutionary song "Daloy Politsey," which has lyrics like:

> Hey, hey, down with the police!
> Down with the Russian ruling class!

> Brothers and sisters, all gather round
> Together we are strong enough
> To bring this tsar down!

> Cossacks and gendarmes,
> Get down off your horses!
> The Russian tsar is already dead and buried!

The band went to play a show in Moscow, where people kept asking if the "Kiev fascists" assaulted them when they heard them speaking Russian. Mitya's bandmates started arguing with the audience members; they couldn't believe that these Russians were so brainwashed by government propaganda. After that experience, the whole band started wearing Ukrainian ribbons.

Tanya translated "Daloy Politsey" into Ukrainian and sang it with Mitya on Maidan, with Svoboda members serving as security guards for the stage. Then Mitya and Seryozha the Gypsy played some klezmer songs together. A Ukrainian and a Jew and a Rom together on the main stage, the crowd applauding—this couldn't be a fascist revolution. I allowed myself to be reassured.

The government set up an anti-Maidan camp with paid protesters, and acts of violence against Maidan activists proliferated. An anticorruption activist was shot in Kiev, his car set on fire. On December 25 Tetiana Chornovol, a well-known investigative journalist, was chased down in her car, beaten, and left for dead. Her dashcam video was soon online. It was terrifying to watch the road as she tried to outrace her pursuers, and as she was cornered on the dark roadside. You couldn't see her, only hear her gasping; the video ended before the beatings started.

On January 16, after yet another huge protest, the Yanukovych administration passed laws making it illegal to blockade government buildings, wear masks or helmets, install tents and stages without permission, or slander government officials. Suddenly everyone on Maidan was a criminal. These "dictatorship laws" prompted yet another enormous protest, which included an appearance by Tetiana Chornovol, her face still battered.

"After Yanukovych passed the dictatorship laws, we knew that even if he cleared Maidan, there would be repressions, arrests, disappearances—we had no choice but to get him out," Tanya Batanova told me.

Full-blown riots erupted outside the government buildings on Hrushevsky Street, near Maidan. Two protesters were shot dead—it was unclear by whom. The first, Serhiy Nigoyan, was a twenty-year-old Armenian-Ukrainian from a village south of

Dnipropetrovsk. With his thick black beard, long face, and fine features, he looked like he'd stepped out of an Orthodox icon. Thousands of people wept over his photo and over a YouTube clip of him reading a Taras Shevchenko poem. The second person shot was Belarusian. The fact that the first casualties were not full-blooded Ukrainians was taken as proof of the revolution's ability to transcend ethnicity or nationality.

Activists who went to hospitals for treatment started vanishing. Two kidnapped activists, Igor Lutsenko and Yury Verbitsky, were found in the woods a day after their disappearance. Verbitsky, a seismologist and mountain climber who had just completed a PhD in physics, had frozen to death after being tortured. I spent a long time looking at his picture; he had a kind, bearded face. The revolution had its first clutch of martyrs.

PartKom, a gallery owned by Lena Grozovska and her husband, where I'd often hung out with musician friends, turned into an underground infirmary. Alik started carrying a guidebook on wartime field surgery—he was following in his grandmother's footsteps, sort of. At one point he stitched up a nationalist with a swastika tattoo on his back.

"You know I'm a Jew, brother?" he asked his patient.

"Oh, I don't hate Jews," the wounded man replied. "Only niggers."

Alik's war surgeon grandmother wouldn't have been impressed by Maidan's gender politics, either. The front line was a world of men, with women appearing only occasionally, to help the wounded or offer food or drink. When fighting started, women were asked to leave or simply hustled off, even if they were journalists. One sign on Maidan announced, "Men are needed for the night guard on the barricades. Women are needed to keep watch by the mobilization tent, to keep order, to make tea and food for the guards and to spread information, leaflets and perform other mobilization work." Another sign put it less politely: "Dear women! If you notice any mess, tidy it up. It will be nice for the revolutionaries."

Some of the Maidan protesters had formed *sotni*—literally, "hundreds"—and these units had combined to form Maidan's self-defense force. In medieval times, Kiev's population had been divided into *sotni* (singular: *sotnya*) that provided a basis for raising a militia, collecting taxes, and completing public works. But Maidan's *sotni* were more like the Cossack squadrons, also called *sotni*, which survived until the Russian Revolution.

In many ways, Maidan looked like a premodern rebellion, the past rising up to conquer the unhappy present. People built a wooden catapult meant to hurl flames at the police, and fought in suits of armor that made them look like medieval knights. But these technologies were more romantic than effective. The catapult didn't work, and one young rail worker who reenacted medieval battles in his free time arrived at Maidan in a suit of armor, only to be shot dead by a sniper.

Other parts of Maidan resembled a postindustrial dystopia. Protesters piled tires into barricades many feet high; these were later burned, producing clouds of thick, stinking smoke, so the police couldn't see what was going on. The square was guarded by a ring of fire. Eventually the tire-barricades were reduced to tangles of singed wire.

From the first weeks of Maidan, it had been clear that not all the protesters were content with the peaceful methods of the

Orange Revolution. On the night of November 29, Right Sector members in masks were spotted carrying truncheons, ready for a fight. The next day they organized a training on how to counter police attacks using impromptu weapons; Dmytro Yarosh later said that this was when Right Sector was truly born. Nationalist groups on social networks shared information on how to make your own arms and armor.

On December 1, on Bankova Street, just above Maidan, a group of protesters commandeered a bulldozer and tried to pull down the fence around the Presidential Administration building, though some prominent figures, including MP Petro Poroshenko, the "Chocolate King" who had once sparred with Yulia Tymoshenko, tried to stop them. Some protesters threw bricks, and masked men threw Molotov cocktails; police responded with stun grenades and smoke bombs. That night a group of radical nationalist protesters used sticks, stones, and ladders to attack Berkut officers who were guarding the Lenin statue at the end of Taras Shevchenko Boulevard. The officers responded with tear gas and flash grenades. The protesters managed to push Berkut back, but two officers were left behind and beaten by the mob.

Opposition leaders were eager to maintain Maidan's reputation as a purely nonviolent movement that deserved the wholehearted support of the West. They disavowed the violent protesters, calling them provocateurs: agents of Russia or of the Yanukovych administration, trying to discredit the demonstrations. Maidan's "self-defense force" patrolled the square all night, making sure there weren't any drunk people or drugs, hoping to head off any future "provocations." (One of the most obvious marks of Maidan's extraordinary nature was the absence of intoxicants.) But in a grassroots protest movement that was largely spontaneous, it's hard to understand how opposition spokespeople could know that violent protesters weren't authentic; they never presented any evidence that the masked men with Molotov cocktails were paid, for example.

Right Sector had made little effort to conceal its fondness for physical confrontation. Dmytro Yarosh's paramilitary nationalist youth group, Tryzub, published an article online entitled "Confessions of a Provocateur," saying, "On December 1 we struck first. And what happened next? The acts of the real provocateurs"—presumably the Yanukovych administration—"acted as a catalyst for the psychology of victims, and they started calling us 'provocateurs.'" This article was soon removed, but the next day the website published another called "Glory to Ukraine! Glory to the 'Provocateurs'!," expressing similar sentiments without admitting to any specific crimes.

Still, the EU and the United States continued to refer to Maidan as an entirely nonviolent movement. It was funny, with memories of Occupy Wall Street still fresh, to imagine what the United States would have done if protesters had occupied New York's City Hall, thrown Molotov cocktails at police, and made a barricaded tent city in Times Square. There was a measure of truth in the Russian government's accusations of Western hypocrisy.

Russian official media seized on every instance of violence on the part of the protesters, portraying Maidan as a CIA-sponsored coup against a legitimate government. It was true that Yanukovych had been elected fairly, even if he was a criminal and his police had attacked peaceful protesters without provocation. Russian accusations of American involvement gained momentum after

181

someone (probably Russia) leaked a phone conversation between Victoria Nuland and Geoffrey Pyatt, the American ambassador to Ukraine, in which they discussed how power should be distributed after Maidan. Nuland didn't want Klitschko in the government, because of his lack of experience, or Tyahnybok, presumably because of his fascist politics. She wanted Yatsenyuk, the experienced politician. One of Putin's advisers promptly told the Ukrainian press that the United States was spending $20 million a week on Ukrainian opposition groups and on arming and training "rebels."

On January 22 the police were authorized to use water cannons, though Prime Minister Azarov promised that Berkut was not permitted to use live ammunition. By now protesters tossed Molotov cocktails freely, repurposing Kiev's empty vodka and beer bottles for revolution. Women formed lines, pulling up cobblestones and passing them along to be thrown at the enemy. Klitschko announced that the protesters would attack if their demands weren't met within twenty-four hours. The far-right Ukrainian National Assembly–Ukrainian People's Self-Defense called on all Ukrainians with guns to defend Maidan.

At first only extremists had been willing to resort to force; now, outraged at the government's willingness to torture or kill unarmed citizens, many people were coming around to the idea of armed resistance. The uncompromising men of Right Sector began to look like heroes rather than provocateurs.

Sasha, my Russian FrontAIDS activist friend, had moved to Kiev, where she was living with her Ukrainian boyfriend.

In the years since I'd first met her in 2006, many of her fellow Russian activists had died of AIDS-related illnesses or overdoses, often because of Russia's refusal to provide decent medical care. Sasha was furiously in favor of Maidan, working at one of the first aid points. After the police turned violent, she wrote on Facebook,

> Rights are not given, but taken. Sometimes roughly. The government has a monopoly, a mandate on the use of violence. As citizens, we delegated that right to the government. But not for use against its own citizens. So we're retaking the right to self-defense from the government, with cobblestones in hand.
>
> When I was undergoing an NGO audit in Russia, answering endless questions about our protest, as I came out of the Ministry of Justice I cried, wrapping my arms around an ancient oak tree near the park where I grew up, where I went swimming in the Neva River with my parents when I was a child. Because it's my land, my city, and it's under occupation, and I can't do anything about it. I spent half my childhood with my grandma in Chernigiv [in Ukraine]. Here I can do something. And I will.

Pasha Skala described seeing a man plant himself in front of Berkut with a shovel and say, "I have nothing but this shovel, but I will use it to protect my family." People had started carrying baseball bats as a matter of routine. A friend told me about seeing a man at a supermarket carrying a pitchfork. (In the nineteenth century, Galician peasants were notorious for stabbing their

183

Polish landlords with pitchforks.) Others announced their willingness to die for the cause. One protester's plywood shield bore the message, MOTHER I WILL DIE FOR YOU BUT I WILL NOT GIVE UP IN SHAME HERE. FOR OUR UKRAINE AND FOR OUR FOREFATHERS I WILL NOT LEAVE MAIDAN WITHOUT VICTORY. His full name and phone number followed, so that his message would make it back to his mother even if he didn't.

In other cities, especially in western Ukraine, protesters were seizing control of government buildings, often facing little or no resistance, and demanding that Yanukovych-appointed officials resign. Maidan was a nationwide movement, with more than two million Ukrainians participating in protests.

Yanukovych offered a compromise: Yatsenyuk would be prime minister, Klitschko would be vice prime minister in charge of humanitarian affairs, and there would be an amnesty for protesters who left occupied buildings. But the crowds on Maidan were vehemently opposed to any compromise, and Yatsenyuk didn't accept. Prime Minister Azarov resigned, and Yanukovych's Party of Regions revoked most of the antiprotest laws, but this wasn't enough. Yanukovych went on sick leave.

Dmytro Bulatov, a leading Maidan organizer, was found badly beaten, soaked in blood, with an ear cut off and his hands pierced by nails, as if he'd been crucified. Missing for eight days, he'd been left to freeze to death in the forest outside Kiev. The police suggested, astoundingly, that he had faked the whole thing. They tried to arrest him in the hospital but were stopped by protesters.

On February 18 there was another huge protest, this time in favor of restoring the constitution to its pre-Yanukovych form. It became a pitched battle.

"We were called to go to the Parliament," Vakhtang said. "I was very opposed—I thought the Maidan camp was established, and moving to the Parliament was very dangerous. But I went along with everyone else, unarmed, without special clothing or armor."

"On the eighteenth of February I was sick with a temperature," Lena Grozovska told me, "but I went out anyway and passed stones. I stood there for eight or nine hours. When I finally went home, I saw a big band of thugs waiting, already shooting. They shot at our car, but we made it through. I sat all night looking out the window on our balcony, watching them shoot at people. If I'd had a gun, I would have shot them. Your brain changes."

"I spent the night on Maidan," Vakhtang told me. "The Trade Union House was set on fire. Berkut tried to set fire to the medical point in the musical conservatory across the street, too—they threw Molotov cocktails on the roof, and people threw them off." The Trade Union House burned down, with protesters trapped inside it. Snipers appeared on rooftops, shooting to kill.

When the violence began, Laima Geidar had started working as a medic. She wanted to rush to Maidan on February 18, but the police had closed the bridge across the Dnieper, blocking crowds of people who, like Laima, were trying to get across to help. Laima went to a hospital in her neighborhood; a crowd of people was outside, preventing the police from arresting wounded protesters. Laima helped organize a medical point at the Greek Catholic church for people who weren't too seriously wounded.

People would get stitched up and want to return immediately to Maidan. "Give me a pill for concussion," said one man who'd been beaten with a truncheon. Even a man with two broken hands wanted to go right back.

During the next two days, Laima's medical team found more than nine people who'd been shot in the left eye: evidence of the coldest and most expert sniper fire.

Olga Vrovke, whom I'd met at the mushroom festival in Vorokhta, saw a man shot by a sniper, then watched a doctor save the man's life in the Hotel Ukraina. On her way home she was chased by a thug with a tire iron. But soon she was back to practical business, coordinating things on Facebook. Did anyone know the entrances to underground tunnels? she asked. Or did anyone have a military map? The snipers were probably using them to get into buildings without being noticed. Mountain climbers were needed to hold the roofs.

Olga's Facebook organizing wasn't unusual—much of the coordination of Euromaidan went on through social media. Unless you were throwing Molotov cocktails or shooting from rooftops, there was no thought of secrecy: this was the "Revolution of Dignity," a public movement whose central tenet was transparency.

On February 19 I watched on the live feed as priests and an imam prayed on the Maidan stage, surrounded by flames. The protesters kept up a steady, dull drumbeat, banging on shields and anything else available. This was the music of revolution: a clatter, a din, anonymous musicians cloaked in smoke. From across the ocean, it looked like the end of the world.

A video showed bodies splayed across the street where my friend Julia Y. had once walked her Labrador, Darcy. Men in camouflage and an older woman in a headscarf helped carry people, bloody and dazed, to an ambulance, as a priest in a black gown and green helmet talked to a crowd of injured people.

A medic did chest compressions on a man who seemed, to my untrained eye, to be obviously dead. The cameraman lingered until the medic said, "Don't stand here!"

"A person is dying!" another man said angrily.

The cameraman retreated. Next, he approached a young, fair-haired man spread-eagled on the muddy ground. His eyes were closed.

"Are you alive, brother? Hey, what's your name?" The blond man didn't answer. The cameraman took his pulse and stepped back, lingering on the body before hurrying down the path at the edge of the park.

He saw another man and repeated his question: "Are you alive, brother?" This time the man in question nodded. His eyes were open, and his face was covered in blood. "Alive, that's good!" the cameraman said, and hurried along. The crowd was roaring in the distance. Kiev was at war.

I was terrified, but everyone told me that it was less frightening to be there than to watch it on television. "When Maidan was going on," Mitya said later, "it felt like the only safe place; it was like a centrifuge. At the center you're safe, but anywhere else the force will send you flying." Yury, one of Alina's colleagues, told me, "It was scary to watch Maidan on TV, but it wasn't scary when you were there—you felt the power of numbers." He said that the more dangerous it got, the more people went to Maidan. After the snipers appeared, Yury said, "We knew that if we didn't go, it was over for Ukraine."

The city was disfigured by violence, but it was transfigured by solidarity and compassion. A stream of people went to

St. Michael's Monastery to offer help, donations, medicine, food. Blood collection centers had to turn people away. On Facebook, Andrei Mikhalevsky, who had been sorting donations at St. Michael's, described an elderly woman who arrived, silent and flustered, and handed him a hand-made cloth bag. When he opened it, he found that it contained 200 grams of sugar, an orange, an onion, three heads of garlic, two pieces of candy, a half-full bottle of vinegar, and five hryvnia (less than a dollar). She had given everything she could.

People sent their children to stay with nannies and asked older children to make themselves dinner as they worked around the clock. At the All-Ukrainian Network of People Living with HIV, many of my old public health colleagues were volunteering to provide emergency medical care, since the hospitals weren't safe for protesters. It was hard to perform surgeries at the network's office—they didn't have proper equipment for anesthesia and had to operate on conference tables. But, miraculously, there were no infections. The doctors removed a blunt, round bullet from one man's neck. Like many patients, he wanted to go straight back to Maidan.

On February 20 I spoke to Alina on Skype. She was rumpled and panicked, like so many other people in the city. The metro had been shut down for two days, there had been runs on groceries, gas, and cash, and martial law seemed imminent. "This is the sort of thing that you should only see on television," she said, looking like she was about to cry. Her mother, who worked as a custodian at a military hospital, said they'd let the staff go home and were preparing for an emergency. The place was covered in blood. She'd seen a very young policeman, a boy, almost, carried past with his insides hanging out; later she saw him being taken to the morgue. On a list of the dead released that day, the oldest reported casualty was born in 1949, the youngest in 1996.

On February 21 Yanukovych signed a deal with opposition leaders: there were to be constitutional changes and elections by the end of the year. But the protests didn't subside, and an impeachment bill was introduced in parliament.

Julia Y. gave a friend of a friend a ride to the morgue; he had to retrieve the body of his father, who had been shot on Maidan the day before.

Pasha Skala put on his beret and went to talk to the line of Internal Troops behind the blue and gold barricade in front of one of the government buildings. They recognized him, and a general came out and told him they wanted to be given a corridor to leave. A bus full of troops was taken hostage by the crowd, but eventually a passage was formed to let them leave Maidan. The government was retreating.

On February 22, after two months of protests, Yanukovych fled Kiev. Parliament declared him unfit to fulfill his duties. His mansion opened for tours; the people flooded through the gates. He left behind a number of incriminating documents, including a handwritten receipt for $12 million and a list of journalists and activists—including Tetiana Chornovol—with photos and license plate numbers. Protesters still in helmets, still carrying shields, their faces still smeared with soot, started playing golf on Yanukovych's private course. There were calls to make the

189

mansion into a Museum of Corruption. It felt like a miracle, like the joyful ending of a film.

But more than a thousand people had been injured, and more than a hundred had been killed. The dead protesters were named "the Heavenly Hundred," the Nebesnaya Sotnya, the divine regiment. Some were carried across Maidan in open caskets, through a crowd of thousands of people who were weeping, singing, praying, and chanting, "Heroes don't die."

"When Yanukovych left, there was huge euphoria," Vakhtang said. "But soon enough, people had to face the fact that they were fighting Russia now."

Chapter 12

Masks and Monuments

In late February, as the violence peaked, someone on Twitter posted a video with the note, "This is the worst so far." I clicked, and saw a dark-haired woman in Khmelnytsky, a town in western Ukraine, being shot in the head by a sniper. She had been protesting outside a government building. Her blood was very bright as it flooded the pavement. A couple of people screamed, but the rest remained calm, and surrounded a passing trolleybus. I wondered if they were trying to get on, to escape the sniper, but they hauled the trolleybus over to block the entrance to the government building. It looked easy, because there were so many people pushing.

At the time I was deeply moved by this display of strength in numbers, which seemed a physical embodiment of the power of ordinary people to overturn an unjust social order. The video—wherever it came from, whoever had filmed it—fit neatly into the narrative of Maidan that I'd accepted, that most of my Ukrainian friends had accepted: it was a good kind of revolution, one that gave you hope for the future. But not everyone believed this story.

Conspiracy theories proliferated. Many were clearly false, generated by Russia's hyperactive propaganda machine. But there were legitimate questions about what exactly had happened in Ukraine that winter. Why had the special police attacked student demonstrators without provocation, an act that was bound to discredit Yanukovych's administration and give new strength and purpose to the protest movement? To what extent (if any) had opposition parties and their oligarch backers planned and funded the protests? Who was responsible for the kidnapping and torture of activists? Who were the masked men who had attacked the police in the early days of Maidan? Who had shot at the police during the final battles, and who, if anyone, had ordered them to do so? And most importantly, who were the mysterious snipers on the rooftops? None of these questions were fully answered in the weeks and months after Maidan. Many of Yanukovych's officials and police had fled, destroying evidence as they went, and the post-Maidan government did a poor job of investigating the crimes perpetrated during the protest, prompting suspicions of a cover-up.

In fact, many officials in the new government were hold-overs from the old one; they'd simply changed sides. It was easy to guess that these seasoned politicians might not be enthusiastic about a thorough investigation into the bad deeds of the old government. The new government also had obvious reasons to cover up any crimes committed by Maidan protesters, who were now heroes. Some evidence suggested that there had been antigovernment as well as government snipers on Maidan in February. (Two men would later admit to journalists that they had intentionally shot police from the windows of the occupied Kiev Conservatory, off Maidan.) Had the attacks and murders been provocations meant to legitimate the overthrow of the government—perhaps by extreme nationalists, or by oligarchs who wanted Yanukovych out because he'd been plundering their treasure chests? You could take your pick of plots. They were all hopelessly confusing, without enough hard evidence to make them credible; but the official story about Maidan was confusing too, with pieces that didn't fit.

Conspiracy theories fell on fertile ground in the post-Soviet world, where plots, double agents, and provocateurs had a long and lurid history. In the late nineteenth and early twentieth centuries, Russian security forces planted police informers throughout worker and revolutionary organizations. Informers didn't just spy on the revolutionaries and labor unions; they participated actively, rising through the ranks and taking part in assassinations and bombings. Soon the revolutionaries planted their own agents in the police service. Informers from both camps were embedded for so long that they often seemed to forget which side they were on.

Traitors made their way to the very top. In 1908 the revolutionaries exposed Yevno Azef, a high-ranking Socialist Revolutionary terrorist who had been on the secret police payroll for some fifteen years, during which time he had helped plan the successful assassination of the minister of the interior. Azef's unmasking was followed by that of Roman Malinovsky, a prominent Bolshevik, close associate of Lenin, and the Russian Empire's highest-paid agent after he was flipped by the secret police in 1910. The information he provided helped send Stalin and other Bolshevik leaders into exile; by 1913 Malinovsky was the only high-level Bolshevik running free in Russia. Lenin put him in charge of the entire Bolshevik operation inside the Russian Empire. When Malinovsky was denounced, Lenin refused to believe it. By then the professional revolutionaries felt so paranoid that, as Bukharin put it, they "looked in the mirror and wondered if they themselves were provocateurs." In the midst of this pervasive double-crossing, the term *provocateur*

193

became one of the worst of all slurs, as it was on twenty-first-century Maidan. In an instant, a familiar face could become an object of revulsion.

In order to justify the hardship and oppression faced by its citizens, the Soviet Union had to unmask its enemies again and again: capitalists, the bourgeoisie, kulaks, nationalists, saboteurs, provocateurs, spies. In the 1930s Stalin built his purges on staged trials, fictional confessions, fantastical conspiracies. Routine unmasking required the steady fabrication of plots. Even as they seethed with hatred for external and internal enemies (as they did again in the post-Soviet period), Soviet people learned not to trust the news, to read between the lines. Some dissidents spoke about the truth that would emerge once the authoritarian monster had been slain, its propaganda machine shut down for good. But many Soviet citizens were skeptical of anything they hadn't seen with their own eyes or heard directly from a friend. (As Bulgakov put it as early as 1923, "Kievans don't read newspapers, being firmly convinced that they print lies. But since a person can't live without information, they get their news from the Jewish bazaar, where old ladies find it necessary to sell their candelabras." The rumor mill produces fantastic, almost mythical tales.) In the Soviet Union, it was assumed that politicians were liars; that was their job. It was taken for granted that governments used the language of idealism to mask sinister motives; that was how governments worked. Many post-Soviet politicians confirmed these principles with their corruption, lies, cover-ups, double-crosses, and frame-ups.

Even if you weren't susceptible to conspiracy theories, there were aspects of Maidan that didn't gibe with the rhetoric about a nonviolent "Revolution of Dignity." Not every bit of ugliness could be blamed on provocateurs.

When I saw the documentary *All Things Ablaze*, which was filmed by three Ukrainian journalists on the front lines of the fighting from the beginning to the end of Maidan, I realized that there were many versions of Maidan. The film shows the heart of Kiev in flames, full of angry mobs and meaningless violence. As in reality, it isn't clear who started the violence, or who's fighting for what, exactly. It often seems that people may be fighting just for the sake of it.

Protesters parade a bloody pro-government thug down the street, screaming that he's a traitor. They beat a Berkut officer who's lying on the ground, as some onlookers try to stop them. Men smash what they take to be a Party of Regions car. As its alarm wails, someone asks, "Why are you doing that? Do you even know whose it is?" A young man wrapped in a Ukrainian flag announces, "The smell of smoke and tear gas is the smell of freedom. Glory to Ukraine! Ukraine over all!" People set themselves on fire while trying to light the Molotov cocktails that they're heaving at the police. A masked man shoots a rifle as someone plays the "Ode to Joy," the EU anthem, on a bagpipe. When the masked man hits his target, which we cannot see, he high-fives his friend.

Oleksandr Techinskiy, one of three directors of *All Things Ablaze*, is a dark-haired man in his thirties, well educated, well traveled, polite. Originally trained in medicine, he went on to become a photographer and a stringer for foreign journalists, mostly Germans. Demographically speaking, he was the kind of person who would support Maidan. And he wasn't against it; he was just skeptical. What he'd seen didn't line up with the stories people were telling.

"When I was on Institutska [one of the streets where heavy fighting took place], I didn't see any self-defense squads," he told me, a year after Maidan. "I saw a lot of lost people. Boys in ski jackets." For him, the story of the heroic self-defense battalions was a myth; the truth was sad and scattered.

Techinskiy believed that one of the biggest mistakes made during Maidan was the choice of some protesters to start hiding their faces. "When this is all over, will we build monuments to men in masks?" he asked.

It was a good question. I thought of all the Maidan protesters who had put themselves in danger by organizing openly, believing wholeheartedly in the "Revolution of Dignity." I remembered Sasha, my Russian AIDS activist friend, whose great act of bravery had been to take off her mask and speak publicly about having HIV. Shouldn't a just revolution show its face? What were the masked men of Maidan hiding?

In *All Things Ablaze*, as Kiev burns and both sides fire, a priest waves a cross and Bible and shouts, "Don't throw stones! Don't shoot!"

Some protesters run over. "Get away," they tell him, "it won't help, those souls are lost."

Many of my friends and acquaintances who'd been on Maidan had spoken about how inspired they'd felt at the sight of ordinary ladies in office clothes prying up cobblestones with their manicured fingers, passing them down a line. Most of the press accounts I'd seen of this, too, portrayed it as a miracle of spontaneous mass organization—a hive of righteous protesters. But people power can be hard to distinguish from mob violence.

All Things Ablaze lingered on the faces of the police who'd had cobblestones thrown at them. Many of them were very young, and they looked terrified. For much of the time they weren't allowed to shoot, and they made it clear that they felt this was unfair. Didn't they have the right to defend themselves? Many of the soldiers on Maidan were conscripts, completing their compulsory military service. Was it glorious to throw stones at them? Was it right to call people—even Berkut officers—"cockroaches" or "black caviar" or a "horde"?

On December 8, 2013, after a huge rally, Maidan protesters toppled Kiev's Lenin statue. The international media were delighted, mostly ignoring the fact that the topplers were far-right nationalists. (The Svoboda party took credit.)

In *All Things Ablaze*, the fall of Kiev's Lenin has an emotional tenor completely different from that of Western news stories covering Ukraine's "Goodbye, Lenin!" moment. It's nighttime, and a mob is taking turns smashing Lenin's body with a sledgehammer. A young man shouts hoarsely, "Outsiders don't forget, Ukrainians are in charge here!" An Orthodox priest takes a turn with the sledgehammer as the mob fights for fragments of the statue. Then the camera discovers Lenin's head in the darkness. With its stone eyes, it looks like the head of a man who is sleeping or dead. Soon the mob finds it, too. A grinning blond girl poses beside it: a bizarre, postmodern Pietà.

The camera moves to a silent middle-aged man in a black fur hat. Looking dazed, he wraps his arms around Lenin's body, pressing his own body against it. He is an old Communist from the Institute of Physics. The crowd is shouting at him, taunting

197

him, taking his picture. Everyone tells him to get away from the statue so they can continue destroying it. One man tells him he ought to hang himself. A woman, obviously afraid he'll be injured, tries to persuade him to leave.

Men drag him away, but he returns to Lenin, still silent. "Don't hit him," someone says. The old Communist looks like he's being torn away from the corpse of a loved one.

"You're the last like this in Ukraine," a man in the mob says. "When you're dead, there will be no Communists left."

But the man in the fur hat wasn't the last Communist in Ukraine, not by a long shot, and many Ukrainians, even those who weren't Communists, were displeased at the country-wide "Leninfall" triggered by the downing of Kiev's monument.

In Dnipropetrovsk in February, someone got up on the pedestal of the city's steel Lenin statue and put a harness around it. The crowd pulled in unison, as if in a tug-of-war with the past, but they weren't strong enough; finally someone arrived with a truck and toppled the leader at last. Lenin fell directly on his head, which broke off. People started beating him.

In the morning, when the ardently pro-Maidan journalist Marina Davydova arrived, Lenin's head sat on the pavement, a noose around his neck, his eyes still wide open. (His head was eventually moved to the Dnipropetrovsk Historical Museum.) Marina managed to get a chunk of Lenin as a souvenir. She later described her ecstasy, on that sunny day, at the destruction of this "symbol of a totalitarian regime," as she called it. "I thought it was a victory, the beginning of a new world," she told me, "though I didn't know what kind of new world it would be."

A group arrived carrying Orthodox icons and asking for the body of their leader. (Communism and religion had reconciled long ago.) One man made a YouTube video showing his fellow citizens hacking away at the steel body. The crowd is much calmer and less menacing than the one shown in *All Things Ablaze*.

"Here are the results of yesterday's vandalism," the man with the movie camera says dolefully. "People are still trying to get their little piece of the monument." His tone becomes sarcastic. "So, we'll live well now that the monument has been knocked down. Everything will be great in our country."

Chapter 13

Reunion

During an all-night meeting on February 22, Putin and his security officials discussed what was to be done with the disgraced, oafish Yanukovych. They decided to give him safe haven in Russia. At the end of the meeting, Putin reportedly announced, "We must start working on returning Crimea to Russia."

Yanukovych's flight from Ukraine set in motion a plan that worked so smoothly that it must have been made long in advance. On February 23 there were pro-Russian demonstrations in the Crimean city of Sevastopol. On February 27 "polite little green men," soldiers in unmarked uniforms and masks, appeared on the peninsula, seizing the Crimean parliament building and other state structures. (As an "autonomous republic" within Ukraine, Crimea had its own parliament and prime minister.) The little green men faced very little resistance from Ukrainian security forces, many of whom promptly defected to the Russian side. Crimea's occupied parliament dissolved the sitting government and replaced Crimea's prime minister with a member of Crimea's Russian Unity party.

The little green men were happy to pose for photos with children and pretty girls, but they refused to explain where they'd come from, saying only, "We're simply trying to prevent violence." Neat, professional, and well behaved, the little green men made a dramatic contrast with the "Crimean self-defense force," a motley assortment of local men in camouflage, athletic wear, and

Cossack costumes formed to defend the peninsula from Kiev's new "fascist junta," as the Russian media called it. Putin denied that the little green men were Russian soldiers, suggesting that they were Crimean self-defense forces who had bought their own uniforms. By then he was just teasing.

Russia's strategic interest in Crimea was obvious. After Ukrainian independence, Russia's Black Sea Fleet had remained in the port city of Sevastopol, which, with its prime military and trading position, has figured in many wars over the centuries. Russia had made clear that it was unwilling to give up Sevastopol under any circumstances, and the ousting of Yanukovych posed a clear threat. After Ukrainian troops on the peninsula had been converted or contained, a referendum was organized for mid-March; the inhabitants of Crimea were to determine whether they would become a part of Russia.

In early March the Crimean journalist Aleksandra Dvoretskaya took part in protests supporting the Ukrainian soldiers who were blockaded in their military quarters. The Crimean self-defense forces shoved the protesters and seized their flags and signs as the police looked on.

As the activists planned a gathering in honor of Taras Shevchenko's birthday, March 9, two of them were arrested and handed over to Crimea's Russian Unity party. They were held prisoner for two weeks, and one of them was shot in the arm and leg. The protesters learned that there would soon be a larger repression of local activists, and that the self-defense forces and special forces were looking for Dvoretskaya. A few days before the referendum, she got on a train to the mainland. "Every stop, every open door was torture—I thought someone was going to capture me," she recalled in an interview with a Ukrainian publication. In Kiev, she started an organization to provide assistance to other internally displaced Ukrainians.

Dvoretskaya was a journalist, an activist, a public figure. But some ordinary people fled, too. On the night before the referendum, Natasha Abrosimenkova, who was twenty-five, decided to flee her village, Lenino. She was frightened by the armed people who had suddenly filled the streets, and she didn't want Russian citizenship. She'd studied Ukrainian history and culture at university and attended a Russian-language secondary school with a Ukrainian curriculum. The Ukrainian government had provided social support for her three children, but the payments had stopped when the little green men took over. She and her husband had worked as traders in the local market: she sold underwear and he sold hats. But they'd gotten the clothes from Ukraine, and with transport cut off, they didn't know what to do.

Soldiers turned many cars back from the cordon, especially trucks. They searched Natasha's family's car but saw that they had three children, and let them through.

For the Abrosimenkov family, the flight from Crimea meant losing almost everything. Their bank accounts were blocked. Friends and relatives rejected them, adding them to the list of personae non gratae: traitors, Nazis, Banderites.

The Crimean Tatars protested vigorously and boycotted the referendum, to no avail. Crimea's new government claimed that it planned to treat the Tatars well, but many Tatars fled the peninsula, remembering Stalin's mass deportation. Their leader,

Mustafa Dzhemilev, left Crimea to attempt to meet with US vice president Joseph Biden; he was refused reentry. Thousands of Crimean Tatars went to the border crossing point to meet Dzhemilev, breaking through lines of Russian troops and saying that they would return to Crimea only if Dzhemilev was with them. But the Crimean Tatars had been written out of the new narrative of Crimea. Their small-scale occupations of land and property, their protests and half-built shacks were dwarfed by Russia's overnight occupation of the entire peninsula. Crimea's acting prime minister, Sergei Aksyonov, said that any Tatars who were displeased with the new situation should leave if they didn't like it; many followed his advice. Authorities banned the Tatars' annual commemoration of their 1944 deportation.

The Tatars, and people like Dvoretskaya and Abrosimenkova, were in the minority. Official reports of 83 percent turnout for the referendum, with 97 percent voting to join Russia, were certainly exaggerated. But many Crimeans truly did want to become Russian—or rather, to return to the Soviet Union, the country in which many of them had been born. They hoped to be rescued from the uncertainty of post-Maidan Ukraine, to receive higher pensions, and to exit a nation in which they'd never really been at home. Many Crimeans couldn't speak Ukrainian even if they wanted to, and they had long been angry that Russian wasn't a state language. There had been periodic bursts of separatist feeling, especially under Orange Revolution president Yushchenko. In 2006, during an election campaign, young people with shovels gathered on the isthmus of Perekop, which connects Crimea and Ukraine, to dig a symbolic trench.

The Crimean government had supported Yanukovych from the beginning of the Euromaidan protests. Many Crimeans watched Russian television, which whipped them into a frenzy of fear over the "fascist" Maidan movement. Dmytro Yarosh, the leader of the ultranationalist coalition Right Sector, was Russia's favorite bogeyman; though Right Sector remained a fringe group, the Russian media made it sound like the Fourth Reich. The Ukrainian government gave plenty of fodder to the Russian propaganda machine, too. In February 2014 the Ukrainian parliament had voted to cancel a 2012 law that allowed for official bilingualism (Russian and Ukrainian) in regions in which more than 10 percent of the population identified as Russian. Interim President Turchynov refused to sign the bill, but the damage was done. Many Russian-speaking Ukrainians became convinced that the post-Maidan government planned to strip them of their rights.

Yaroslav Pilunskiy, a cameraman in his late thirties, had filmed the Maidan protests as part of a documentary filmmaking collective called Babylon '13, which formed, in Pilunskiy's words, to "help in the information war." Many members were people from the student movement of the 1990s, the sorts of people who'd participated in the Orange Revolution.

Yaroslav was born in Crimea, in Simferopol. At the time of the referendum his father was still a deputy in the Crimean parliament, a vocal advocate for Ukrainian unity. Before the referendum he appeared on live Russian television, where, according to Yaroslav, "they cut him off because he was telling the truth." People on the street called him a traitor. Fearing for his father's life, Yaroslav went to retrieve him, accompanied by Yura Gruzinov, another member of Babylon '13. Yaroslav brought his camera and money he'd collected from Maidan activists to purchase groceries and other supplies for friends in Crimea.

Yaroslav and Yura were trying to film surreptitiously outside a police station when the self-defense patrol, a group of Crimeans with automatic weapons who'd been assigned to guard the area, caught sight of them. Yaroslav and Yura didn't have any press accreditation; the patrolmen seized their camera and brought them in for interrogation.

"I was interrogated first," Yaroslav told me. "We decided together that it was a misunderstanding, we hadn't filmed anything anyway, and they'd just take our memory cards and let us go. But then they interrogated Yura, and while they were doing that, a guy came in who knew my father. He recognized me and said, 'We need to hang on to this guy.' Then there was a call on my cell phone. It was a comrade from Maidan who was entered in my contacts as 'Regiment Assistant.' And that was it—they thought we were Right Sector. We were just enemies to them.

"They cuffed our hands behind our backs, blindfolded us, and put us in a basement room that was meant for kitchen storage, with a tiled floor. There was blood splattered on the tiles. The only objects in the room were a mattress, a bottle of water, and a bottle for urine. We couldn't hear anything. In the wall between the rooms where we were being held there was a hole, and we could see each other's eyes—that helped. We were panicked, of course. But we had to pull ourselves together, and we did.

"After twenty-four hours a military commander came into the next cell. He was a Ukrainian who'd been detained. We whispered to each other, and I saw the fear in his eyes, even though he was a military man, ten years older than I am. He said the main thing was to survive. We wondered who'd come to interrogate us—Russians, or Cossacks with long beards, or Berkut. But it was three young guys, maybe thirty years old at most, in masks. And then we felt better, because we knew they weren't going to kill us—you don't need three guys in masks for that.

"They tied my arms behind my back again, put a towel over my head, and took me into the next room. I asked them if they planned to beat me, and they said they did. I asked what for, and they said they were going to find out when Right Sector was going to show up in Crimea. I told them we should just talk, that I had nothing to hide. But they said there was only one way this could go.

"They put me in a chair and kicked me in the chest, then hit me with a pipe, put a pistol in my face. And they were asking absolutely stupid questions. I could tell they'd learned them from films or from a book. They demanded addresses, safe houses, passwords. From the beginning, they were convinced someone had sent us—some senior member of the Maidan self-defense force. They wanted to know who'd paid us. We kept insisting we didn't represent any armed forces. I realized that the Crimean peninsula had been closed off, and a sort of collective unconsciousness had taken over . . . . So I talked to them and tried to make them think with their own minds. Sometimes I'd make progress and we'd start arguing—but then they'd revert, saying, 'Fascist, Banderite,' and so on.

"One of them said, 'You're my enemy. Because your camera is stronger than my weapons.' I was in ecstasy—I wanted to applaud. It was so unreal. For them, every person with a camera is an enemy. I think it's because they know that what they're doing is criminal, and they're afraid of being caught and tried for separatism, which is a crime. But when they're in masks, in big groups, and feel protected by Russia—then they're not afraid.

"We had a conversation—of course, in those conditions it could hardly be called a conversation, but still—and we found out we had relatives from the same place, Kamenets-Podilsk, and I found out he had two degrees from institutions of higher education—though maybe they were in physical education, I don't know. He was very Orthodox. He looked for a cross under the neck of my shirt, and when he didn't find one, he said, 'Are you a Jew?'

"When he held the pistol to my head, it meant he wasn't beating me, so I could relax a little. That was when we talked. 'Who gave you the money?' he asked. I told him that I'd gotten it from donations, from people on Maidan. People who want to get criminals out of power. And then he put the pistol down. He didn't point the pistol at me anymore, he didn't beat me anymore. When I said, 'get criminals out of power,' I was talking directly about him. His brain had gone on, he'd started thinking. He asked me about Right Sector, and I explained what they do, and how they weren't going to come to Crimea, because they had their hands full in Kiev."

Yaroslav and Yura were in the basement for six days before they were released. They were the subjects of many news stories, the first hostages in what was now an open conflict between Ukraine and Russia.

Putin presented Russia's annexation of Crimea as a generous response to the long-standing desire of the Crimean people to "return" to Russia, their native land. He later said that with the referendum, Crimeans had "shown that they remain true to the historic truth and our forefathers' memory." Putin wasn't alone in this rhetoric of reunion. "Step by step, we have led Crimeans to realize their dream of returning home to Russia," said the speaker of the breakaway Crimean legislature. Khrushchev's symbolic gift of Crimea to the Ukrainian Soviet Socialist Republic in 1954, the culmination of a large-scale Russian-Ukrainian friendship campaign, was a mistake that had finally been corrected. The Russian media called the annexation "the third defense of Sevastopol," showing shots of the battle for Crimea in the Second World War.

Putin's annexation picked up a long-running narrative thread in Russia's history. In April 1783, after complicated political negotiations with the Ottomans who then controlled Crimea, Catherine the Great had annexed the peninsula without firing a single shot. Russian poets interpreted this victory as a sign that Crimea was a natural extension of the Russian Empire. Gavrila Derzhavin, Russia's greatest poet at the time, wrote,

> Which god, which angel
> Which friend of mankind
> Crowned us with bloodless laurels,
> Gave us trophies without battle?

Russia has always been worried about its origins, its authenticity. It was late to adopt Christianity, to develop a written alphabet and a literary language, to modernize. Russians imported innovation from abroad, and they suffered acute anxiety of influence. But if God had given the Russian Empire

Crimea, cradle of ancient cultures, surely Russians had no need to worry about being newcomers to European civilization. By absorbing Crimea, imperial Russia was able to associate itself with the ancient world and with Christian Byzantium; by defeating the Ottoman Empire's Muslim Turks and Tatars, it put itself on the side of Europe and Christianity rather than Asia and Islam.

The medieval Kievan Prince Vladimir's conversion to Christianity at the Crimean city of Khersones was the foundation of Catherine and Prince Potemkin's Greek Project: Crimea was the place where Rus had become Christian. In a letter to Catherine after the annexation of Crimea, Potemkin called Khersones "the source of our Christianity and of our very humanity." Catherine, whom her poets called Minerva, would break pagan spells and resurrect the glorious ghosts of the peninsula, exceeding even Homer's glory. Court poet Derzhavin wrote,

> Circe howls in vexation,
> All her magic reduced to nothing.
> The Achaeans, turned to beasts,
> Are made human again by Minerva.
> Smiling, Pythagoras is amazed
> To see the transmigration of souls:
> Homer appears where a dragonfly had been
> And with his thunderous voice,
> He sings not fables, but the truth.

Catherine and Potemkin were never able to fully realize their Greek Project; there was soon another Russo-Turkish War, Potemkin died in 1791, and Catherine herself died in 1796.

But the Russian scholar Andrei Zorin writes that the Greek Project "remained in Russian culture as an intention, a lost possibility, a latent—but for that all the stronger—realm of attraction." The loss of Crimea, its ancient paradise, its creation story, haunted post-Soviet Russia; the possession of Crimea was "the crown of Russia's historical mission, its civilizing task." The symbolic meaning of the peninsula lingered in its rough, dry hills and ancient caves, and in the shining Black Sea, whose depths preserved the wrecks of ancient Greek ships.

Putin picked up where Potemkin had left off. In 2011, as Russian scientists excavated the ruins of an ancient Greek city off the coast of Crimea, Putin had himself filmed in a wetsuit, retrieving two broken amphorae from shallow waters nearby. It was clear to everyone that the amphorae had been planted there, just as it had been obvious to Catherine during her Crimean tour that Potemkin's villages and Amazons were just for show. Like Catherine, Putin was staging a play that would allow him to lay claim to a history that wasn't his own. After he'd annexed the peninsula, he echoed Potemkin, announcing that Crimea was "the spiritual source" of the Russian state, because it was in Khersones that Prince Vladimir had been baptized before bringing Christianity to Rus. This gave Crimea "invaluable civilizational and even sacral importance for Russia, like the Temple Mount in Jerusalem for the followers of Islam and Judaism." Never mind that Vladimir was prince of Kiev, long before the modern Russian state existed.

Ukraine's acting president, Oleksandr Turchynov, said that Ukraine would never recognize the annexation. (For their part, many eastern and southern Ukrainians, as well as Crimeans, did not recognize Turchynov as legitimate, considering Maidan a coup.) The United States, the EU, and others condemned the annexation, which had been unconstitutional, and imposed sanctions in retaliation. There were somewhat hysterical comparisons, both inside and outside Ukraine, to Hitler's annexation of Austria in 1938. Was Putin now willing to invade any country he pleased? Was he planning to devour Ukraine piece by piece, and then move on to the other post-Soviet states?

But no one was ready to fight Putin for Crimea. The interim Ukrainian government was in no position to wage war, with a dysfunctional army, an empty treasury, and central Kiev still covered in ashes. The US and the EU would not support Ukraine in a war for Crimea.

Despite their outrage at Putin's insolence, Ukrainians were well aware that Crimea's integration into independent Ukraine had been an accident of history, an uneasy coupling. Crimeans were portrayed as Soviet-style freeloaders, living on summer vacation earnings and causing trouble in Ukraine's national politics, preventing Ukraine from realizing its European (as opposed to Soviet, or Russian, or even Ottoman) destiny. Ukrainians didn't like the annexation, but some were willing to acknowledge that it might be for the best.

After the annexation there was peace in Crimea, but there was also rampant inflation and a loss of access to banks and credit cards. That summer the seaside was nearly empty. There was talk of schemes to make Crimea into a casino paradise, or a giant military base, or some combination of the two, but Russia's economic slump and Western sanctions put plans for a Russian Las Vegas on hold. Ukraine stopped running trains from the mainland. There were plans to build a bridge across the Strait of Kerch, to connect Russia and Crimea, but it would be hugely expensive and take years to complete.

My friend Olga and her husband Sanya continued to spend every summer on Meganom, taking a ferry from Russia now that it was no longer possible for them to drive through Ukraine. They were well aware of the bad effects of annexation on the economy, but they couldn't help enjoying the tranquillity brought by Crimea's new isolation. Olga told me that Meganom seemed to be cleaning itself, as if in preparation for some great event, and that she'd never seen so many stars, soaring and falling. When she went up the cliff, above the seashore, the canopy of stars was reflected in the water; it looked as if there weren't any sea, only the starry heavens, embracing the earth.

Chapter 14

The Wild Steppe

Ukraine was soon distracted from its outrage over Russia's annexation of Crimea. In early March, pro-Russian protesters started taking over government buildings in the eastern Ukrainian regions of Donetsk and Luhansk, co-opting Maidan's narrative of righteous occupation and demanding referenda like the one in Crimea.

In early April, protesters occupying the Donetsk Regional State Administration Building proclaimed the Donetsk People's Republic, asking Russia to send "peacekeepers" to protect them from Kiev. The protesters went on to seize the Ministry of Internal Affairs and to take control of buildings in a number of other cities in the Donetsk region. Protesters in Luhansk occupied the local security service building, calling for a "people's government": federalization within Ukraine, or incorporation into Russia. They went on to declare the Luhansk People's Republic. As in Crimea, many local officials and police in Donetsk and Luhansk went over to the separatist side. Others were beaten, taken captive, or killed.

Like Crimea, Donbas, the area that includes Donetsk and Luhansk, is a place with a potent myth. In the Russian and Ukrainian imagination, Donbas signifies both freedom and the threat of foreign invasion, a place where coexistence explodes easily into violence.

Donbas, whose name comes from "Donets River Basin," is located on the vast steppe that stretches from Moldova to Kazakhstan. The medieval Slavs stayed away from this "wild field," which had few freshwater lakes or trees. The only people who felt at home on the steppe were non-Slavic nomads, whom the Christian chroniclers of Kievan Rus considered harbingers of the apocalypse, barbarians who slept with their step-mothers and ate carrion and prairie dogs. The Slavs and the nomads fought, but they also traded together and formed political alliances.

Too flat and wide to be defended, the steppe made good on its apocalyptic potential in the thirteenth century, serving as a highway for the Mongol-Tatar invaders who sacked Kiev. The Slavs eventually regrouped and began to expand their areas of control, but much of the steppe remained beyond their reach. Early Slavic steppe dwellers were fugitives: criminals, victims of religious persecution, escaped peasants or serfs. The Orthodox Christian Cossacks, masters of mounted warfare, fought endless battles with the non-Christian steppe nomads. Sometimes the Cossacks fought on behalf of the Russians or Poles; sometimes they simply robbed and looted as they saw fit.

In the eighteenth century, as the Russian Empire became more powerful and more Westernized, its rulers worked to bring the steppe under control. Catherine the Great renamed the region north of the Black Sea—now southern and eastern Ukraine—Novorossiya, "New Russia." Like the annexation of Crimea, the colonization of Novorossiya was part of Russia's impe-rial glory and "civilizing task." In 1786 Prince Potemkin wrote to Catherine, "This country, with your care, has been turned from a place of uninhabited steppes into a garden of abundance, from a lair of beasts to a pleasing refuge for peoples from all countries." As usual, Potemkin was indulging Catherine's fantasies. New Russia wasn't uninhabited, and it was no "garden of abundance." Many of the settlers Catherine sent soon died, while others led hardscrabble lives, on the brink of starvation.

In the nineteenth century, industrialization brought a new kind of misery to Donbas. Wealth was discovered beneath the steppe, in the form of coal and steel, and foreign industrialists arrived to exploit these natural resources. The most famous was the Welshman John Hughes, who built a steel plant and several coal mines in Donbas in the late nineteenth century. He gave his name to Yuzovka, the city that is now Donetsk. (From 1924 to 1961 it was called Stalino.) Travelers reported that the flat, colorless landscape was so monotonous that it could drive you insane. In the towns, mud swallowed pedestrians and horses during spring floods. Workers lived in filthy, damp, flea-infested barracks; some lived in dugouts unfit even for livestock. Then as now, air pollution from the mines and factories was so severe that it made people sick. The Kiev-born Soviet writer Konstantin Paustovsky wrote of Donetsk during the First World War, "Greasy soot dripped from the sky .... The curtains, pillowcases, and sheets in the hotel were gray, all shirts were gray, even horses, cats, and dogs were gray instead of white."

Donbas coal miners worked in miserable, dangerous conditions and looked forward to summer work above ground, in the sunny fields. But seasonal labor was bad for industry, so Hughes held workers' passports in order to prevent them from leaving. Workers were flogged, sometimes to death. There were periodic uprisings, riots, and looting, often fueled by vodka. The coal miners did their best to drink away their misery; sometimes they were simply paid in alcohol. The lack of clean drinking water led to epidemics of cholera, which soon spread to other regions. Donbas became not only the gateway for the Mongol Horde, but a source of infection.

According to Marxist logic, Donbas workers should have been ripe for revolutionary mobilization. They were certainly angry. One Russian engineer compared armed workers in Donbas in December 1905 to insurrectionary Cossacks, "a large crowd of people armed with the most incredible weapons—home-made pikes, shotguns, even scythes." But it proved difficult to organize the largely illiterate Donbas coal miners, who were more inclined to drunken riots and Cossack-style spontaneous self-government than to political campaigns and lessons in class consciousness. After the revolution of February 1917, the coal miners demanded an eight-hour workday and attacked or arrested many higher-level mine employees. Miners formed "comrades' courts," which tried and sentenced supervisors and other white-collar work-ers. Sometimes *samosud*, a village tradition of spontaneous trial, ended in property seizure, a beating, or a lynching; in other cases, the accused would be required to beg the workers for mercy.

The region was taken and retaken during the Russian Civil War, with each new army slaughtering its enemies en masse. Charismatic leaders rose out of nowhere, amassed followers, then were killed or driven out. The region's Cossacks were among the fiercest opponents of the Bolsheviks and were nearly extermi-nated as a result. Later, Donbas's rebellious residents fought bitterly against Stalin's agricultural collectivization, which brought mass starvation and violence.

Donbas maintained its reputation as a wild, half-barbarian place. Under the Soviets, Donbas workers continued to be exploited and abused, but they found little sympathy from Soviet dissidents. In the 1970s, mounting efforts at labor activism in Donbas were always crushed, the leaders sent to psychiatric hospitals, the standard treatment of political dissidents at the time. The Soviet dissident intelligentsia, however, had little interest in labor organizing, which demanded better pay and working conditions rather than a wholesale political transformation or democratic liberalization. Donbas labor organizers were second-class dissidents.

In 1991 Donbas workers voted overwhelmingly in favor of Ukrainian independence, hoping that it would bring economic prosperity. They were soon disillusioned. Not only did they find themselves exploited by post-Soviet oligarchs; Ukrainians in other regions continued to see them as unlettered, materialist barbarians. In Donbas, Russian was the primary language of the cities and of many villages. As the Soviet Union collapsed, Donbas had rejected Rukh, a party that promoted a Ukrainian identity based largely in the Ukrainian language and called the choice of Russian over Ukrainian "cowardly and mistaken." One Rukh leader called the Donbas miners "sausage people" after a miner announced, "It's all the same to us what language we speak, as long as there's sausage." For nationally minded Ukrainians, Donbas's focus on material needs seemed petty, the concern of people who had stomachs where their souls should have been.

In public health work in Ukraine in the twenty-first century, I heard a lot about the former regions of Novorossiya, southern and eastern Ukraine, which became the center of Ukraine's HIV epidemic as unhappy residents sought comfort in hard drugs. In 2007 a study found that a staggering 88 percent of injecting drug users in Kryvyi Rih, a mining town in the Dnipropetrovsk region, were HIV positive. In 2011, 3 percent of the town's total population was registered as HIV positive, a rate comparable to that in West African countries. A Ukrainian colleague told me that the pollution from the mines in Kryvyi Rih was so bad that a white shirt was stained red by the end of the day. A Canadian colleague who did a workshop there felt certain that it was the worst place on earth.

Originally from northwestern Ukraine, Natalia Yurchyshyn, a student at the Kiev-Mohyla Academy, was active in the Maidan protests. When things went wrong in Crimea and then in eastern Ukraine, she told me, she started thinking about how little contact she and people in her social circles ever had with people who lived in Crimea or, especially, in Donetsk and Luhansk, places that most Ukrainians went out of their way to avoid. In April 2014 Natalia decided to go and visit these regions: better late than never, she thought.

Natalia may have been one of the only tourists ever to visit the polluted, decrepit post-Soviet industrial city of Sloviansk, which had recently been taken by separatists. As she stood in the center of the city, taking a picture of a blue garbage can near a blue door, a man wagged his finger at her. She assumed that he thought she'd been photographing him, so she came over and showed him he wasn't in the frame.

He took her iPhone and tried to delete her photos, but he didn't know how. Giving up on the unfamiliar technology, he asked, "Why are you photographing that?"

"It's an interesting color combination," she replied. She was telling the truth.

The man summoned two armed, masked separatists, who took her to a police station they'd seized. The men who interviewed her there were almost friendly. "Are you drunk?" they asked her.

"No," she answered.

"Then why are you talking like that?"

"I probably have a different accent than you have in Sloviansk," she replied. Though her interrogators were Ukrainian, they didn't recognize her western Ukrainian accent.

They called a nurse to check her eyes for signs of drug intoxication, but the nurse confirmed that Natalia was sober.

"Why do you want to be in Russia?" she asked them.

"Because in Russia the pay is higher," they answered, like good sausage people.

Natalia talked about Yanukovych's palace, about the way he had stolen from Ukrainians. She explained that people in Kiev were against the current government, too, and were demanding new elections. "Let's work on this together!" she said, optimistically.

But the separatists just shook their heads. By then they'd taken off their balaclavas and were speaking frankly. "It's hopeless," one said. "The politicians will just steal everything, like they always do."

They gave Natalia lunch and told her she was free to go.

After failed attempts to reach a peaceful political solution, Ukraine's prosecutor general declared the People's Republics of Donetsk and Luhansk to be terrorist organizations; the fight against them was dubbed the "anti-terrorist operation," or ATO. But the Ukrainian government was unable to quash the rebellion, in part because Ukraine's army, hollowed out by years of corruption, didn't have enough equipment or supplies, or enough competent soldiers and officers. Ukraine resorted to crowdfunding. Patriots made donations through the electronic kiosks that took payments for cell phones, Internet service, and the popular *World of Tanks* video game. Bands held fund-raising concerts, and cafés and restaurants had jars for donations. "Volunteer battalions" were raised, many of them based on Maidan's regiments (the "hundreds"), many of them funded by oligarchs. The nonprofessional "fighters" in these battalions were often the fiercest combatants and the first on the front lines. Some came from far-right movements, from Svoboda and Right Sector and paramilitary groups that had long been hoping for a chance to fight.

Ukraine insisted that Russia was orchestrating the separatist movement, though Russia vehemently denied this; locals gave conflicting reports. It became clear that there were a number of Russian, Chechen, Serbian, and other foreigners fighting with the separatists—mercenaries, volunteers, Russian soldiers who claimed to be on holiday—but it was hard to know the precise proportion of covert Russian invasion to local rebellion. As during the civil war a century earlier, military leaders kept appearing out of nowhere, with nicknames like "Demon," "Bogeyman," and "Ghost." Some were imported from Russia, but others were homegrown. Several were Cossacks who rejected both Ukrainian and Russian authority, hoping to revive the old statelessness of the steppe. The separatists resurrected the old tradition of "people's trials": in the Luhansk People's Republic, an accused rapist was sentenced to death after a show of hands.

*

On May 11, 2014, the Donbas separatists held referenda. Voters answered yes or no to a simple yet ambiguous question: in Donetsk, "Do you support the declaration of state independence of the Donetsk People's Republic?" and in Luhansk, "Do you support the declaration of state independence of the Luhansk People's Republic?" There was little discussion of what a yes would mean in practice. There was also massive election fraud, leading many observers to dismiss the landslide votes in favor of independence. Only Russia recognized them as legitimate. But as in Crimea, many people in Donetsk and Luhansk truly did want to distance themselves from Kiev's new government and to put themselves under Russian protection.

The Donetsk People's Republic and the Luhansk People's Republic formed the Novorossiya confederation, which they hoped would eventually include most of southern and eastern Ukraine. Russian Orthodoxy would be the official religion, and industries would be nationalized. Like Putin's annexation of Crimea, Novorossiya was an idea that could be traced back to Catherine the Great. But the new Novorossiya's ideology also drew on parts of the Soviet legacy, with its rhetoric about the people's control of the state and key industries.

Like the Maidan protesters, the Donbas separatists were history buffs. One separatist recruiting billboard announced, "The fate of the Russian people is to repeat the feats of their fathers, defending the motherland," showing drawings of soldiers in 1918, 1941, and 2014. The new Donetsk legislature was called the Supreme Soviet, and the Soviet Victory flag flew over battle scenes. Separatists appropriated a Soviet tank that was on display at a museum. The first leader of the Donetsk People's Republic was the former Russian intelligence officer Igor

"Strelkov" Girkin, who had seized Sloviansk. Girkin's hobby was historical military reenactments. (He had also fought in real-life Chechnya, where he was accused of disappearing Chechens, and in Bosnia, where he was accused of taking part in a massacre.) Old photos online showed him in grassy fields, dressed in a dapper olive uniform, pretending it was the Russian Civil War. He usually played a White Army officer, an enemy of the Bolsheviks. As a student, he had been an outspoken monarchist.

The Western media, which knew virtually nothing about Ukraine, spoke casually about a deep-rooted conflict between "ethnic Russians" and "ethnic Ukrainians," evoking the Balkan wars and ignoring the fact that cultural, linguistic, and political identities in Ukraine were far too complex to be reduced to a simple pair of eternally incompatible "ethnic" groups. Meanwhile, the Western political establishment often portrayed the separatists not as a people's uprising, but as Russian pawns. This narrative fit well with the logic of the "new Cold War," as people had started calling it: a fight between justice-loving Westerners and barbarian tyrants from the East.

It was true that eastern Ukrainians were doused in Russian propaganda, and it became increasingly clear that Russia was supplying fighters, arms, and instructions to the separatists. But eastern Ukrainians were also culturally and economically isolated from the rest of Ukraine. They were anxious about the shift of political power away from the east and toward the west. They were worried about their economy, which was dependent largely on trade with Russia, and afraid of austerity measures that would follow the new Kiev government's deal with the IMF. They were fearful and angry at the possibility of a "national idea" that would treat Russian speakers, or people who did not reject

Soviet history wholesale, as bad Ukrainians. They were upset because they were poor and under-educated and unemployed and sick and despised by their own countrymen.

Many of the separatists I saw in pictures and videos looked familiar; these were the same sullen, sunken-eyed young men I'd encountered at harm reduction centers, partial to homemade amphetamines and opiates brewed from Ukrainian poppies. But now they had guns; now they were heroes.

Part IV

War and Peace

Chapter 15

Heroes Don't Die

In May 2014 Halyna, the woman who looked after the apartment, let me into my old place on Bohdan Khmelnytsky Street. She looked the same as always, strangely ageless. But she had a new manic sparkle in her eyes as she told me to be careful at night and not to allow anyone to follow me into the building, because there were bands of disreputable characters roaming the streets.

"Every second person in Donetsk is a separatist," Halyna said with a hard smile. "*Lumpen.* Do you know what *lumpen* means? They just want to drink and steal, they don't want to work." She was referring to the Marxist term *Lumpenproletariat*, which described the dregs of the lower classes, the criminals and degenerates who would never achieve class consciousness.

The apartment was as I remembered it, only more decrepit. Halyna told me that it had been empty all year, which wasn't surprising. It was now in such bad shape that it was hard to rent out; the building's plumbing was rotten. The poorly lit vestibule and chipped marble staircase, once so familiar, had become menacing. At the all-night convenience store around the corner, the place where my friends and I had often bought supplies for late-night parties, a chalkboard announced a sale on vodka and beer. A building down the street had been turned into Right Sector headquarters, its front balconies draped in Right Sector's colors: red for blood, black for earth.

It was Kiev's most beautiful season, the one I'd encountered during my first visit seven years earlier. Khreshchatyk Street, the wide boulevard that leads to Maidan, bore no resemblance to what I'd seen in the live feeds and videos I'd spent the winter watching from New York. Then everything had been snowy, barren, charred, and clouded with smoke from open fires and burning tires; now it was leafy and green, just coming into blossom. There was pouring rain almost every day, as if the sky were trying to wash away the pain and destruction of the preceding months.

Khreshchatyk was still closed to cars, though, and the protesters' tent city was still standing. I passed some scary-looking guys in fatigues. One was wearing a balaclava and pointing a very old rifle at his friend's head, apparently as a joke. In front of the central post office, I watched a disheveled man in fatigues buy a cloud of cotton candy. Someone had painted pink polka dots on the burned-out Trade Union building, giving it a strange, cartoonish look. Maidan protesters had often talked about their desire to live in a "normal European" country, but nothing was normal or European about this scene; neither was there the mild, friendly mood that had made me fall in love with Kiev on my first visits.

The people still camped on Maidan were the most marginal protesters, the ones who had no jobs to return to and no kitchen gardens to tend, who hadn't chosen to go and fight in the east. They'd settled into domestic life on Maidan, a cozy permanent revolution. People were cooking, couples were arguing, and music played from boom boxes. A man fed pigeons, and a toddler in a motorcycle jacket poked his head up above the wooden boundary of the encampment. A banner with photos of a Maidan martyr cried, "Revenge the death of the great knights!" The tents were marked with the names of *sotni*, regiments: a city name, or "OUN," for the Organization of Ukrainian Nationalists, or "Hutsul," for the Carpathian cowboys.

A sidewalk exhibit showed homemade bulletproof vests, leg shields, and armor. There were a number of small altars with photos of the dead, candles, and flowers. People watched news about the war in the east on a giant screen. Down the street, a man in a sailor's hat was playing a cheesy song in English about a miracle. The blue and gold Maidan piano had fallen terribly out of tune.

As I passed a young man wearing a shirt with an eagle on the front and "SS" on the back, a guy in a horse costume came and put his arm around me.

"Take a picture with a horse," he said, "It will be fun!"

The horse was not alone. Khreshchatyk was swarming with Mickey Mouses and giant green insects and people inviting you to pose for photos with dingy doves. Vendors sold golden loaf magnets (a golden loaf of bread was one of the scandalous arti-facts discovered in Yanukovych's mansion), T-shirts showing Cossacks and the nationalist hero Stepan Bandera, and various items shouting FUCK PUTIN, alongside the usual cheap, mass-produced embroidered peasant blouses and plastic garlands of blue and yellow flowers.

As the center of Kiev's downtown, Maidan had always been full of furries and vendors. The tourist trade had persisted even as the coffins of the dead were carried through the square. But now it was different: everyone was in costume, and it had become hard to distinguish the amateurs from the professionals. There were would-be soldiers with their uniforms and antique rifles,

Cossacks with billowing pants, high boots, and swords, and girls dressed as village maidens of the past, in embroidered blouses and red beads. Many people were wearing blue and gold outfits. In a way it was touching, but it was also intolerably kitschy, as if Americans all decided one day to go around dressed as pilgrims. The overt theatricality gave the proceedings an air of insincerity that was the very opposite of Maidan's famous ocean of shining eyes.

My clarinetist friend Mitya told me that Maidan had been a theatrical performance from the beginning. At one point, he said, he'd been kept waiting for a long time to perform on the main stage. As he stood in the wings, he watched a man yelling into the microphone, sounding very aggressive, exhorting the crowd. Mitya thought he had the mannerisms of a fascist and assumed he was an orator, a political figure. But when he came closer, Mitya saw that he was wearing eyeliner; he was an actor. This was Evhen Nishchuk, Maidan's unofficial MC. The role came easily, since Nishchuk had also helped run the Orange Revolution. He was a professional.

"He's not an orator, or a politician, or a revolutionary," Mitya said. "He's more like a *tamada* [the person, in Georgian culture, who leads toasts] or like Father Christmas." Post-Maidan, Nishchuk had been made the interim minister of culture.

Mitya put me in touch with Taras Kompanichenko, a latter-day Ukrainian bard. When I met Kompanichenko on Khreshchatyk, he was dressed in full Cossack regalia: loose *sharovary*, pants suitable for riding on horseback; long, pointy shoes; and a tie woven in a traditional Ukrainian pattern. His hair was closely shaved except for the Cossack *oseledets*, or "herring," a long, gray-ing plume on the top of his head. For convenience, he'd wound his forelock around his ear. His thick, dark brown mustache curled up at the ends. This wasn't a protest costume, or a means of attracting tourists; this was how he got dressed for work.

He kissed my hand and escorted me past a group of boys breakdancing to techno music, into Puzata Khata, a chain that offered Ukrainian cuisine at fast food prices. (The name trans-lates to something like "Belly Cottage.")

When the chivalrous Kompanichenko brought me tea and a slice of cake, I noticed that he had the long nails required to play the *kobza*, the lute used by the Ukrainian minstrels known as *kobzari*. The *kobzari*, who were usually blind, roamed Ukraine for centuries, relying on the generosity of their listeners. Their songs often dealt with religious and historical topics. As vectors of Ukrainian national feeling and as wandering mendicants, *kobzari* were repressed first by Russian imperial authorities, then by the Soviets. According to a story in wide circulation in Ukraine, Stalin summoned all the Ukrainian minstrels to a conference in Kharkiv in 1939 and had them shot. State-sanctioned *kobzari* endured, however, as a part of Soviet Ukraine's institutional-ized folklore. The *kobzar* tradition gained new life after Ukraine became independent, as part of the effort to recover and purify the nation's identity.

A professional musician and composer, Kompanichenko played very old songs, some of them dating back to the seven-teenth century. He had made his whole life into an embodiment of the Ukrainian national idea, a romantic fantasy of Cossack heroes and pastoral patriots. It was fitting that he shared his first name with Taras Shevchenko, the poet-prophet of the Ukrainian nation, who wrote a book called *Kobzar* and was often called a *kobzar* himself, though he was not a musician. In the nineteenth century Taras Shevchenko had wept over Cossack burial mounds, writing poems that glorified a mythical Ukrainian past; now Taras Kompanichenko was carrying on this tradition.

As Kompanichenko spoke, he stroked his forelock, which he'd unwound from his ear. He was the most earnest person I had ever met. I was moved by his gentle sincerity, but I couldn't help finding him a little ridiculous, like a museum exhibit that had come to life and wandered out into the streets.

In the early days, Kompanichenko said, the Maidan protests had been something like a people's national liberation festival. The music had been acoustic, and there was only one microphone. Maidan's musicians had acted as private citizens, as protesters. They hadn't been detached from reality, hadn't been stimulated by alcohol, fame, or money; they had participated because they cared about their country. This sense of a higher purpose had given Kompanichenko an almost superhuman strength, he said, enabling him to play endlessly in the rain or snow, long after he'd lost his voice.

Then Svoboda, the ultranationalist party, got sound equipment. Everything became much more formal. There was a long line to perform, and the political parties took turns running the show. Some musicians were paid by political parties; Kompanichenko was concerned about the spiritual as well as financial corruption that this had caused.

"Our weapon is our soul," he told me. "Music is magical. It can carry ideas into the heart, by giving them the wings of emotions. But it has to be sincere, not manipulative. It has to search for the truth, for universal human values."

During Maidan, Kompanichenko and his Cossack choir made a point of performing only familiar songs so the crowd could sing along. They were reinforcing the true national archetypes, Kompanichenko said: not *salo*, Ukraine's traditional cured lard, or *horilka*, Ukrainian vodka, but freedom, and "the fundamental values of European civilization." They sang a Ukrainian version of Beethoven's "Ode to Joy," the EU anthem, over and over. Once the first people were killed, Kompanichenko and his Cossacks started playing memorial songs for the dead.

By February 19 performers were being shot with rubber bullets. The only person onstage who had a bulletproof vest was the MC. Kompanichenko continued singing, though he was consumed by the fear that a bullet would fly into his open mouth and pierce his throat.

By this point in our conversation, Kompanichenko was close to tears. Daft Punk's latest single was playing in the background.

"Did my music provoke violence?" he asked plaintively. "It raised the protesters' spirits. They were so brave. They didn't know how terrible the consequences could be."

At the gallery PartKom, I struggled to imagine the white space filled with wounded people, just as I had struggled, while standing on Maidan, to imagine the many thousands of peaceful protesters who had been gathered there a few months earlier.

I was looking for my friend Seryozha the Gypsy; instead I found Okhrim, a violin player I knew through Toporkestra. Okhrim was the oldest of the group, an inveterate carouser with a gray pageboy haircut and bottle-cap glasses. My first memory of him was from a party where he'd leaped onto a table and played an exuberant fiddle version of a 1980s underground pop song, "A Romantic's Walk," howling out the sweet lyrics:

> There's thunder through the windowpane
> The streetlights shine and the shadows are strange
> I look into the night, I see that it's dark
> But that won't stop a romantic's walk.

Having finished his song, Okhrim fell asleep in the corner; someone had to play a tuba in his ear to wake him up. Despite his passion for cheap Armenian cognac, he was nice, in an obscene sort of way.

Okhrim specialized in Ukrainian folk music and had played on the Maidan stage several times. On February 22 he and Taras Kompanichenko had played a funeral march in honor of the Heavenly Hundred, the martyred protesters.

"Topor said Maidan was a circus, and he was glad he missed it," Okhrim reported. Topor, our Moldovan bandleader friend, had spent the winter in Goa with some of his fellow musicians. "But I was glad I was there." Okhrim's tone was solemn. "I'm a new person now. When you saw the look in people's eyes after Maidan, you saw that they were new people, too. We had to sit in silence for a while, absorbing it all. Ever since Maidan I don't go on drinking binges. I just drink sometimes." He was smoking a cigarette and drinking a bottle of beer as we spoke, early in the afternoon. I suspected that not even a revolution could make Okhrim get sober for good.

*

I went to an artists' talk, curious about whether revolution had given new vitality to the Kiev art scene. Everyone was supposed to be speaking Ukrainian, partly out of patriotism and partly because one of the panelists was Polish and understood Ukrainian but not Russian, but people kept forgetting.

"I don't understand everything," the Polish panelist said pleasantly, when one Ukrainian, Liza Babenko, criticized another, Larisa Venediktovna, for speaking Russian. Venediktovna spoke Ukrainian for about thirty seconds, then returned to Russian as she discussed the fact that the future was simultaneously now, never, and always.

Denis, a very young leftist activist, said in Russian that he had been preparing for the revolution for his entire life. He had the feeling that time was leaping forward; perhaps it was getting ahead of itself. "I have arrived in the future," he said ecstatically. He had an artistic it-boy look, tall and skinny, with a strong chin, a straight nose, and hollow cheeks.

"Has the future passed?" an audience member asked.

Denis thought for a while.

"The future has come," he announced. By then almost everyone had given up and switched to Russian, though most of them didn't seem aware of what language they were speaking. Only the poor Polish woman toiled on in Ukrainian, and had to keep asking clarifying questions. She asked one woman to translate a word into Ukrainian; the woman, who was Ukrainian, had to ask another panelist. It was all very symbolic, this disjunction between intentions and inclinations, this literal failure to find a common language.

"The future is the bottom," someone opined. At the exhibit that accompanied the talk, I had seen a large square of black paper taped to the floor; perhaps, I thought, this had been the future.

Actually, Venediktovna said, history was an endless stack of paper in a bottomless hole.

"Then what is the paper at the bottom of the pile?" a man in the audience asked. He broached the idea of the end of history.

"No, no, no," Venediktovna said impatiently, in English for some reason.

"Maybe the future is a swimming pool," someone suggested. By then about half the panel had gone out for a cigarette.

While the leftist artists were preoccupied with the future, Laima Geidar, the lesbian activist who'd worked as a medic during Maidan, was interested in the past. When I asked to interview her, she wanted to meet at the McDonald's on Khreshchatyk, a place where she'd spent many hours during the protests and battles, getting warm.

When we started talking, I was surprised to discover that Laima had become an avid proponent of the Ukrainian national idea. This was remarkable not only because she was a lesbian feminist—not exactly part of the usual nationalist demographic—but because she was a Russian speaker whose mother, with whom she was no longer on good terms, lived in Siberia. The Ukrainian and Russian national ideas were at war in her head.

"The murder, the suffocation of Ukraine—this is part of Russia's national idea. Now, analyzing all these events, I think Yanukovych was Putin's project," she said in Russian. "They decided to find a jailbird, make him a governor, make him prime minister, and then he could become president. His only interest was in stealing. He had no national idea—just murder and kitsch, like at his mansion.

"During our revolution, I discovered our classics—our prophet, Taras Shevchenko, Lesya Ukrainka, Ivan Franko, writers who taught us about the *moskali*"—the derogatory Ukrainian word for Russians—"about their lying, thieving ways, about their amorality in the pursuit of their goals . . . and only now, surviving all this terror, I understand the greatness of these poets, these prophets. Shevchenko wrote something like 'It's all the same to me which God a boy prays to. But it makes a difference to me when evil people lull Ukraine to sleep, and Ukraine wakes suddenly from her dream in the middle of a fire.'"

After Laima finished crying, we walked around Maidan. Laima wasn't the only one with Taras Shevchenko on her mind; there was Shevchenko graffiti everywhere. On one wall, Shevchenko was a Marvel-style superhero with a purple mask and a bulging groin. Another mural showed him in an embroidered Ukrainian blouse and an orange helmet, the kind popular on Maidan, with red and black Molotov cocktails forming X's on either side of his face and the words OUR WHOLE LIFE IS WAR in a banner over his head. In yet another painting, he wore a red and black nationalist bandanna over the lower half of his face, scowling above the words THE FIRE DOESN'T BURN THOSE WHO HAVE ALREADY BEEN TEMPERED IN THE FLAMES. Nationalism was a cult of war, a cult of death, a cartoon.

Laima pointed out some girls in hijabs, saying they were resettled Tatars from Crimea. She described treating a man whose stomach had been slit open, and others who had been shot in the head by snipers on the rooftops, and she showed me the place where her fellow medic, a young woman, had been shot through the neck by a sniper. (In the hospital, the woman had tweeted "I'm dying" and then gone silent, prompting an Internet furor. She survived.)

Laima was furious with Germany and the United States for not helping Ukraine to defend itself against Russia. "They don't know who they're dealing with—you can't put on a tie and talk to these people," she said. "You have to pick up a stone and throw it." Maidan's cobblestones, once torn out and thrown at police, were now piled in neat stacks.

We looked at the displays in some of the tents.

"'A good Communist is a dead Communist,'" Laima read approvingly from a sign above a hanged mannequin. Another hanged effigy was dressed in a red snowsuit decorated in hammers and sickles.

Someone was drumming inside the music conservatory just off the square. Laima stopped to enjoy the rhythm; she didn't seem to notice the foul smell in the air. Maidan stank, like an infected wound.

"I don't like to go to Maidan anymore," Mitya told me later. "It's like a corpse—the body is there, but the soul is gone."

With war erupting in the east, the euphoria and solidarity of Maidan had been replaced by grief and anger. Fear contorted faces that I'd always known as friendly and calm, and the air was thick with suspicion. Anna, a young woman I knew from AIDS work, another person who'd helped coordinate medical care for wounded protesters, told me that she believed rumors that Right Sector was a Kremlin project and that Tyahnybok, the leader of Svoboda, was on the Russian payroll. Yulia Tymoshenko had never actually been in prison and was paid by Putin; it had all been an elaborate plot so that she could become president. Anna had heard from a person who worked for Vitaly Klitschko, one of the opposition leaders, that some people were paid by opposition political parties to stay on Maidan—to live there. "Otherwise who would stay on Maidan for months?" she asked. "And they were so well organized." The first clearings of Maidan had been done to provoke further protests—it didn't make sense otherwise. Anna couldn't say who'd brought in the snipers, though. Maybe Tymoshenko, maybe the United States, maybe Russia. She was convinced that China was involved, too.

By the time she was finished, I felt dizzy. I asked what she thought about the situation in the east.

"I am supporting the idea of exterminating separatists," she answered casually. (We were speaking English.)

"Exterminating?" I asked, shocked.

"I would deport them, I mean. I would buy them tickets myself."

Anna's attitude was not unusual. Many otherwise pleasant people had concluded that the only answer was to excise a certain portion of Ukrainian society, cutting it off like a gangrenous limb. No one had ever liked Donbas much anyway; wasn't it just Soviet deadweight in a Ukraine eager to flee westward, into Europe and the future?

*

241

I met up with Topor, at Bessarabsky Market, near where the statue of Lenin had fallen. People had covered the empty pedestal with Lenin posters and pro- and anti-Soviet propaganda. A glued-on picture showed Lenin sitting at his desk, reading a book and drinking tea, looking thoughtful. Someone had scratched out his face, but his reflection was still visible in the window beside him. At a restaurant across the street, a chalkboard advertised a new dish: "marinated Yanukovych ears." (I think they were mushrooms.)

Topor's beard had grown very long and bushy, and his dark hair was turning gray. As we stood on the street eating bad shawarma, a drunken bum approached us. Mistaking Topor for a priest, he tried to kiss him on the cheek and asked for half his sandwich. Topor brushed him off good-naturedly.

Topor had notoriously perverse political views. We'd once had a long argument about who killed more Soviet citizens, Stalin or Gorbachev. His position was that Gorbachev was the guiltier of the two, because under Gorbachev people starved to death, while Stalin killed people who were guilty—or who would have done something wrong if they'd lived long enough. There was an element of irony in Topor's argument, but it was also clear that he had been marked by the trauma of perestroika and its aftermath.

On another occasion he reminisced fondly about his time on a student exchange in Kentucky. "It was very good there," he said, "like Moldova under Brezhnev. Very calm. Everyone had a house, a car, a wife, and a mistress." That was Topor's ideal: peace, and moderate prosperity.

"I'm against Maidan!" he exclaimed before I'd even asked. "Why should I die for a national idea? What am I, a sucker? Anyway, it's not my nation. You know, the *titushki*"—pro-government thugs—"were the Ukrainian people too. Why doesn't anyone ever talk about that? They were the ones acting rationally—they were the ones who got paid!"

I mentioned my conversation with Okhrim about Maidan.

"Okhrim killed people! You know why? Because he encouraged them with his music. If he hadn't stood on that stage playing, maybe they wouldn't have gone and fought!"

I couldn't tell whether he was being facetious.

"But on the other hand," he continued, "I'm for Maidan! Now the police are afraid of the people, which means they're afraid of us, too. We can play on the street as late as we want. And who'll complain about street music after they've heard the sound of snipers? They're happy to hear us playing. That's why I'm for Maidan."

As we drove around in his van, he delivered a virtuoso account of conflicting Maidan conspiracy theories, one of which revolved around the mechanics of porta-potties.

"What did they do with all the shit?" he cried, thumping the steering wheel. "Where did it all go? If it was really there, why didn't they use it to make barricades?" Then, twisting the knife, he gave me a lecture about how AIDS didn't exist.

"So you're writing a book about us? Making money from our suffering? Where's my money?" he asked as we pulled up in front of my building.

I staggered out of the car and went straight to bed. The shawarma had upset my stomach.

The night before the presidential election on May 25, there were campfires on Maidan. If something went wrong, people were ready to protest again.

I had dinner with Alina and Igor, our friend from Rakhiv. Always a font of insider information from mysterious sources, Igor gave me the rundown on all the presidential candidates and what would happen next. He said that Ukrainians looked favorably on the expected winner, Petro Poroshenko, the "Chocolate King," because he came from a relatively well-to-do family; unlike most Ukrainian oligarchs, Igor said, Poroshenko didn't use the ruthless tactics common among those who became rich in the lawless 1990s. But Poroshenko wouldn't be able to salvage the situation. Igor predicted that there would be blood.

On the restaurant's television, we learned that Russian TV viewers were getting a different picture of the Ukrainian elections: Russia's Channel 1 reported that Dmytro Yarosh, leader of Right Sector, was in the lead, with 37 percent of the vote. In reality, Yarosh won less than 1 percent. Russian propaganda had sailed into a world of pure fantasy, and somehow it was bringing much of the Russian population along with it.

During my short walk home from the Maidan metro station that night, I saw at least four men lying on the sidewalk, drunk to the point of unconsciousness. They didn't look like bums.

I spent Election Day walking around the sunbaked, half-deserted streets. Many people feared that there might be a terrorist attack, or "provocation." When I walked by the Central Election Commission, I saw that it was guarded by police with a bomb-sniffing dog. Farther down the street, a bus had let out a crowd of young policemen who were sitting in the grass, eating sunflower seeds and drinking kvas.

Outside Volodymyrskoye Market, an old lady held three empty glass jars. In Russian, with her Ukrainian accent, she called, or maybe begged, "Please buy a jar. Not expensive, not expensive." Ukraine's currency, the hryvnia, had lost half its value over the last year; revolution hadn't been good for the economy. Inside the market, shoppers and vendors asked one another, "Did you vote? Did you vote?"

All over the city, Kievans were standing in the longest lines they'd ever seen at a polling site, with waits of up to two hours in hot, stuffy rooms. Many voters wore embroidered Ukrainian blouses to show their patriotism. They were sweaty, dizzy, and tired, but they waited, and cast their ballots. "My hands were shaking as I voted," Alina told me later. "I felt such a heavy responsibility."

The self-appointed leaders of Donetsk and Luhansk were willing to do whatever it took to prevent the elections from taking place in their regions. Separatists abducted and threatened election officials, seized election offices and voting records, destroyed ballot boxes, and set fire to an election commission office. The police didn't intervene; in some cases, they even helped the separatists. The overwhelming majority of polling stations were closed, and voters were afraid to visit those that were open. One election commission member in Artemivsk, north of the city of Donetsk, said that his commission had decided not to hold the vote. "If we have elections tomorrow, they will kill us," he said. This obstruction meant that Ukraine's new president would have little legitimacy in the east, no matter who he was.

Poroshenko won the election, with an absolute majority that precluded a runoff. Most of the people I had spoken to in Kiev had said that they planned to vote for Poroshenko because, given the current crisis, Ukraine needed a new president immediately. Poroshenko was the lesser evil. He spoke fluent English and had proven himself on Maidan, appearing regularly and doing his best to defuse violent situations, as when he tried to talk down the masked men in the bulldozer. Russia seemed to have a relatively conciliatory attitude toward him; at a press conference the day before the election, Putin had indicated that he would respect the results of Ukraine's election and work with the new government, though he still considered Yanukovych to be Ukraine's legitimate leader.

Poroshenko's campaign slogan, "A New Kind of Life," was less than convincing; he was a politician who'd survived many different political periods in Ukraine, making all the necessary deals and compromises. Under Orange Revolution president Yushchenko, Poroshenko had vied with Yulia Tymoshenko for the position of prime minister, but he had also helped found Yanukovych's Party of Regions. Given Poroshenko's deep roots in Ukraine's corrupt status quo, it was unlikely that his presidency would mark a new epoch for Ukraine. Three months after the end of Maidan, Ukrainians had drastically lowered their expectations.

After the election, the Kiev city administration made a desultory attempt to clear Maidan, removing the makeshift museum exhibits and sending the campers and souvenir vendors packing. Many Kievans wanted life to go back to normal, to be rid of the stench of Maidan's corpse, the suspicious characters, the spectacle of lawlessness. But some believed that the campers should be allowed to stay. Hadn't they fought for Maidan? Would the revolution be over when they left? Going back to normal was frightening; Maidan had been about overturning the status quo and making a new reality, and at present reality didn't seem very new at all.

When I took a final stroll on Maidan before flying home, I found the campers burning tires. Men in fatigues and balaclavas stopped cars on Khreshchatyk, checking their trunks. The occupiers were reluctant to give up their territory, to remove the costumes that had invested them with the power of history.

Old ladies were berating these dregs of the revolution, telling them to get off Maidan so it would be clean again. Grubby little men in camouflage sat on a tank parked in the square, along with a girl who was playing old Russian rock songs on a guitar.

A one-eyed drunk danced ecstatically.

"Glory to the nation!" he cried.

Chapter 16

Crashing

On July 17, 2014, Malaysian Airlines flight 17 was shot down over eastern Ukraine. The flight had been traveling from Amsterdam to Kuala Lumpur, and many of the passengers were going to the International AIDS Conference in Melbourne; I recognized the names of two of the victims. My ex-boyfriend Kotik, with whom I no longer spoke, emailed me to say he hoped I hadn't died.

Hundreds of corpses lay bloating in the sun. Armed separatists, along with journalists, volunteers, and others, walked through waist-high wheat and sunflowers, contaminating evidence, if not stealing it. A *New York Times* reporter described watching a group of separatists picking through the crash victims' possessions: one of the men had never seen a boarding pass and asked what it was. One of the first photographers to arrive at the scene found a naked body that had fallen through the roof of a dilapidated house with faded blue woodwork, the kind you saw all over Ukraine and that seemed to have been there forever, remnants of a pastoral life.

Ukraine released a recording of three phone calls it said it had intercepted. In them, separatists expressed some dismay at the fact that MH17 was a passenger flight rather than a Ukrainian military plane, as they'd thought when they took the shot. But not all of them felt guilty. Igor "Strelkov" Girkin promoted the theory that the plane had been loaded with frozen corpses and flown over Ukraine on autopilot, part of an incredibly elaborate setup to frame the separatists and Mother Russia. This conspiracy theory, along with several others, made the rounds of Russia's state-controlled media.

The corpses were put on a train that sat in the station of a small coal-mining town, emitting an unbearable stench. This process was supervised by armed masked men, some of whom seemed to be drunk. The Donetsk billionaire mining tycoon Rinat Akhmetov (who some believed had financed the separatists, only to lose control of them, much to his own detriment) ordered his miners to join the Ukrainian police on patrol, and a local boss sent his miners to help clear the corpses. "I wouldn't call this volunteer work," one of them told a journalist. International monitors were allowed only to peek in at the bodies on the train. Volunteers and locals were still trudging through the fields, collecting body parts and whole corpses. The *Guardian*'s Shaun Walker described a scene reminiscent of Greek tragedy: not long after the crash, a man brought the corpse of an Asian child to a local hospital. His own son was the same age, about six or seven, and the man wanted to keep the body from being eaten by stray dogs.

For many Ukrainians, and for many others, the shooting down of MH17 was the decisive moment in which the separatists and their supporters lost any remnant of humanity and became monsters, excommunicated from the civilized world. A Ukrainian blogger wrote, "No, these aren't people, they're some kind of vampires . . . . Now there is truly no compassion. See a Colorado—kill him."

The term *Colorado* was a recently coined slur for pro-Russians. It was inspired by the Colorado beetle, which destroys potato crops and has stripes that resemble the black and orange

St. George ribbon, a symbol of Russian patriotism. Calling people Colorados made them into pests, insects to be crushed underfoot. The term's most notorious usage occurred on May 2, 2014, when forty-eight anti-Maidan protesters were killed and some two hundred wounded in Odessa's Trade Union building. After attacking a pro-Maidan demonstration, apparently with the blessing of at least one police officer, the anti-Maidan protesters fled to the Trade Union building and barricaded themselves inside, as a throng of pro-Maidan protesters stood outside, shouting threats. The building caught fire, most likely from one of the Molotov cocktails being thrown from both sides. The police stood and watched, and firefighters took an hour to arrive. Maidan protesters had been burned alive in Kiev's Trade Union building in February; now, in an eerie parallel, anti-Maidan protesters were burned alive inside Odessa's Trade Union building. Though some Maidan supporters helped rescue people from the burning building, others reportedly chanted, "Burn, Colorado, burn." Some beat people who escaped from the burning building, or shot at those inside. The "Odessa massacre," as it came to be called in Russia and eastern Ukraine, became a central justification, in the Russian media and popular imagination, for Russian intervention in Ukraine. Some volunteers in the separatist forces cited the incident in Odessa as the principal reason they'd joined up.

On Ukrainian Independence Day in August 2014, Kiev proudly displayed the weapons with which it was bombarding its eastern regions. Donetsk held an "anti-independence" parade, marching Ukrainian POWs down the street at bayonet point, past the statue of Lenin, then hosing down the street behind them. "Fascists!" bystanders shouted at the prisoners.

Iryna Dovhan, a pleasant-looking blond woman accused of being a Ukrainian spy, was wrapped in a Ukrainian flag, made to hold a printout that said SHE KILLS OUR CHILDREN, and tied to a pole in a traffic circle. In a widely circulated photo, she squeezed her eyes closed as a middle-aged woman in sandals and a glittery black spandex top kicked her, smiling like a goblin. (Under pressure from journalists, Dovhan was released by the separatists a few days later.) Both sides fired on civilian areas, and towns lost electricity and access to medicine, food, and drinking water.

When the Donetsk and Luhansk People's Republics held general elections in November 2014, voters were greeted at polling stations with plates of pierogis and huge mesh sacks of potatoes and cabbage, welcome gifts at a time when food was increasingly hard to come by. People scrounged for coal in abandoned mines, desperate for something to sell. When the shells and artillery fire started, they took refuge in their basements and in World War II-era bomb shelters. Some of the elderly women who sat in the shelters had survived that earlier war, or even fought in it. The present scurried down into the dank, subterranean spaces of the past.

Though it continued to fight for its eastern territories, the Ukrainian government chose to treat the regions as enemy ground. Kiev stopped funding government services (including hospitals and clinics) and providing social benefit payments in separatist-controlled areas. This meant that residents had to travel to government-controlled areas to receive their pensions, which were often their only source of income. In January 2015 the Ukrainian government placed limits on travel, requiring civilians to get a special pass to allow them to move between separatist- and government-controlled areas. Many of the people who needed government pensions and social benefits were unable to travel; they didn't have the money, they were sick or disabled or very old, they couldn't wait for ten hours in line, they had to care for family members. Some were simply too afraid to travel or even to leave their basement shelters—which was reasonable, considering the frequent bombardment of civilian areas. The travel permit system caused interruptions in supplies of medicine, including HIV and tuberculosis medications. Hospitals started running out of gauze and bandages.

The Ukrainian government's logic was that anything sent to eastern Ukraine would only help the separatists survive longer. As for the civilians who would starve alongside the separatists—well, if they were still in the east, they were separatists, too: sausage people, pests, filth. Let Russia feed them. (But Russia didn't feed them.) In keeping with long tradition, the people of Donbas were once more considered an infection, a barbarian horde. A pro-Ukraine police official in the Donetsk region later wrote, "I call on public organizations and activists in Kiev to block the movement of buses between Donetsk and Kiev, which allow for the spread of the terrorist plague and filth across the territory of Ukraine. If I had my way I'd just shoot these tourists to the Donetsk People's Republic, these lovers of referenda and parades of Ukrainian prisoners of war." Never mind that some of these "tourists" were bringing food and other supplies to relatives and friends unable to leave the region. Journalists and commentators who tried to call attention to the growing humanitarian crisis in eastern Ukraine (including me) were accused of spreading Russian propaganda.

*

In *White Guard*, Aleksei Turbin dreams about a fellow officer, Zhilin, who died in the First World War. Zhilin explains that his regiment was allowed to march into heaven with its armor, horses, and comfort women. When he learned that there was a starry crimson mansion awaiting even the Bolsheviks who would be killed in the civil war, he asked God how atheists could have a place in heaven.

"So they don't believe—what can you do?" God shrugged. "Somebody believes, somebody doesn't, but you're all at each other's throats. As far as I'm concerned, you're the same—men killed on the battlefield."

Chapter 17

New Year in Kiev

As the months of fighting wore on, I got used to thinking of Ukraine as a war zone, a landscape strewn with corpses, a place where people did terrible things to each other. But when I returned in December 2014, the Kiev airport's arrivals hall was the same as usual. For a moment I thought that maybe everything hadn't gone to hell after all.

Then I heard a group of men on the other side of the customs booth singing the Ukrainian national anthem.

Souls and bodies we'll lay down for our freedom

"Listen to how soulfully they sing!" said a middle-aged woman standing behind me in line. She'd been speaking Russian with her grown daughter, but now she started drifting into a mix of Russian and Ukrainian. "Can you imagine them singing the Russian national anthem in Sheremetyevo?" Sheremyetevo is an international airport in Moscow.

Her daughter murmured in agreement.

Glory to Ukraine!
Glory to heroes!

"Ukraine has so many beautiful things, doesn't it?" the mother mused. "Like sarafans." A sarafan is a traditional dress, a bit like a jumper.

"My ears ached on the plane, the whole way," the daughter said.

"Why didn't you put drops in?"

Glory to Ukraine!
Glory to heroes!

"Ukraine is a European country," the mother said happily. By the time we made it past customs, the singing patriots had dispersed.

On the way into the city, I passed the big soccer ball that had been placed there in honor of the Eurocup. It was right next to the Kiev city limits sign, which had the words HERO-CITY above it: this was the official Soviet designation for the cities that had suffered most during the Second World War. Graffiti along the highway shouted, THIS IS OUR GOD-GIVEN COUNTRY! My driver turned up the volume on the radio every time the news came on.

I'd decided that my old apartment on Bohdan Khmelnytsky had become uninhabitable, so I was staying with Alik. It was already dark when I arrived at his apartment in Podil. He heated up a carrot "cutlet" for me—a vegetarian variation on the Eastern European staple, the *kotlet*, a meat patty made of ground meat, breadcrumbs, eggs, and onion.

"Just like Tolstoy ate," Alik told me. "He invented them."

Like Tolstoy, Alik was a pacifist: he couldn't understand why anyone was volunteering to fight, especially people with children.

Any mention of the war made him snarl with anger and disgust. Alik was a humanitarian; he had no interest in national ideas.

Alik took me to visit his friend Jacques, a French artist who'd been living in Kiev for a year. Long-haired and skinny, in white jeans and huge plush slippers bought at a market stall, Jacques talked about every kind of event with the same sarcastic, self-deprecating humor. He told us about his love interest; the night before, he said, they'd had a whole bottle of vodka, but she still wouldn't sleep with him. In the same tone of amusement and feigned outrage, Jacques spoke about his experience of Maidan. He'd moved to Kiev just after the protests started, and he'd been living right off Khreshchatyk Street, on Ivan Franko Square. When the barricades went up, he'd been almost trapped in his apartment. Soon he didn't want to leave anyway, because of all the fires and explosions. Snipers were shooting from just above his building. "I mean, fuck, man," he kept saying, as if he were complaining about a traffic jam or being kept on hold while he called customer service.

Now Jacques was back to the expat good life, in a huge under-priced apartment with mirrored walls and ceilings and northern and southern views. The revolution had caused some stress, but the resulting collapse of the Ukrainian currency had made the expat good life even better. Jacques said that he liked Ukraine because it was a really free country, not like France or England or the United States. In Western Europe, he said, there were too many rules, and everyone was always asking questions. Here you could do as you pleased, especially if you were an expat. He said he was working on a nude portrait of Trotsky's great-granddaughter.

*

The Opera was decorated with a huge banner that said WE WELCOME THE HEROES OF ATO. (Everyone referred to the antiterrorist operation by its initials.) Despite this warm reception, many would-be heroes were still wearing their masks. At the Christmas fair on St. Sophia Square, Santas posed for cash while men in camouflage and balaclavas collected money for the Azov Battalion, the volunteer battalion with the strongest neo-Nazi tendencies. The previous summer Azov members had told the *Guardian* that once the war in the east was over, they'd "bring the fight to Kiev" and that they wanted to install a strong military leader, perhaps a dictator. They didn't think it would be very hard. "What are the police going to do?" asked one Azov fighter. "They couldn't do anything against the peaceful protesters on Maidan; they'll hardly withstand armed fighting units." Azov used a modified version of the Nazi-era Wolf's Hook as their insignia; like the ultranationalists of the 1990s, they said it represented the words "Idea of the Nation." Azov was funded by Ukraine's most prominent Jewish oligarch, Igor Kolomoysky. Nothing was surprising in Ukraine anymore.

My old friend Zakhar, the proprietor of the underground art gallery-garage, invited me over to his house. I took a taxi; at the new exchange rate, I was suddenly very rich.

When I arrived, Zakhar and a friend were watching an American romantic comedy dubbed into Russian. We were soon joined by Zakhar's long-suffering girlfriend, Alla.

"What's new?" I asked, though I knew this was a fraught question.

"I have no news," Zakhar answered, in his usual bantering, slightly deranged tone. "I haven't done anything for an entire year—that's a record for me. I've just been monitoring. During Maidan I lived in the gallery so I could monitor the revolution more closely." (His gallery was a short walk from Maidan.) "Sometimes I didn't leave the garage for three days at a time. Alla was the only one who knew I was there—she'd come and make me go outside. You could eat well on Maidan! We used to line up for borscht, didn't we, Alla?"

Alla rolled her eyes.

Zakhar and his friend, an unpleasant man with a pointed nose, beady eyes, and long, greasy hair, started talking about the war. Everything came down to money, they said. People joined the Azov Battalion for the money—and no wonder, now that there were no jobs. Zakhar and his friend discussed a rumor they'd heard about how you could make big money by buying weapons in the ATO zone and selling them for twice as much in Kiev. The problem with this otherwise appealing plan was that it required going to the ATO zone.

Ukraine had reintroduced conscription the previous May, and a new wave of troop mobilization had just been announced for February.

"Don't you understand that we could be drafted at any time?" Zakhar's friend said, his voice shrill with anxiety. "I don't want to be cannon fodder!"

"You think they want *me* in the army?" Zakhar said ironically.

Alla and I laughed at the idea of drafting an emotionally unstable, alcoholic bohemian with a penchant for public nudity.

"They could take you," his friend insisted. "They can take anyone, whenever they want."

*

Although many people spoke loudly about their support for the war, far fewer intended to go and fight. Friends shared strategies to avoid being drafted; to many, the draft seemed like a form of human sacrifice. An estimated fifteen hundred servicemen had been killed during nine months of fighting, but evidence suggested that the real death toll was higher, that the government was trying to conceal the scale of its losses.

Misha Friedman, a Russian-American photographer, invited me to meet Sveta, a longtime AIDS activist from Donetsk, and her husband, Aleksei, a fighter who'd just been released in a pre-New Year's prisoner exchange. Both Sveta and Aleksei were HIV-positive former drug users. When Sveta had started her AIDS NGO, Aleksei had been on the board of directors, but he'd soon grown tired of the paperwork and become a mechanic. For him the war was personal: he'd lost his apartment in Donetsk, his work, his hometown. He volunteered early for the Donbas Battalion, which was on the front lines from the beginning. When he joined up, it wasn't even a proper battalion, just a band of patriots without a name.

Misha had told me we were going to a party for the released prisoners, and I'd imagined a big event, a noisy hall full of men in fatigues. But it was only a few close-mouthed couples at Il Patio, a faux-Italian chain restaurant on Bessarabska Square. Aleksei had the high, stripped cheekbones that you often see among people who take HIV medications, which change the distribution of body fat. With his glassy, beatific green eyes, he was beautiful in a way peculiar to some drug users and people with HIV or TB, people who seem to have one foot in the next world. He and Sveta were already on intimate terms with Misha; they'd even let him photograph them in bed on the first night after their reunion, as they lay in the dark, staring at their phones and frowning. I had the impression that they were relieved to have an intermediary.

In August, Aleksei had been captured in the battle of Ilovaisk, a strategically important town between Donetsk and Luhansk. Pro-Ukrainian volunteer battalions managed to raise their flag in Ilovaisk without any casualties and were said to be clearing the city of terrorists. But then the separatists appeared. There were battles in the streets, with many casualties. Ukraine promised to send reinforcements, government troops, but these never arrived: a terrible betrayal. The pro-Ukrainian fighters in the city were surrounded. After several days, the separatists agreed to allow them to retreat via a "humanitarian corridor," but the retreating battalions were ambushed, killed and captured. Survivors reported seeing not only separatists but also Russian troops. Before Ilovaisk, it had seemed that Ukraine was about to win the war.

As prisoners, Aleksei and his fellow fighters had been beaten, made to confess, and paraded for Russian news cameras. Eastern Ukrainians like Aleksei usually tried to hide their origins, so that the separatists could think them natural enemies from the west rather than traitors, who might be treated even more cruelly. But the separatists weren't always strict. People in Ilovaisk had written letters asking the Donetsk People's Republic for POW labor, and the people's republic had complied. Aleksei and some other POWs were assigned to do repairs in a woman's house. The woman felt sorry for Aleksei, and let him Skype with Sveta.

The families of the exchanged prisoners hadn't been informed in advance about where the men would arrive; President

Poroshenko kept all the joy for himself, having the prisoners deposited on an airstrip at night. He was the only one photographed greeting them. The wives were furious.

Now Sveta looked anxious and happy, her eyes open as fresh wounds. Aleksei was drinking a half-liter glass of beer; he had been sober for ten years before the war, but he'd gotten smashed on his first night as a free man.

During his four months in captivity, Aleksei had shared a bed with a friend, who was also at the table with us. The friend was only twenty-four, and his fur hat with its earflaps askew made him look like a little rabbit. He and Aleksei and the other men muttered in their guttural Donetsk accents, showing each other war videos on their phones and discussing military equipment. Aleksei's eyes lit up at the talk of weapons.

"I don't think he'll be a mechanic again," Sveta said. "Look— he already misses his gun." I made some anodyne comment about the need to organize help for the fighters who returned with PTSD; Sveta snorted. No one was going to help these men.

Il Patio closed, and the party was over. I arrived at the Maidan metro station just before the train stopped running for the night. Men in camouflage and balaclavas were wrapping up a drunken fight out front; empty beer bottles were scattered on the ground.

Not all the volunteer fighters were motivated by political ideals or national ideas. For a certain type of man, the war offered an opportunity to recapture a sense of potency and significance, whatever the cost. In a society in which so many men were adrift, war had appeal, especially if it paid.

Oleksandr Techinskiy, who made the Maidan documentary *All Things Ablaze* and went on to work with a number of foreign journalists covering the war in eastern Ukraine, put it more cynically, saying that many of the guys who were fighting were just "looking for an excuse to get away from their wives, stop showering or changing their underwear, and get drunk."

Once the country had taken up arms, it was hard to put them down. "People have gone over to war now," Techinskiy told me. "They've gotten used to it, they're comfortable there, and they don't want to leave."

"At one point I was in Piski, near Donetsk, with Right Sector. A Right Sector guy asked a Right Sector girl if she had ten towels. 'I do,' she said, 'but what will you give me in return?' He traded her a hand grenade—an F1, a kind of grenade that was invented in the Second World War."

Weapons became playthings, sometimes literally: two Luhansk separatists and a couple of bystanders were injured after the separatists tried to bowl with grenades. Weapons offered relief first from the boredom of everyday life, and then from the boredom of war.

"You spend hours just sitting around waiting, with nothing to do," Techinskiy told me. "Fighters are fun people—they know how to keep themselves occupied. One fighter once said to me, 'Oh! You're a journalist! Want to throw a fly?" *Mukha*, or "fly," is the nickname for a Russian rocket launcher developed in the early 1970s. When Techinskiy declined, the fighter shot the rocket launcher himself, just to keep busy.

*

Olena, an acquaintance from my public health days, told me straight off that the last year had almost killed her. During Maidan she had coordinated medical aid to the wounded, sending people to clinics and buying medicine, equipment, and prosthetic limbs. In August her husband, father of her nine-year-old daughter, had been drafted. Olena hadn't wanted him to join up. She knew that there were plenty of ways to get out of the draft; after all, this was Ukraine, still one of the most corrupt countries in the world. Even military personnel, she'd heard, were managing to escape mobilization. But Olena's husband said he wanted to defend his country. He had no real military training, only some theoretical knowledge of artillery.

The impoverished Ukrainian army provided almost no equipment to its conscripts, so Olena and her husband scrambled to purchase several thousand dollars' worth of gear and medical supplies with assistance from friends and colleagues. Through personal connections, Olena was able to obtain prescription painkillers, another thing the government didn't provide. (The government was shocked to discover that because of its own labyrinthine requirements for opioid prescription, it was unable to procure painkillers for its own soldiers.) After just three weeks of training, Olena's husband was sent to Donbas. When Olena and I met, he had been on duty for three months without any break or hope of rotation. He was already used to killing people, and to people trying to kill him.

Olena said that Maidan had "crystallized" civil society, proving that self-organization was far more efficient than anything orchestrated by the corrupt, useless, badly managed state. But the story was no longer an inspiring one. Olena and her husband had been lucky to have the money and connections to get the necessary equipment and supplies, but they couldn't do anything about the broader problems: lack of equipment, training, and experience, and incompetent officers who exposed soldiers to unnecessary risks.

"Many people are killed because of pure stupidity," Olena told me. "My husband and many others are hostages of this situation—they cannot escape. Or if they do, they'll be criminals." Her husband was one of the many people who predicted that the soldiers would come back very angry at the government, with their own military equipment and fighting experience, and that Ukraine would become even more dangerous than it had been in the 1990s.

Alik's friend Spinner (pronounced "Spee-nehr") came over to visit. Spinner was an extremely good-looking raver. He was thirty but seemed younger, with a boyish face, yellow-tinted glasses, baggy camouflage pants, and brightly colored high tops. His outfit was perfectly normal for a raver, and I wouldn't have looked at it twice in New York in the 1990s. But in Kiev in 2014, when every underpass held a cluster of shady, unshaven men in fatigues, Spinner's outfit seemed more than outdated.

Spinner stood in Alik's living room, looking in the mirror, admiring himself, practicing his dance moves. "I'd like a car and an apartment on Bessarabska Square and a pistol," he said dreamily.

"Why do you want a pistol?" I asked.

"I like pistols," he said. "There are weapons everywhere now."

"The nineties are coming back," Alik said.

"We have to be ready!" Spinner laughed.

*

At a trendy new café off Khreshchatyk Street, I interviewed Nikita, the eccentric harm reductionist I'd first encountered several years earlier. Huge, broad-shouldered, and bald, in a red-and-white-checked cowboy shirt, Nikita was out of place, out of proportion, out of time. American Christmas music was playing in the background: Bing Crosby's "Jingle Bells," "Last Christmas" by Wham!, and "All I Want for Christmas Is You." Nikita looked around with impatience, declined a coffee, and told me about the Soviet Union.

"We had a very tough country. You had to wait in line for two hours to buy underwear. There was food to eat in the capitals—in Kiev, Moscow, Tallinn. But not in other places. Every Saturday and Sunday people rode on the train to buy sausage. On Sundays in Kiev, you'd have to wait in line for four hours. People stood and read, wrote whole dissertations, while they waited to buy sausage." He laughed. "So anyone who robbed the government was a saint. Now it's the same way."

He told me about working as a black marketeer in the 1980s.

"I'd go up to a foreigner who's visiting. 'How's life, kid? Give me a T-shirt or some underwear. Or dollars.' For dollars you got eight years.

"Russia wants to bring us back to Soviet times. But Putin has given us a nation. I used to be closer to Donetsk in spirit. But now I'm not close to Donetsk at all. I would never invite Putin to come to Ukraine. I'd get a gun and shoot him instead." He said this in a very casual way.

I asked him about anti-Semitism in Right Sector and Svoboda. (Nikita was half Jewish, which was part of the reason I'd wanted to interview him.)

"Svoboda works for the KGB," he said.

"What makes you think so?" I asked.

"I don't *think* so. I *know*."

"You *know*?"

"I'm an old Jew, what do you want? I know everything," he said, and laughed.

Because drug treatment with methadone or buprenorphine was illegal in Russia, all Crimean programs had stopped; the UN had recently announced that of the eight hundred Crimean drug users who'd been receiving substitution treatment before the Russian annexation, an estimated one hundred or more were now dead, mostly of overdoses or suicides. Others had moved to parts of Ukraine where treatment was still available. There were drug users and HIV-positive people among the refugees from the east as well. Nikita had new harm reduction clients, but he didn't like them much.

"The good ones from the east or Crimea are somewhere else, doing something else," he said. "They're not the ones who came here. The ones I see want to take with both hands—they have Russia in their heads." In his opinion, although all drug users were tricky, the HIV patients and drug users who had moved to Kiev from Crimea or the east were more cunning, more dishonest than Kiev natives.

"People from Donetsk come and think we owe them something. So you're a drug addict, so you're HIV positive—go ask Russia for help. Why are you coming here? Maybe you shouldn't have been waving those flags and begging Putin to come."

On New Year's Eve, Alina and I went to visit Alina's colleague, Yury, and his wife, Yulia. (Alik had disappeared.) Yury and Yulia were good-looking, charming, successful people in their thirties, with a beautiful blond son about five years old. They lived just off St. Sophia Square, in a high-ceilinged, Euro-renovated apartment furnished with white IKEA furniture.

We drank champagne and ate ham that Yury's mother had baked.

"Why don't you show us your present?" Yury asked his shy son, who was playing quietly in the corner. The boy's eyes widened, and he ran into his bedroom. When he came back, he was holding a huge black air rifle, as big as his body.

"He was begging for it for six months!" Yury said, laughing. "It's real—it works. But there are no bullets in it, of course."

Kiev residents traditionally celebrated New Year's Eve on Maidan, but now there were too many painful memories; the festivities had been moved to St. Sophia Square. When it was almost midnight, we went downstairs. Bundled in our parkas, scarves, hoods, hats, and gloves, watching our breath in the night air, several hundred of us greeted a new year. Everyone was eager to chase away the old one.

In the morning, Kiev's snowdrifts were strewn with empty bottles of cheap champagne. ("Soviet Champagne" was one of the most popular brands.) While nursing my hangover, I saw on Twitter that Evgeny Feldman, a Russian photographer, was at the annual torch march in honor of the nationalist hero Stepan Bandera's birthday, January 1. Feldman's pictures were ominous; a mass of torches burning in the night, the marchers almost invisible. I headed to Maidan.

A man was leading a pony through the Maidan underpass, and drunk men in Winnie-the-Pooh costumes were propositioning laughing women who shoved them away. The menacing, torch-wielding hordes of Feldman's photos, which had already been retweeted again and again by those who were concerned, or who wished to seem concerned, about Ukraine's far right, had dispersed. All that remained was a small group of flag wavers. About half the flags were blue and gold Svoboda flags; the others half were red and black, for Right Sector and other nationalist groups. Passing clusters of men in fatigues, some of them in balaclavas, I stopped behind a family.

"It's not too scary for you?" the father asked his children, laughing. The children seemed unconcerned. Their father was showing them a historical curiosity, a zoo exhibit.

A group of pensioners were wearing traditional Ukrainian clothing; one babushka wore a woven headband covered in pom-poms and little pins with portraits of Bandera. Small children slid across the icy cobblestones. An attractive blond woman had Right Sector's black and red flag painted on her cheek.

"Glory to Ukraine!," the group shouted. Only a couple of people yelled "Death to enemies," and they didn't sound convinced.

On a small stage, a pretty woman stood and smiled radiantly, holding a portrait of Bandera. An old man held a Ukrainian flag and a portrait of Taras Shevchenko. An Orthodox priest made a speech, and then everyone sang a song. As the rally's speakers stepped down from their little stage, they clustered around Oleh Tyahnybok, the leader of Svoboda, asking him to pose for photos with them. Robust and photogenic, he towered over the crowd. He looked like a real politician, but if this was his constituency, he was in trouble. The crowd was full of people who were one-eyed, disabled, elderly, visibly marginal. It was hard to take them seriously as a neofascist menace. Feldman, the journalist, said the march was smaller than it had been in previous years; maybe this was because the young and able-bodied had gone to fight in the east.

On the steps leading up to the square, some young men in camouflage were clowning around, waving flags and singing some kind of nationalist limerick. Suddenly a few of them began to shout "Glory to Ukraine! Glory to heroes! Death to enemies!," the guttural chant tearing out of their throats. This time it sounded genuinely frightening.

At the Bulgakov Museum, housed in the novelist's childhood home, a sign on the door announced, "The entrance into our museum of individuals who support the military occupation of Ukraine is not desired." Inside, one of my fellow tourists was wearing a Right Sector scarf.

I could tell that the tour guide, a well-kept woman in her fifties or sixties, was the kind of person for whom literature is a religion and a favorite writer is a messiah. Though she spoke quickly, her voice had the modulation of a professional actress's, and she looked very dignified in her black cardigan sweater with its grid of thin white lines. It was clear that current events had inspired her with new fervor, new grief.

Speaking Russian, she told us grimly that by 1918 this house had become a communal apartment; Bulgakov couldn't go home again. The world of his childhood had vanished. He lived in Moscow for a while but soon returned to Kiev, because it was freer there.

"That was a hundred years ago," she said meaningfully.

She led us through the living room, where there were two pianos and a Christmas tree—which would not, she pointed out, have been allowed during Soviet times—and then into a painstaking reconstruction of Bulgakov's sisters' bedroom. With great ceremony, she opened the wardrobe to reveal an apartment door with a tablet that read "50." This was apartment 50 on 302-bis Bolshaya Sadovaya Street, the Moscow communal apartment where Bulgakov lived with his first wife. He hated the apartment and made it the site of the dance of the unclean spirits in *The Master and Margarita*.

We walked through the wardrobe into Bulgakov's room in Moscow, then into a final sitting room, back in Kiev. The guide lined us up in two rows, shortest to tallest, in front of a mirror.

"This room can never be peaceful," she said, "because it is full of doors. There is another room where peace can be attained, but we cannot reach it; I can only show it to you."

She turned off the lights and pressed a switch. The mirror became a window, and instead of our own reflection, we saw a ghostly white bed, a bookshelf, and a cluttered writing desk that seemed to be suspended in the air, trembling. We gasped. Then she flipped another switch, and we saw nothing but stars.

"Why do we look at the night sky so seldom?" she asked. She was referring to the famous last lines of *White Guard*:

> All this will pass. Suffering, sorrow, blood, hunger, and mass death. The sword will vanish and the stars will remain, long after the shadows of our bodies and our

affairs are gone from the earth. There isn't any man who doesn't know this. So why are we so reluctant to turn our gaze to the stars?

"Thank you for coming to our beautiful city," our guide concluded, "where, as you can see, there are no fascists or Banderites."

Chapter 18

Rocket City

The first time I traveled through the Dnipropetrovsk region, which lies between Kiev and Donetsk, it was the winter of 2007. The landscape was half charred and half aflame; farmers were burning the fields to make them fertile again. Soviet statues of muscle-bound proletarians stood among half-built concrete buildings, abandoned factories with smashed-in windows. Rusted pipes loomed like obelisks, and Lenins waved at no one. In Pavlohrad, a small city in the region, I interviewed harm reduction workers in an unheated room with a pool table, and then interviewed a madam, a *mamochka*, on the street. Everyone kept asking if I'd seen the *rakyeta*. I didn't understand what they meant until they brought me to the edge of a gray field and pointed at a small, lonely rocket.

Dnipropetrovsk, the region's capital, was once nicknamed "Rocket City." As a center of the Soviet arms and space industries, it was closed to visitors. Today Dnipropetrovsk still seems to negate human presence: the streets feel too wide and too empty, and the heavily ornamented buildings on the main stretch, Karl Marx Avenue, are designed to intimidate.

When I visited Dnipropetrovsk in January 2015, Vitaly, the husband of Olga Belyaeva, one of the harm reduction colleagues I most admired, met me at the train station. I hadn't seen Vitaly for years, except in the pictures he'd posted on Facebook. In December he stood on the Maidan barricades, wrapped in a

Ukrainian flag. In February he posed in Kiev in a military helmet, and posted pictures of burnt-out stairways and Molotov cocktails. In June he stood in front of a tank in a sunny green field, dressed in camouflage, holding a big gun; I deduced that he had joined up. Now he was going to show me around Dnipropetrovsk's war operation, along with a vivacious, orange-haired journalist named Marina Davydova. Apart from his camouflage and a new tightness around the mouth, Vitaly looked the same as he had when I'd first met him eight years earlier: tall and well built, with dark, friendly little eyes. In the back of his black SUV, I saw a Ukrainian flag and a baseball bat.

As separatism had gained momentum after Maidan, the local oligarch Igor Kolomoysky, who was worth an estimated $1.6 billion, had been made governor of Dnipropetrovsk. He soon started funding volunteer battalions—among them the Dnipro Battalion, which was to defend Dnipropetrovsk (and Kolomoysky and his business interests) from separatism. Dnipropetrovsk borders the Donetsk region, and Dnipropetrovsk, like Donetsk, is a primarily Russian-speaking city with a distinctly Soviet feel. Dnipropetrovsk might therefore have been expected to harbor separatist sympathies, but it remained firmly pro-Ukrainian. Marina, an avid patriot, told me that Dnipropetrovsk had once been full of "cotton," a slur for pro-Russians (who had cotton for brains), but now all the separatists had gone back to their "burrows." There were rumors that Kolomoysky's antiseparatist tactics had included marches to the woods and summary executions.

Vitaly and Marina took me to a "logistical center" where volunteers collected supplies for the fighters being sent to the east. The official story was that the Ukrainian army, now under the command of a new, more honest post-Maidan government, was struggling to recover from decades of corruption, and ordinary Ukrainians were doing their best to fill the gaps with donations and volunteer work. Volunteers were even welding metal plates onto vans—makeshift tanks—and learning online how to build drones. I'd decided to visit the logistical center partly because of an article I'd read in the *New York Times*, a feel-good story about how volunteers, mostly women, were using their knack for handicrafts for the good of Ukraine. A certain Natasha Naumenko, a travel agent who organized the center, was quoted as saying, "Our guys, our men, are defending the country, our country, and everything depends on them. They need a strong spirit. We want to give them the warmth of home, let them feel they are not standing there for nothing. Their wives, their mothers, their daughters have made them borscht." As in post-Soviet hard times, it seemed, women were using their skills and ingenuity to save the collective, whether within the domestic sphere or as NGO workers. But now men had a very clear role to play, one that was traditionally masculine and highly prestigious: they could go to the front.

The *New York Times* article glossed over an important question: who was in charge of the fighters who were receiving assistance from these plucky volunteers? Homegrown ingenuity was supporting not only Ukrainian soldiers but also the fifteen to twenty thousand fighters in the volunteer battalions: Dnipro, Donbas, Azov, and all the rest. The donations were not simply bolstering an impoverished army and bankrupt government; volunteers were running a war that was largely independent of the state. The Maidan movement, President Poroshenko, and Western politicians and pundits in favor of arming Ukraine referred, over and over, to Ukraine's commitment to "European values." But a country full of volunteer battalions funded by oligarchs, political parties, and donations looked more like premodern Europe than like a potential EU member.

The logistical center was located in the government's House of Scholars, in a couple of basement rooms with a little kitchen. These premises were the government's only contribution to the center. The basement flooded periodically, which was why the supplies—winter boots, coats, helmets, and homemade, though very professional-looking, bulletproof vests—were stored on shelves raised above floor level. There were piles of brightly colored single-use boxer shorts, many in floral or psychedelic patterns; these were sewn by Swedish women, the "Swedish battalion," from scrap material. Now that it was winter, volunteers were sewing white helmet covers and robes, so fighters could blend in with the snow. A large Right Sector flag hung on the wall.

Roman, a small, laconic man in his thirties, was a former mechanic, one of about one hundred volunteers working at the center. He and Natasha the travel agent, a jovial, matter-of-fact woman in a checked scarf, showed me the food packets that volunteers made for soldiers: nuts with ginger, honey, and lemon; dried borscht; and *salo*, cured lard with garlic. The center was stacked with donations: huge mesh bags of beets and potatoes, countless jars of preserves. One clever babushka brought her preserves wrapped in Styrofoam to keep them from breaking.

Other donations were less useful. One old lady had donated a large box of raspberry branches to stir tea, to ward off illness. (I remembered my Russian teacher Lena, with her endless supply of food-based folk remedies.) Someone else had donated an orange and white electric razor that, judging by the design, had been bought in the 1970s. Another had contributed the fourth volume of the collected works of Robert Louis Stevenson, with a handwritten letter wishing the soldiers victory and expressing the hope that the book would bring them comfort. One woman, Natasha said, had offered to sing to the soldiers. She had three numbers: "New York, New York," a song by Whitney Houston, and an aria from the operetta *The Circus Princess*.

"People give what they have. We put everyone to work," Natasha said, laughing. "We had one reporter peeling carrots. He loved it."

The volunteers showed me the "mini-pharmacies" they'd made, little first-aid kits that were, they said, the same as those used by NATO. But while in Europe such kits cost 100 euros each, these cost only 300 hryvnia, which was then about 17 euros.

"The government doesn't buy supplies because it doesn't have any money," Roman said. Then he seemed to contradict himself, saying, "They're bureaucrats, people who should be sent to jail and have their property confiscated. They drive around in Mercedes while soldiers are hungry and cold."

I asked him why he had chosen to volunteer.

"Each person does what he can do, what he has to do. The government isn't going to do it," he replied. In a bitter, muted tone, he continued, "This center has only enough supplies for fifty people. It's just a drop in the bucket. There isn't enough of anything, and everything's figured out along the way. No one knew, at first, except maybe the occasional medic, what Celox was, and why it's needed to stop the bleeding on a torn-off leg." Celox is a brand of hemostatic gauze. "No one knew anything about night vision goggles. Now they know. But it's all trial and error. Volunteers are doing the work of the Ministry of Defense.

One general said the Ministry of Defense was providing clothing for the soldiers, that volunteers weren't doing anything. I'll show you what kind of clothes he gave us."

Roman's face had brightened with anger. He looked almost happy as he searched through a heap of clothing.

"Here's one," he said, bringing over a jacket. Its lining was in tatters, eaten by mice. Next he showed me a helmet that was dented and riddled with bullet holes, its edge torn by an explosion.

Natasha and Marina showed me bracelets of woven ribbon, some blue and gold, some red and black. Children had made them for the center.

"Take one!" Marina said. "The red and black ones are the very best, and the blue and gold ones are also good. We're already on the second level," she said, and showed me her own red and black friendship bracelet, the thread kind I used to make in elementary school.

When I picked a red and black bracelet, Marina, Natasha, and Roman were visibly pleased. By then a tall man dressed in camouflage had appeared; he was pleased, too.

"You're one of us!" Marina said, or maybe it was Natasha. The tall man showed me his Right Sector ID card. Marina put it in my hand and took a picture of me. I hoped she wasn't planning to post it on Facebook.

As we left, Vitaly and Marina told me that they worried that soon the volunteers' money would run out. Military aid went to the Ministry of Defense, they said, and most of it was stolen; nothing went to the volunteers who were running the war effort.

The other worry was that the government would arrest the members of Right Sector once the war was over. In November, Ukraine had incorporated the volunteer battalions into the

National Guard, thereby legalizing them and bringing them under at least nominal control (and also providing them with more weapons). Dmytro Yarosh, the head of Right Sector, had been making efforts to pass legislation legalizing Right Sector's military wing, but he continued to reject its integration into government forces; he wanted it to operate independently. He also wanted the government to help arm his men, who were fighting with whatever weapons they could find, such as those captured in battle. The government was in no position to refuse assistance, and Right Sector was protected by wide popular support, but Right Sector's actions were technically illegal. Many of its fighters were in possession of weapons that would be hard to control or confiscate once the conflict was over. Officials were afraid that Right Sector would rise up against them.

"And," Vitaly said grimly, "they have good reason to rise up."

Dnipropetrovsk's center for displaced people was near the train station, on Karl Marx Avenue. The word used to describe these displaced people was *pereselentsy*, "resettlers." When I said "refugee," people often corrected me, perhaps because they didn't want to acknowledge that the east was experiencing a full-fledged war. (The Ukrainian government never declared war, for political and financial reasons.) But *pereselentsy* was also a charged term; in the Soviet Union, it was a euphemism to describe deported ethnic groups such as the Crimean Tatars.

The center was housed in the kind of faceless, run-down Soviet institution familiar from my visits to drug treatment centers and hospitals, but it was obvious that this building was inhabited by energetic new occupants: the stairs were a fresh pink, the walls a fresh green. The red and black Right Sector flag hung beside the blue and gold Ukrainian one.

After some searching, we found Lyudmila Khapatko, the director, a small, thin middle-aged woman in a beige vest. She had been educated as a chemist and had worked in finance until she dropped everything, as she said, "to run to Maidan." Her ferocious, friendly energy was almost equal to Marina's.

Lyudmila took us to a bright room full of attractive furniture and children's toys, with flowered wallpaper and a row of new sewing machines donated by the UN. More than two thousand people had passed through the center; at the moment about thirty were staying there. Most of the people who stayed in the center were there for only one night, stopping over en route to regions that were not yet overflowing. Dnipropetrovsk had been closed to resettlers long ago, being completely full, as had Kiev, Vinnytsia, and other more populous and desirable places. It was hard for the resettlers to find housing; sometimes eight people would live in a single room. The government was doing a miserable job of supplying its soldiers, but it was even worse at handling the flood of displaced people. Here, again, volunteers had leaped forward to fill the gap.

Lyudmila was doing admirable work, but she had few tender feelings for the people she was helping.

"The patriots left long ago," she said, "but there weren't many of them anyway." She estimated that 80 percent of Donbas people hated the people of Dnipropetrovsk.

"Donbas people have a strong sense of entitlement. They're aggressive, so people in Dnipropetrovsk don't like them, don't want to hire them," she told me. "But if they would behave, they could find work."

Given Ukraine's financial crisis, I had my doubts.

It was hard, she said, for the center to find volunteers. Of every kind of volunteer work available in Dnipropetrovsk, helping displaced people carried the lowest prestige; volunteering to help soldiers was far more popular.

I asked why the resettlers didn't help run the center.

"No resettler can be a coordinator—it's out of the question," she explained. "It's not just a matter of mentality—they're simply another kind of people. They'd start trying to act like kingpins. Their first commandment is not to be too trusting, not to be gullible.

"Most people come to the center for concrete assistance. But eventually, we would like to make it a social center. . . . You can't just give people some groceries and say goodbye. You can't let them be enemies. They'll start to form self-organizations that might be anti-Ukrainian. Organizations of people from Luhansk helping people from Luhansk, people from Donetsk helping people from Donetsk."

There were suspicions, she said, that some people were playing a double game, taking aid while engaging in antigovernment activities. Donetsk and Luhansk People's Republic graffiti had started to appear in Dnipropetrovsk.

Lyudmila said she often couldn't stand the parents, but she loved the children. After all, they hadn't chosen where they'd been born. She showed me some of the stuffed animals she'd sewn herself. One was a smiling cat, red and black for Right Sector. A child's drawing, posted on the wall, had a picture of a polka-dotted tank flying a Ukrainian flag, and GLORY TO UKAINE GLORY TO HEROES MAKSIM DANETSK [sic] written in crooked blue and gold letters. Nearby hung a portrait of Roman

Shukhevych, the Ukrainian ultranationalist who was involved in terrorist attacks against Poles in western Ukraine in the 1920s and '30s. Made a "Hero of Ukraine" by Orange Revolution president Yushchenko in 2007, Shukhevych, like Bandera, soon lost his posthumous title under Yanukovych.

At an American theme bar called the Cotton Club, on Sholem Aleichem Street, in a blizzard, I interviewed Tanya Savchenko, who'd run the harm reduction NGO I'd visited in Pavlohrad in 2007, and her husband, Andrei, a Luhansk native. Tanya had moved from Pavlohrad to Luhansk and, once the war started, to Dnipropetrovsk.

No two people could have borne less resemblance to the aggressive, self-pitying, conniving Donbas residents that Lyudmila Khapatko had described. It was hard, Tanya admitted, to go from being the one who helped others to being the one who was helped, but she and Andrei had already found work and a place to live, and now they were doing what they could to help other displaced people. The members of the Luhansk community, they said, supported one another. This didn't sound like a sinister cabal. When I asked about discrimination, they admitted that Andrei, who worked in trash collection and recycling, had been denied a contract in Zhytomyr, in western Ukraine, because his potential employers believed that all eastern Ukrainians were terrorists. But such cases were rare, Andrei and Tanya insisted.

Tanya gave me a trident pendant and a knit floret pin in blue and gold; I had the impression that she and Andrei took pains to display their patriotism whenever they could. They were working hard to improve their Ukrainian.

When it was time for me to get on the train back to Kiev, Tanya and Andrei gave me a ride. They took the long way in order to show me the Hotel Parus, which had been under construction for nearly forty years. *Parus* means "sail" in Russian, and the hotel billows out over the Dnieper River. A grandiose plan of the Brezhnev period, the hotel, on the Lenin Embankment, was under construction throughout the 1970s, but financing slowed to a trickle in the 1980s and ended for good in the 1990s. Everything that could be stolen from the building—doors, windows, wiring—was taken. Only a concrete shell remained.

The city had painted the side of the thirty-two-story building with Ukraine's blue and gold trident, the largest in Ukraine. Now the hotel would have to be finished; demolishing the building would look like the destruction of Ukraine itself.

Chapter 19

Victory Day

On May 9, 2015, Donetsk celebrated in the rain. It was Victory Day, the annual commemoration of Germany's surrender to the Soviet Union in 1945. Aleksandr Zakharchenko, the prime minister of the Donetsk People's Republic, stood in the drizzle and made a speech. There were dark circles under his eyes, and he slurred his words; pro-Ukrainians later accused him of being drunk, but maybe he was just tired. Seventy years ago Soviet heroes had defeated the fascists, he declared, and now their children and grandchildren were fighting fascists once again; the generation of victors had raised a generation of heroes. The past bled into the present, as the victories and losses of the Second World War mingled with those of the "antiterrorist operation."

Onlookers stood under umbrellas, cheering "thank you" and throwing flowers at the stony-faced new heroes of Donbas. Men with noms de guerre like Givi and Motorola held their white-gloved hands in fixed salutes as they rode past on tanks. In the evening there were fireworks, as is customary on Victory Day, though one might have expected the residents of Donetsk to be tired of explosions after nearly a year of intermittent shelling.

In Russia, a spokesman at the Federal Agency for Air Transport announced that a group of planes would be ready to attack any Victory Day rain clouds with cement particles and silver iodide. When Putin made his speech on Red Square, he was surrounded by foreign dignitaries from China, Uzbekistan,

Turkmenistan, Zimbabwe, Cuba, and Egypt, as well as Winston Churchill's grandson, a Tory MP. Most European leaders skipped the parade in protest of Russia's actions in Ukraine. To many Russians, it looked as though the once-Allied countries had forgotten that it was the Soviet Union that had rescued them from Nazism. Intercontinental missile carriers rolled through Moscow's streets, and fighter jets formed a huge 70 in the sky.

Russia was eager to claim the heroes of the Second World War, but Russian soldiers who'd been sent to eastern Ukraine were another story. Putin made military deaths a state secret even in peacetime, an obvious attempt to conceal Russian casualties in Ukraine. Sometimes Russian soldiers were required to "retire" just before their deployment to Ukraine. Russia disavowed two of its soldiers who were captured in Luhansk. From a Kiev hospital bed, Aleksandr Aleksandrov, one of the two prisoners, said he had been unable to reach his wife for weeks, and begged a Russian journalist to tell her he still loved her. He couldn't believe his country had abandoned him.

SEVENTY YEARS OF VICTORY!, posters all over Moscow cried as if victory were not a historical occurrence but a permanent state of exaltation. The orange and black St. George ribbon snaked across walls, windows, cars, trains, lounge chairs, bread loaves, dog collars, vodka bottles, flip-flops, fingernails, and even sex toys. On my train from the Moscow airport, the conductor wore a floppy St. George's bow that covered half her breast; the ribbon was unnaturally large, too big for a human being. In the metro I bought a ticket from a glowering, beribboned woman with horn-rimmed glasses, smeared pink lipstick, and a military hat decorated with a hammer and sickle pin. On the metro platform, a man who looked like he might be Kyrgyz or Kazakh was wearing a St. George ribbon like a bolo tie.

As I waited for a friend outside the Belarus metro station, I watched two vagrants trying to smash each other's heads against the plastic walls of the metro entrance. They were too drunk to succeed. Beside them, a dog whined in protest; she was chained up and guarding a puppy. My friend arrived, and we went into a Georgian restaurant around the corner. A St. George ribbon flapped on our waiter's chest.

The Moscow art group Blue Horseman satirized the ribbon cult with a private exhibit called "We Won." Works included a faucet spouting ribbons as tiny toy soldiers looked on from above, a man vomiting ribbons into a metal basin, and a black and orange meat-grinder. The leader of the Blue Horseman, Oleg Basov, had previously knelt on a Ukrainian flag in front of the security service building and bathed himself in stage blood. In another action, he splashed holy water on Lenin's Tomb, intoning, "Arise, and get out."

Law enforcement agents confiscated the Blue Horseman's work, detained the artists, and sealed the gallery. When Basov refused to give them his passport, they beat him. He screamed for help, hoping that the police and members of the government press in the next room would hear him, but no one even knocked on the door. A Russian television station began its story on the exhibit with the line "On the eve of May 9, the police liquidated a Nazi lair in the very heart of Russia." Swastikas were removed from historical exhibits, and toy Nazi soldiers and copies of Art Spiegelman's *Maus* were pulled from stores.

When I passed the Ministry of Defense in Moscow, I saw that the lawn had been decorated with artificial roses as tall as electrical poles. Their plastic leaves waved in the breeze.

Rapidly escalating tensions between the United States and Russia, wild threats and accusations from both sides, had led to a predictable uptick in anti-American feeling in Russia.

"Sanctions are a form of collective punishment," said Dmitry Muratov, editor of *Novaya Gazeta*, one of Russia's last independent newspapers. "They're aimed not at the people who are responsible for the war in eastern Ukraine, or at the people who financed it, but at the whole country. A tremendous amount of diplomacy has tried to make the West not an enemy, to make Russia part of the world—and now these efforts have been derailed. The Russian authorities can now explain any mistakes and failures—for example, unsuccessful medical or educational reforms, or the awful state of agriculture—by blaming our enemies. It's a blockade mentality. People aren't touched by sanctions in a substantive way, but propaganda has convinced them that we live in a world of enemies."

I asked him about the involvement of Russian soldiers in Ukraine; *Novaya Gazeta* was one of the only Russian outlets reporting on it. Very discreetly, he indicated that he couldn't talk about it; he didn't want to add fuel to the fire. Suffice it to say that *Novaya Gazeta* was against war, against killing.

He gave me butter cookies in a Victory Day tin and two pastel mugs made to look like rusting tin army cups, decorated with the words WE WON! and NOT ONE STEP BACK! As I left, he showed me the desktop computer of the murdered journalist Anna Politkovskaya. It sat in a display case in the newspaper's front hall.

Moscow was bloodthirsty and cheerful. Tricolor Russian flags waved beside red Soviet Victory banners, and kiosks sold T-shirts showing Putin dressed as a Soviet soldier. On Arbat, a touristy pedestrian street, I stopped in front of a stage where people were doing Victory Day karaoke, right across from the American chain restaurant Shake Shack.

"Death is not frightening!" a man sang off-key. Everyone applauded.

Walking farther down Arbat, past the Moscow Torture Museum and a long series of souvenir shops, I saw an enormous mural of Marshal Zhukov, one of the generals who led Russia to victory in World War II. The marshal's chest was plastered in medals, and his shoulders were too wide to fit on the wall. The painting was the work of United Russia, Putin's party, which claimed that it was the largest Zhukov portrait in the world: 250 square meters. United Russia member Andrei Metelsky, a deputy in the Moscow city council, had explained that the portrait was "our small 'thank you' to veterans." It was also, he added ominously, "a warning to those who have forgotten what war and victory are."

I wandered through Muzeon, the sculpture garden where Soviet monuments were brought to rest. Lenins led the way and Brezhnevs scowled. One Stalin had no nose and looked less like a worn Roman statue than like the victim of a terrible accident. Yakov Sverdlov, a Bolshevik leader who died under suspicious circumstances in 1919, looked jaunty, with riding boots and a popped collar. It was hard to discern the features of Feliks Dzerzhinsky, the founder of the Soviet secret police, because his pedestal was so high. Protesters had had to use a crane to topple him in August 1991.

The Muzeon lawn was populated not only by political figures, but by monuments commemorating the Second World War. In one statue from 1950, a woman with a baby released a dove. Behind her stood an armless veteran and a Chinese woman holding the corpse of her own child. WE DEMAND PEACE! declared the statue's inscription.

On November 7, 1941, the twenty-fourth anniversary of the October Revolution, Stalin held a parade that was filmed and shown around the world. Troops marched directly from Red Square to the battlefields. With the Germans just outside Moscow, the stunt was an extraordinarily risky way of raising morale and cowing the enemy.

In his speech, Stalin invoked the great minds of Russian art and science and Russia's national heroes: Aleksandr Nevsky, who defeated the Teutonic Knights in 1242; Dmitry Donskoy, who defeated the Tatars in 1380; Minin and Pozharsky, who defeated the Poles in the seventeenth century; Suvorov and Kutuzov, who defeated Napoleon in the nineteenth century. The symbolic union of the USSR with imperialist-Orthodox Russia was uncongenial to some revolutionaries, but it was a reliable crowd-pleaser. To win the war, Stalin harnessed the energy of all the victories of the Russian

Empire. It didn't matter that the revolution had promised to abolish the imperial system for good. The old heroes and gods were too potent to be discarded.

After the war was won, the metro's hammers and sickles were joined by artwork celebrating the greatest victory of all. Now these works were reminders of a state that had once been much more than just Russia. In Moscow's Kiev metro station, mosaics showed the liberation of Kiev in 1943. A Lenin mural in another station read THE FRIENDSHIP OF THE PEOPLES IS THE STAUNCHEST BASTION OF A FREE FATHERLAND, a line from the Soviet anthem. Victory could not be separated from the memory of the days when Ukraine was part of the Soviet Union; many of the war's key battles occurred on Ukraine's black earth. After the Nazis captured Ukraine, Crimea, and Donbas, the three territories were won back at the cost of millions of Soviet lives. Stalin described the Red Army as the defender of "peace and friendship between the peoples of every land." Ukraine was at the heart of this friendship; Ukraine was at the heart of Victory.

After the war, the Ukrainian Republic played a correspondingly important role in the emerging Victory cult. War commemoration was incorporated into coming of age rites, wedding processions, and national holidays. This helped to counteract the wartime surge in Ukrainian nationalist sentiment, some of which the Party had encouraged for reasons of morale. The Victory cult also helped dull the memory of agricultural collectivization, which had killed millions of Ukrainians. According to Party rhetoric, Victory was final proof of the necessity of uniting the family of Soviet republics; all the sacrifices had been worth it.

*

When I arrived at Boris Kagarlitsky's office at the Institute of Globalization and Social Movements, where he was director, the only person there was an acned, overweight young man who had just finished a meal from McDonald's. As we waited, I looked at the books on the shelves: the *Soviet Encyclopedia*, the collected works of Marx and Engels. A poster for *Rabkor*, the institute's online journal (the title is a Soviet abbreviation for "worker-correspondent," the name for freelance contributors to worker publications), showed a bullhorn in the shape of a revolver. Kagarlitsky, a Marxist theoretician and sociologist, was one of many Russian leftists who had embraced the idea of Novorossiya. In late 2014 he told a journalist that the Cossack separatist leader Aleksei Mozgovoi was the "best show in town from a left point of view." Mozgovoi was later assassinated, perhaps for this reason.

Kagarlitsky walked in, accompanied by a dark-haired man in a limp suit.

"One of my friends said it very well: the liberals want to make it look like Putin is Hitler. But Putin isn't Hitler, he's Chamberlain," Kagarlitsky told his friend, an exiled Moldovan leftist politician, who laughed knowingly. Enjoying their own performance, the men discussed the crisis in Ukraine and made analogies with the Russian Civil War, using Soviet terms like "antipeople" and asking questions like "Will it be red?" The room reeked of political conviction.

"When Brezhnev's generation died—the generation of leaders who actually fought in the war—the legitimacy of the Soviet government disappeared with it," Kagarlitsky told me once the Moldovan was gone. "Now Putin's government is trying to establish legitimacy not based on any real historical experience, but by using late Soviet style and aesthetics. On television, you see dancing girls in uniforms of the Second World War. Half the girls with the red Soviet flag, and half with the tricolor Russian flag. The message is very clear: Russia is the successor of the Soviet Union, the heir to Victory. It looks like a mockery, a way of hiding the fact that the war was won by a different government, a different political and social system. They're claiming a historical inheritance to which they don't have sufficient rights."

"Do you think the government is using Victory Day to prepare the population for war?" I asked.

"No. On the contrary. They do everything they can to make the people feel that they are *not* on the verge of a serious armed conflict. The Russian regime isn't ready to fight with anyone. It's ready to make friends with the West; it's the West that doesn't want to make friends with Russia. That's Russia's big problem— unrequited love for the West. The Putin regime is just trying to keep what it has. A dog has been hunting, and if you take away its kill, it starts to growl. That's its dinner. Isn't that right?"

Ukraine was trying hard to distance itself from the Soviet past. It declared May 8 "Victory in Europe" Day and replaced the Soviet term "Great Patriotic War" with "Second World War," in keeping with European practice. May 9 became "Victory Day over Nazism in World War II," a solemn rather than a festive affair. Kiev's traditional Victory march was replaced by a peace march, without fireworks. The Motherland statue was crowned with a garland of red poppies, which are used in Europe to commemorate the war dead. St. George ribbons were frowned upon, or worse. A video circulated of two Svoboda members berating an older man who was trying to leave his home wearing a ribbon on his lapel; when he refused to go back inside, they doused him in kefir.

Shortly after Victory Day, Poroshenko signed new laws that attached criminal penalties to the display of Soviet and Nazi symbols in almost any context, and prohibited any denial of the "criminal character of the communist totalitarian regime of 1917–91 in Ukraine." A second law, written by Yury Shukhevych, son of Ukrainian Insurgent Army general Roman Shukhevych, recognized the Organization of Ukrainian Nationalists and the Ukrainian Insurgent Army as "independence fighters" and made it a criminal offense to question the legitimacy of their actions. Shukhevych was leader of one of the groups that had joined Right Sector; his law realized a cherished dream of Ukraine's far right, enshrining the controversial nationalists as heroes. (Shukhevych had a life story that could have radicalized anyone: because of his father's past, he was deported to Siberia at age eleven along with his mother, then sent to an orphanage for children of enemies of the people; at sixteen, he was sentenced to hard labor. He spent more than thirty years in Soviet camps and was blind by the time he was released, in the 1980s.)

The laws didn't only affect discussion of the past; they also effectively banned Communism in contemporary Ukraine. The "memory laws" were criticized by historians, Poles, Jews, leftists, and advocates of free speech, among others. In its strenuous effort to break with the Soviet past, Ukraine was using Soviet-style tactics: the suppression of political speech and debate, and the imposition of an official version of history. The new laws were an act of symbolic violence against the civilization in which many Ukrainians grew up, and for which millions of Ukrainians lost their lives while fighting the Nazis. They were also an enormous waste of money at a time of economic collapse. Thousands of signs had to be changed and monuments removed, replaced with the heroes of the moment.

I went to visit my old friend Max, the truck driver from Meganom, at his house in Dreamtown, a gated community outside Moscow. (The first time I'd visited him there, he crowed, "Well, what do you say? Is this Switzerland or what?") Max had just returned from several months in Vietnam. When I had written to tell him I was coming, he'd joked, "You're our only chance to tell the world that not everybody in Russia is a Putinoid." Max didn't like taking sides. It upset him when people turned into "Putinoids," as most of his relatives and neighbors had, but he was also unhappy when his Ukrainian friends turned into "Maidanuts." Either way, they lost themselves and became impossible to talk to. The Ukrainian contingent from Meganom no longer communicated with him, he said, except for his sometimes-girlfriend, Alyona, who had moved back in with him as soon as things got crazy in Ukraine.

But he had new Ukrainians in his life. An old acquaintance from Luhansk had gotten in touch with him over the summer, and Max had let the friend and his family stay with him. Two other families had followed. Max said there were a lot of Ukrainian men living in Russia to avoid being sent to fight in the east. Putin had made it easier for them by changing the rules about how many days a Ukrainian could stay. Max and I agreed that this was one of Putin's better moments.

"Of course a lot of refugees were taken in by Muscovites," Max said. "Why wouldn't they be? It was one country so recently." As a former truck driver, he was opposed to borders on principle.

While Max and I were having dinner, a neighbor named Natasha came over to visit. She was from Mariupol, in the Donetsk region, and had left to get away from the conflict. Now she was living in an unfinished house in Dreamtown. Plump and smiling, with glasses and short dark hair, she exuded the almost desperate cheer and friendliness of the recently resettled; she reminded me of Tanya Savchenko in Dnipropetrovsk. She had brought batter for *syrniki*, fried pancakes made with soft white cheese and raisins. Like a true Ukrainian mother, she fried enough pancakes to last a week. They were delicious.

"What do you think of *Dancing with the Stars?*" Natasha asked me shyly. I told her I didn't watch it but knew what it was.

"Oh, I love it very much," she said. "My favorite is Derek Hough. I can tell from his dancing that he's a good person."

Max said he regretted that he couldn't speak English. "People don't speak with languages, they speak with their hearts," Natasha said, with her sweet smile. This was another way to avoid taking sides, especially important, no doubt, for a Ukrainian refugee in Russia: a denial of boundaries, an all-encompassing kindness and optimism.

Max had been in Crimea in the fall; he reported that everyone there was very happy about Russia, selling Putin magnets with affection and respect. To him it didn't matter whether Crimea belonged to Russia or to Ukraine; he only wished there wouldn't be any more corpses. Crimea had once been the center of his fantasy world, the destination of his life; now it had been replaced by Vietnam.

*

Belgorod, the hometown of Olga and Sanya, my friends from Crimea, was a midsize city twenty-five miles from the northeastern Ukrainian border, just fifty miles from the Ukrainian city of Kharkiv. Because of its location, Belgorod was hit hard by World War II. It was occupied by the Germans from October 1941 until early 1943, then recaptured by the Germans at the end of that year. The Red Army liberated it after the Battle of Kursk, the world's largest tank battle, which saw 863,000 Soviet and nearly 200,000 German casualties. The journalist Alexander Werth wrote that when he arrived in the area north of the city, the earth was dead for miles around, and "the air was filled with the stench of half-buried corpses."

Belgorod's airport was on Bogdan Khmelnitsky Street (the double of my old street in Kiev), just one sign of Belgorod's close ties to Ukraine. In 1918 Belgorod had been part of the short-lived Ukrainian state established by German-backed Hetman Pavlo Skoropadsky. When Skoropadsky was overthrown, Belgorod became Ukraine's temporary capital. Some residents, like Sanya, spoke with guttural accents like those in eastern Ukraine and sprinkled the occasional Ukrainian word into their speech.

Olga and Sanya told me that one Ukrainian friend had disowned her sister for going back to Meganom after it became Russian. Before the conflict, people had moved between Belgorod and Kharkiv with little sense that they were crossing a national boundary. Now a border crossing required time, documents, and money, and people didn't do it unless it was absolutely necessary. Many of those who crossed were escaping the violence in eastern Ukraine. Sanya said there had been long lines at the border at Easter, when people went to visit the graves of relatives killed in the conflict.

*

Olga and I woke up early on the morning of Victory Day to go to Belgorod's Immortal Regiment march. Organized several years earlier by journalists from a respected independent television station, the Immortal Regiment began as a nonpolitical, non-governmental initiative to encourage people to collect and share information about family members who served in the war. Every Victory Day, participants marched carrying pictures of their relatives. The project was an attempt to focus attention on the real people who fought in the real war, on historical reality rather than jingoistic fantasy. Not all of the stories on the Immortal Regiment's website were about heroic feats: one person wrote about how his grandfather arrived late to the draft office and was never seen again.

Belgorod was a relatively small city, and we'd spent the last day and a half wandering through empty streets. Now we were confronted with a sea of faces, living and dead. Olga kept seeing acquaintances carrying portraits of their grandparents or great-grandparents. Many of the portraits we saw were handmade, often with carefully assembled collages of photographs and words.

A group walked by carrying a huge red Soviet Victory banner and a large portrait of Stalin. Nearby, a man in a mass-produced red Stalin T-shirt was waving a Soviet flag and carrying a bunch of red roses. Another man in an identical shirt soon joined him. A heavily made-up young woman paired the same top with red high heels.

"How do you feel when you see people with Stalin's portrait?" I asked Olga.

"I feel completely calm about it," she said resolutely. "I'm not a political person." After a pause, she added, "But I'm surprised to see them at the parade. And there are moments . . . I saw a picture recently online, of Gumilyov"—the poet, husband of Anna Akhmatova, shot by the Cheka in 1921—"after he was tortured. And then I did think about the terrible things that Stalin did. You know, my great-grandfather fought in the war, and came home afterward. He was living in a village outside the city, where it was safer, but someone got jealous of him and informed on him falsely. He was deported to Siberia and shot."

Vendors were selling balloon tanks and helicopters along with balloon SpongeBob SquarePants and hearts that said I LOVE YOU THIS MUCH in English. Men dressed as Cossacks stood on guard, knouts in hand. I bought a Victory Day ice cream bar.

Whole families were dressed in Soviet uniforms or in camouflage. A woman pushing her uniformed toddler in a stroller looked like a parody of a war nurse. Family members of all ages competed to see who could assemble and disassemble a rifle fastest, and posed for photos with an actor-soldier on a vintage military motorcycle. Two tanks swarmed with little children, and a boy in uniform marched in circles on the back of a military truck. A tiny dark-haired girl, perhaps five years old, recited a poem into a microphone held by a man in uniform. It ended, "What is Victory Day? It means there is no war."

An older woman, whose hair was dyed the same shade of purple as her raincoat, told me that she was carrying the portrait of her grandfather, who had been killed just two months before the end of the war, when he was only twenty-three. She looked like she was about to cry.

"I'm tired," she said mournfully. "I'm going home."

Olga and I were also tired; we stopped in a café for a coffee. A grinning man sitting alone at one of the tables said, "Girls, where are your ribbons? Today is an important day! It's our duty to celebrate!" He was visibly drunk, though it wasn't yet eleven a.m.

Every store was decorated in honor of Victory Day, which led to strange juxtapositions like

BELGOROD IS A CITY OF MILITARY GLORY
MEAT
FISH
CANDY
UNDERWEAR

Walking down the city's main stretch, we passed the offices of the Donetsk and Luhansk People's Republics, which did PR and recruiting for the war.

After the parade we met up with Vasya and Misha, a gay couple who were Olga's close friends. The flamboyant Vasya was wearing bell-bottoms, a T-shirt with orange stripes, and a St. George ribbon. Like pretty much everyone else I talked to in Belgorod, he loved Victory Day.

We went over to his and Misha's apartment, which featured velvet curtains and an immense collection of cat figurines. Like Olga and Sanya's apartment, it was lovingly renovated and obsessively tidy. People in Belgorod seemed to devote most of their energy to interior decoration and childrearing. The world outside was too sinister; the only way to find happiness was to turn inward. Your home was your country, as the Ukrainians liked to say.

More friends arrived, and we went to grill sausages and chicken in Vasya and Misha's garage, which was nearly as well decorated as their apartment. The neighbors had disguised their cars as tanks and airplanes, with red stars and hammers and sickles. The back of one car had cardboard rockets and the words TO BERLIN.

Dima, an old friend from Meganom, joined us. He told me that his grandfather had made it all the way to Berlin, where he fell in love with a German woman whom he married and brought back to Russia. They were repressed, sent to the taiga; they were lucky they weren't shot.

Dima had been working in construction, building houses on the Russian-Ukrainian border. Now no one wanted houses there, and he was broke.

"Death to traitors," he said ironically, lifting his glass of vodka, "and to fascists."

We went up to the roof to watch the fireworks, which were just across the street. The blasts were deafening and the air was thick with smoke.

"This is how the universe began," Dima yelled into my ear, "with explosions."

Back in the apartment, Vasya put on a record of patriotic Russian power pop. Olga was telling everyone about how moved she'd been by the Immortal Regiment.

"I had goose bumps! There were tears in my eyes!" she kept saying, though when we'd been there, she'd registered almost no emotion.

By now all the men were extremely drunk. I started drinking vodka, too. The atmosphere of close-lipped happiness in the room, in Belgorod, in Russia, had become too much for me.

"Sophie, let's drink to *Bruderschaft!*" Dima said.

I knew that *Bruderschaft* meant "brotherhood," so I consented. Dima poured us two shots and linked my arm in his. We drank, and he leaned in to kiss me with an open mouth.

I pulled away, laughing awkwardly.

"You ruined the toast," he said. "Now it won't work." I'd hurt his feelings.

I moved over to Lyosha, another friend of Olga's, and asked him what he thought about the conflict in Ukraine.

Leaning in close, he told me he'd been feeling paranoid.

"You know," he slurred, "when I heard about the fire in Odessa, I wanted to drop everything and go and fight for Donbas. But now I think about how I reacted, and I wonder if the whole thing was just a Russian provocation. Sometimes I watch the Ukrainian news and then the Russian news, just to compare. All of them are lying. They tell you everything is black and white, but it's not that way at all. There are no heroes in this. In Belgorod, we all know people who've come from eastern Ukraine. They tell us about being attacked by Ukrainian forces and by the rebels— by both sides. They've been as close to the fighting as we were to the fireworks."

He held his palm up to his face to demonstrate.

"Do you think Russian soldiers are fighting in Donbas?" I asked.

He lowered his voice to a whisper. "I think so. But everyone thinks I'm wrong—even my friends. Even my mother."

We drank to peace, again and again.

A Note on Sources

The following are the major English-language secondary sources that I consulted, and the ones most relevant for those interested in further reading.

Serhy Yekelchyk's *Ukraine: Birth of a Modern Nation* (Oxford University Press, 2007) provides a clear, even-handed overview of Ukraine's fascinating yet complex history. Andrew Wilson's *The Ukrainians: Unexpected Nation* (Yale University Press, 2002) is another concise but detailed history. Michael Hamm's *Kiev: A Portrait, 1800–1917* (Princeton University Press, 1993) is a vivid account of the city's development.

Hiroaki Kuromiya's *Freedom and Terror in the Donbas: A Ukrainian-Russian Borderland, 1870s–1990s* (Cambridge University Press, 1998) tells the violent, painful story of the region that is now embattled eastern Ukraine. Willard Sunderland's *Taming the Wild Field: Colonization and Empire on the Russian Steppe* (Cornell University Press, 2004) is a history of the "wild steppe" that stretches from Moldova to Kazakhstan, and that includes what is now eastern Ukraine. Peter Holquist's "'Conduct Merciless Mass Terror': Decossackization on the Don, 1919,"

Cahiers du monde russe 38 (1997) recounts the Bolshevik attempt to excise Cossacks from the Soviet Union. Terry Martin's *Affirmative Action Empire: Nations and Nationalism in the Soviet Union, 1923–1939* (Cornell University Press, 2001) discusses the Soviet policy of "Ukrainization" in depth. Serhy Yekelchyk's *Stalin's Empire of Memory: Russian-Ukrainian Relations in the Soviet Historical Imagination* (University of Toronto, 2004) analyzes the politics of memory and the "friendship of the peoples" under Stalin. Alexander Werth's *Russia at War: 1941–1945* (Dutton, 1964) provides an eyewitness account of the Second World War in the Soviet Union, including descriptions of several trips to Ukraine and Crimea.

John Armstrong's *Ukrainian Nationalism* (Ukrainian Academic Press, 1990, originally published 1955) was the first detailed study of the Organization of Ukrainian Nationalists (OUN) during the Second World War. Myroslav Shkandrij's *Ukrainian Nationalism: Politics, Ideology, and Literature, 1929–1956* (Yale University Press, 2015) analyzes the writings associated with OUN.

Amir Weiner's *Making Sense of War: The Second World War and the Fate of the Bolshevik Revolution* (Princeton University Press, 2001) examines the experience and legacy of the Second World War in the central Ukrainian province of Vinnytsia. Kate Brown's *A Biography of No Place* (Harvard University Press, 2004) explores the transformation of the multiethnic Ukrainian-Polish border zone into a mostly homogenous Ukrainian "heartland" between 1923 and 1953. Tarik Cyril Amar's *The Paradox of Ukrainian Lviv: A Borderland City between Stalinists, Nazis, and Nationalists* (Cornell University Press, 2015) analyzes the transformation of Lviv from a multiethnic, east-central European border city into a Ukrainian urban center. The collection *Shatterzone of Empires: Coexistence and Violence in the German, Habsburg, Russian and Ottoman Borderlands*, edited by Omer Bartov and Eric Weitz (Indiana University Press, 2013) includes several articles on the clash of empires and communities in what is now Ukraine.

For an exploration of approaches to Ukrainian historiography, see the collection *A Laboratory of Transnational History: Ukraine and Recent Ukrainian Historiography*, edited by Georgiy Kasianov and Philipp Ther (Central European University Press, 2009). On post-Soviet Ukraine's politics of national memory, see David Marples's *Heroes and Villains: Creating National History in Contemporary Ukraine* (Central European University Press, 2007) and Marples's article "Stepan Bandera: The Resurrection of a Ukrainian National Hero," *Europe-Asia Studies* 58, no. 4 (2006). Eleonora Narvselius's article "The 'Bandera Debate': The Contentious Legacy of World War II and Liberalization of Collective Memory in Western Ukraine," *Canadian Slavonic Papers* 54, nos. 3–4 (2012) discusses Lviv's historical theme restaurants, including Kryivka.

Serhy Yekelchyk's articles "The Body and National Myth: Motifs from the Ukrainian National Revival in the Nineteenth Century," *Association for Slavic and East European Studies* 7, no. 2 (1993) and "The Nation's Clothes: Constructing a Ukrainian High Culture in the Russian Empire, 1860–1900," *Jahrbücher für Geschichte Osteuropas*, new series 49, no. 2 (2001), explore the construction of Ukrainian national identity through clothing (notably the *vyshyvanka*, or Ukrainian embroidered blouse) in the nineteenth century. Serhii Plokhy's *Unmaking Imperial Russia: Mykhailo Hrushevsky and the Writing of Ukrainian History* (University of Toronto Press, 2005) discusses Hrushevsky's crucial role, in the early twentieth century, in creating modern Ukrainian national identity. Yekelchyk's "Cossack Gold: History, Myth, and the Dream of Prosperity in the Age of Post-Soviet Transition," *Canadian Slavonic Papers* 40, no. 3–4 (1998) describes the moment when Ukrainians hoped to literally cash in on their history.

Catherine Wanner's *Burden of Dreams: History and Identity in Post-Soviet Ukraine* (Pennsylvania State University Press, 1998) offers an anthropological perspective on the formation of Ukrainian national identity in the aftermath of the Soviet collapse, including a discussion of nationalism in music festivals. On the role of music in the Orange Revolution, see Adriana Helbig's "The Cyberpolitics of Music in Ukraine's 2004 Orange Revolution," *Current Musicology* 82 (2006).

Linguist Laada Bilaniuk's *Contested Tongues: Language Politics and Cultural Correction in Ukraine* (Cornell University Press, 2005) discusses the history and politics of *surzhyk*, the mixture of Ukrainian and Russian. Serhy Yekelchyk's "What is Ukrainian About Ukraine's Pop Culture? The Strange Case of Verka Serduchka," *Canadian-American Slavic Studies* 44 (2010) discusses the political valence of *surzhyk* in the performances of Ukraine's transvestite Eurovision winner.

Vyacheslav Likhachev examines Right Sector's role in Maidan in his article "The 'Right Sector' and Others: The Behavior and Role of Radical Nationalists in the Ukrainian Political Crisis of Late 2013–Early 2014," *Communist and Post-Communist Studies* 48 (2015). Olesya Khromeychuk's "Gender and Nationalism on the Maidan," in *Ukraine's Euromaidan*, edited by David R. Marples and Frederick V. Mills (Ibidem-Verlag, 2015), discusses nationalist attempts to define and constrain women's participation in the Maidan protests. Sarah Phillips's "The

Women's Squad in Ukraine's Protests: Feminism, Nationalism, and Militarism on the Maidan," *American Ethnologist* 41, no. 3 (2014) is an ethnography of the women's squad (or "hundred") on Maidan. For an exploration of Odessa's dating agencies, see Shaun Walker's *Odessa Dreams: The Dark Heart of Ukraine's Online Marriage Industry* (Thistle Publishing, 2014).

Anton Shekhovtsov has written a number of articles about Ukraine's far right, including "The Creeping Resurgence of the Ukrainian Radical Right? The Case of the Freedom Party," *Europe-Asia Studies* 63, no. 2 (2011), on Svoboda, and, with Andreas Umland, "Ukraine's Radical Right," *Journal of Democracy* 25, no. 3 (2014). Alina Polyakova has also written several articles on the subject, including "From the Provinces to the Parliament: How the Ukrainian Radical Right Mobilized in Galicia," *Communist and Post-Communist Studies* 27 (2014). Andrew Wilson's *Ukrainian Nationalism in the 1990s: A Minority Faith* (Cambridge University Press, 1997) explores the phenomenon of Ukrainian nationalism in the years immediately following the fall of the Soviet Union.

Pavlo Zaitsev's *Taras Shevchenko: A Life*, first published in 1955, is an engaging, if somewhat hagiographic, biography of Ukraine's national poet. It is available in an abridged English translation (University of Toronto Press, 1988). George Grabowicz's introductory essay in the catalogue *Taras Shevchenko: Poet, Artist, Icon, 1814–1861* (Ukrainian Museum, 2014) provides a shorter biographical sketch of the poet, with discussion of his importance for Ukrainian national identity. The collection *Shevchenko and the Critics: 1861–1980* (University of Toronto Press, 1980), edited by George Luckyj, shows how interpretations of Shevchenko's life and legacy have changed over the decades.

Yuri Slezkine's *The Jewish Century* (Princeton University Press, 2004) includes a chapter on the position of Jews in the Russian Empire and Soviet Union. Zenon Kohut's "The Khmelnytsky Uprising, the Image of Jews, and the Shaping of Ukrainian Historical Memory," *Jewish History* 17 (2003) analyzes the evolving image of the Jew in early modern Ukrainian historical narratives, focusing on interpretations of seventeenth-century Hetman Bohdan Khmelnytsky's anti-Polish uprising and anti-Jewish pogroms. Rodger Kamenetz's *Burnt Books: Rabbi Nachman of Bratslav and Franz Kafka* (Nextbook, 2010) discusses Rabbi Nachman's pact with God.

Andrei Zorin's *By Fables Alone: Literature and State Ideology in Late-Eighteenth-Early-Nineteenth-Century Russia* (Academic Studies Press, 2014) includes chapters on Catherine the Great's "Greek Project" and annexation of Crimea. Greta Lynn Uehling's *Beyond Memory: The Crimean Tatars' Deportation and Return* (Palgrave Macmillan, 2004) is an ethnography of Crimea's Tatar minority. On the Black Sea region, see Charles King's *The Black Sea: A History* (Oxford University Press, 2004) and Neal Ascherson's *Black Sea: The Birthplace of Civilization and Barbarism* (Vintage, 1996). Gwendolyn Sasse's *The Crimea Question: Identity, Transition, and Conflict* (Harvard University Press, 2007) explores Crimea's political history.

George Young's *The Russian Cosmists: The Esoteric Futurism of Nikolai Fedorov and His Followers* (Oxford University Press, 2012) explores Fyodorov's wild theories and their influence. Irina Masing-Delic's *Abolishing Death: A Salvation Myth of Russian Twentieth-Century Literature* (Stanford University Press, 1992) includes a chapter on Fyodorov in the context of a detailed discussion of the "immortality myth" in twentieth-century Russian literature. Nikolai Krementsov's *A Martian Stranded on Earth: Alexander Bogdanov, Blood Transfusions, and Proletarian Science* (University of Chicago Press, 2011) examines the life and work of the Marxist polymath. Lesley Milne's *Mikhail Bulgakov: A Critical Biography* (Cambridge University Press, 1990) analyzes the Kiev-born writer's work in the context of his life.

On the struggle between Russia's imperial secret police and revolutionaries, see Jonathan Daly's *Autocracy Under Siege: Security Police and Opposition in Russia, 1866–1905* (Northern Illinois University Press, 1998) and *The Watchful State: Security Police and Opposition in Russia, 1906–1917* (Northern Illinois University Press, 2004). Gábor Rittersporn's *Anguish, Anger, and Folkways in Soviet Russia* (University of Pittsburgh Press, 2014) examines the Soviet predilection for conspiracy theories. On the Soviet approach to addiction, see Alisher Latypov, "The Soviet Doctor and the Treatment of Drug Addiction: 'A Difficult and Most Ungracious Task,'" *Harm Reduction Journal* 8, no. 32 (2011).

Charlotte Douglas's *Malevich* (Harry N. Abrams, 1994) includes a sketch of Kazimir Malevich's biography. The Guggenheim Museum's *Kazimir Malevich: Suprematism*, edited by Matthew Drutt (2003) is a collection of essays on his art and writing. Boris Groys's *The Total Art of Stalinism: Avant-Garde, Aesthetic Dictatorship, and Beyond* (Princeton University Press, 1992) includes a discussion of Malevich's ideas and their reception.

The Ukrainian-born writer Konstantin Paustovsky's memoir *The Story of a Life*, quoted here, was translated into English by Joseph Barnes (Pantheon, 1964). Passages quoted from *The Odyssey* are from Robert Fagles's translation (Penguin, 1996).

Acknowledgments

Above all, I am profoundly grateful to the Ukrainian and Russian friends, colleagues, and acquaintances without whose hospitality, generosity, and kindness this book would never have existed. I am also thankful to my colleagues in the international harm reduction and drug policy movements, who taught me so much and gave me many opportunities to explore.

I was lucky to benefit from the insight, close reading, dedication, and encouragement of my excellent editors, Tom Avery at Heinemann and Tom Mayer at Norton. I was also fortunate in my agent, Zoë Pagnamenta. Christopher Cumming, Jeremy Kessler, Orysia Kulick, and Julia Yatsenko provided helpful comments and invaluable moral support. Keith Gessen at *n+1* solicited several articles on Ukraine that later grew into this book. At Columbia University, Boris Gasparov and Tatiana Smoliarova introduced me to many of the literary themes and figures discussed here.

I owe a special debt to my wonderful parents, who instilled in me a lifelong love of literature and supported my sometimes mystifying journeys to foreign lands.

ACKNOWLEDGMENTS

The Institute for International Education provided the grant that allowed me to live in Ukraine for an extended period, and the International Research and Exchanges Board supported my time in Irkutsk.

Short portions of this book stem from articles written for *Foreign Affairs*, *n+1*, *The Nation*, and *The New Yorker*. I am grateful to the editors and other staff who worked with me at those publications.

312